DATE			

Letters to My Children

Letters to My Children

Robert C. Maynard with Dori J. Maynard

Andrews and McMeel

A Universal Press Syndicate Company

KANSAS CITY

Dedication

To all the members of the many branches of our family
and to Bettie and Mr. Potts, who complete our immediate family.

Grateful acknowledgments to Al Neuharth and John Quinn, whose
enduring faith, friendship and support made this book possible, and to
Eric Newton and Rochelle Riley, the best editors a writer could ask for.

Library of Congress Cataloging-in-Publication Data
Maynard, Robert C.
    Letters to my children / Robert C. Maynard with Dori J. Maynard.
       p.   cm.
    ISBN 0-8362-7027-4
    1. Maynard, Robert C.   2. Journalists—California—Biography.
I. Maynard, Dori J.   II. Title.
PN4874.M48393M39   1995
814'.54—dc20   95-3213
                                                                                CIP

Designed by Cameron Poulter
Attention: Schools and Businesses:
Andrews and McMeel books are available at quantity discounts with bulk purchase for educa-
tional, business, or sales promotional use. For information, please write to Special Sales
Department, Andrews and McMeel, 4900 Main Street, Kansas City, Missouri 64112.

Contents

The Right Kind of Father

The News & Observer, Raleigh, North Carolina, Friday, August 20, 1993

Most of the tributes to former *Oakland Tribune* editor and publisher Robert C. Maynard, who died Tuesday of cancer at 56, dwell on the lasting difference he made in opening up U.S. newsrooms to minority journalists.

That would justly make Maynard proud. He himself had blazed the way to the eminence where, as the first black owner of a major general-circulation daily, he could command a hearing for this cause. A bare dozen years after quitting high school to write for a black weekly, he earned a prized journalism fellowship to Harvard. His brilliant newsroom career brought him credibility when he told editors and publishers they were both doing wrong and wasting talent in failing to hunt out promising minority reporters. Most got the message.

News & Observer readers, however, knew Maynard best as a syndicated columnist. Here too he will be hard to replace, for he had a gift unique among current pundits for shrinking massive problems to family size.

Of the scores of Maynard columns this newspaper carried, probably half began with some homely anecdote—a child's dinner-table question, a saying from his Barbados-immigrant mother. He taught his three children and his many readers that today's issues are neither too new nor too complex to yield to old, tested, honorable tools and measures.

Through his writing on matters as widely various as Japanese trade, teen pregnancy and urban riots ran a single strong, enduring theme: the need for individuals, families and communities to take responsibility.

His own family has suffered a great loss in the death of Bob Maynard, who seemed to represent the best meaning of the word "fatherly"—exemplar, teacher, guide and friend. In our degree, so have we all.

Introduction

Still, I can see him, headphones covering his ears, back turned to the room, hunched over his computer, his fingers pounding the keyboard. I don't know if he was listening to his favorite Miles Davis, or simply blocking out the world. Dad was writing his column, and it was best not to interrupt.

My father loved his column. It was born, as he would say, shortly after he was named editor of the *Oakland Tribune* in 1979. Despite the turmoil of the next decade and a half, he didn't miss many columns. He might miss a few meals. He might miss a meeting. But not a column.

Writers have to write, and above all else, my Dad was a writer—an optimistic writer who truly believed in the old-fashioned values of hard work, fairness and honesty. He practiced the intellectual rigor and precision with language he preached. Most of all he simply did not understand the word *can't*.

Once when I was 10, Dad found me reading Sammy Davis Jr.'s autobiography. He threw a fit. He didn't mind me reading about the man. It was the title of the book, *Yes I Can*, to which he objected. "That presumes there is some chance you can't," he snapped. "Hard work will take you further than you think."

Watching him whip off a column in an hour, I once wondered aloud about this notion of hard work. The column, he explained, was the product of many years of writing and even more years of reading, thinking and talking.

"It may appear easy," he said, "because I have already spent time figuring out what I want to say and learning how to say it."

For the first few years his column focused on the media. Slowly, he branched out.

"I began writing about my parents, my siblings and growing up as an experiment," he wrote in a column. "My purpose was to give more of myself to the process. I find little interest in those columns devoid of any of the humanity of the writer."

Six years after beginning his weekly "Letter from the Editor," Daddy signed on to write a twice-weekly syndicated column. His assistant, Janis Snyder, was convinced it would be impossible to carve time out for a new endeavor. If Jan was skeptical, Nancy, his wife and partner of 20 years, was incredulous.

"Now let's add up your jobs," Daddy quoted her as saying. "You're publisher of a major daily newspaper; that's a full-time job. You're editor; that's another one. You're on enough boards and committees to constitute a third full-time job. . . ."

Nancy had just begun law school, and Dad argued that the column would help fill his time while she studied. They need not have worried. The column was his labor of love.

"Still, you could say my national adventure was born in the doghouse, but I am happy to report it now has a room of its own in our house and our lives," Dad wrote in 1990.

It was for Dad what knitting may be for others. His column was the reward at the end of a busy day, an opportunity to focus his thought and share his vision. It was only in the month before he died that he put it aside, taking a leave "until I have recuperated."

In the hospital only weeks before he died, Daddy and I discussed ways to compile his columns into a book. Noting the columns contained much of what he had taught us, Daddy suggested a family theme.

"Perhaps we could call it *Fathers and Sons*," he said to his daughter with a straight face. I was not amused. Later, we settled on *Letters to My Children*, for there in the columns were the values he wanted us to carry into adulthood.

I had followed my father into journalism. For years we had talked about ways we could collaborate. This book, we thought, might be just the beginning.

Daddy died of cancer in the summer of 1993. Jan and I culled through the thousands of columns he wrote while in Oakland. When I was tired and missing my dad, I dreaded facing the mountain of columns, letters, essays and journals he left behind. Then I could see him, wagging his finger at me. "You'll never get anywhere if you let your emotions stop you from completing your task. I thought I taught you better than that," he admonished.

And so here is the book. It contains the wisdom and humor my brothers and I rely on, the lessons of life—of his life, of ours and, now, we hope, of yours.

DORI J. MAYNARD

Life Back Then

My father brought home an old oak partner's desk shortly before he suggested we might work together. The desk reminded Daddy of one he found when he first walked into the Oakland Tribune Tower at the end of August 1979. He could have bought new office furniture. Instead, Pop poked around the aging tower and found a beat-up, old desk that reminded him of his first newspaper job back in York, Pennsylvania.

Two decades passed between Dad's first job with the *York Gazette and Daily* and the day the Gannett Company named him editor of the *Oakland Tribune*. The *Tribune* was considerably larger than the *Gazette*, but it had a considerably smaller reputation. Back in the 1970s, the *Trib* was called the second worst paper in the country. The description didn't disturb Daddy. It only made him love his new newspaper more, for he knew that it would one day earn national respect. Still, I think even he was surprised by what happened next.

Two years later he left the massive two-sided partner's desk for the sleek mahogany desk in the corner office. Many would marvel at his journey from Bedford Stuyvesant to the publisher's chair and from there to becoming the first black man to own a big-city newspaper.

"The first black . . ." That was a description he hated. He had every cub reporter's dream job—running his own newspaper—and that's what he wanted to talk about. There were other firsts for which he was truly proud. He was the first newspaper executive to use a management-leveraged buyout to purchase his paper. Ours was the first family to buy a newspaper from a newspaper chain.

Inevitably, though, the stories focused on the fact that my father was the first African-American to own a major metropolitan newspaper.

Leaning back in his tall desk chair, with his rich, deep voice, he would patiently explain why it was not useful to dwell on his ethnic origin. That, he thought, implied there was something unusual about a black man who was successful in America. What should be explored, he believed, was not what made Bob Maynard successful, but why were there not more Bob Maynards heading the country's major corporations.

He could view the world no other way. The youngest of six children, my father grew up in a household that worshiped God, brain power and hard work.

His parents, West Indian immigrants, Samuel C. and Robertine Maynard, were determined their children would succeed. There were no excuses for doing otherwise. My grandfather often reminded his children that no one's life can be assured against disaster. The challenge is what you do afterward.

My grandparents were thorough in preparing their children.

They read the books their children were assigned. They quizzed them thoroughly on the school day. They designed individual lessons for their children. When the school books were not good enough, my grandparents explained where the authors had lost their way.

They taught Dad that courage can triumph over the most difficult challenges. It was a lesson that saw him through much of his life. When we learned in 1987 that he had inoperable prostate cancer, it was his faith and courage that got us through the difficult times.

It was as he said before his death: "Fear can often defeat the best of goals, but courage can often accomplish what seems impossible. The folks back in Brooklyn used to tell us small fry that you make your own luck most of the time," he wrote.

Even with Dad's almost annual bouts of radiation treatment and drug therapy, my parents saved the *Oakland Tribune* from extinction. The family drew closer than ever.

At the end of 1992, Dad's health forced the family to sell the newspaper. Not long after the sale, Dad brought this partner's desk into the first floor suite of offices at home.

Though not one for living in the past, Daddy believed strongly that we could learn a great deal about our future by looking back. History, for my father, was both the yardstick for the present and the foundation for the future. It was no wonder he loved that big old partner's desk. He saw history in that heaviness along with a promise for the future.

Daddy's health continued to decline. He spent more and more time in the hospital. In the summer, Pop became partially paralyzed. We made sure one of us was with him 24 hours a day.

Daddy kept working—outlining the projects that needed to be done. We would talk a bit about what we had learned from working together. We had a lot to say. Something always had to be left out.

I don't think I ever told him this story. Years ago I dreamt we were having a vigorous father-daughter discussion. I don't remember the details, only that I yelled at him for neglecting to support me sometimes. Standing in his study, my father looked at me as if I had lost my mind. "History," he said, sweeping his arms open, "I have given you your history."

I woke up puzzled.

The older I get, and again as I watch my two younger brothers grow, I realize what a wonderful gift it is. Like this old desk. Even after refinishing, it is still nothing fancy. But it is a solid foundation. A place where people can create something that may be useful. It took awhile, but I finally understand why Daddy bothered to bring it home.

D.J.M.

A Brick and a Family's History

June 23, 1993—The brick is in a place of high honor. It sits on the mantel in my study beside some of my most treasured mementos. I stare at it, lost in wonder. It has the capacity to inspire me and cause my spirits to soar. It can also sadden me deeply. The brick represents so much that was wonderful, so much that is lost. I feel certain my big brother, wise in his ways, knew he was not presenting me with a simple gift when he mailed me the brick.

Why, I wondered as I opened Edward's package that Saturday morning, is my brother sending me a brick? An old, old brick at that? This brick, his letter explained, is all that is left of the old house in Brooklyn. This was the house with the big dining room where we six children received our most basic and our highest education. This was the house in which my parents entertained their many religious confreres from, quite literally, every corner of the globe.

It was here that a visitor from Australia, watching my mother proudly feeding her infant granddaughter, expressed surprise at seeing the baby drink white milk. For some reason, she had it in her head that a little brown child would better tolerate chocolate milk.

This house produced a dozen degrees, including two earned doctorates by the same fellow, Edward. Starting with my mother's easy grasp of Yiddish and my father's brilliant baritone Italian, the collective linguistic achievements at 804 Marcy Ave. gave the place a faint resemblance to the Delegates' Lounge of the United Nations. This was a house, a friend of mine used to say, where you could get cussed out in 10 different languages without realizing you'd been insulted.

Well, some of us would. Insults were a subject to which we were all keenly attuned. Each one of the six children was ready to mount the ramparts at a moment's notice to defend her or his honor. Evenly divided, three girls and three boys (all the girls were older), we were our own built-in gender battleground. Upon reflection, though, brothers and sisters agree there was surprisingly little gender-based conflict at the Marcy Avenue house.

The reason for this, we have since guessed, is the example set by our parents. They were equal partners in business, running the family and every aspect of their lives. They demonstrated in every expression toward each other a profound mutual respect that had no place for artificial gender tensions. My father's regard for the intellect of his daughters was easily equal to his appreciation for that of his boys. Perhaps, because the girls were older, it might have been higher. I cannot once remember an incident in which he displayed a diminished respect for my sisters based on gender.

Indeed, what was so remarkable about 804 Marcy Ave. is that it was a house filled with love, respect and constant mutual affirmation. To live in that house was to be special. As the youngest, the power of that fact became clear to me at an early age. As I grew up and pursued my dreams in journalism, there were many places along the way at which people asked if I didn't doubt if I could do this thing or that. Or they would ask if I were not afraid of failure. It was not always convenient to explain that if your foundation was built at 804, you were unlikely to spend a great deal of time dwelling on doubt.

That is what continues to inspire me. That is what the brick on the mantel represents to me. I can look at it, shut my eyes and relive one or another of 10,000 rich and enriching memories, reflections I share with my children and, once in a while, with my readers.

The sad aspect of the story of the brick is what happened to 804 Marcy Ave. and the entire neighborhood that surrounded it. My brother tried to save the old house from the wrecker's ball to preserve the venue of such a rich legacy. That was the ultimate impossible dream. What happened on Marcy Avenue is the story of the tragedy of the cities of America.

That neighborhood, once the birthplace of thousands of dreams, became a nightmare. Drugs, crime, decay and neglect turned a once-proud community into a shadow of its former self. Our gracious redbrick town house was torn down to save it from further degradation.

It is a story that has been repeated thousands of times across America. Cities that gave much to many have been allowed to rot away in a wave of social chaos. What has been lost can never be replaced. My siblings and I take what comfort we can from our memories and from a red brick that once was a tangible part of a fabulous foundation.

A Triumph of Neglect and Greed

March 11, 1990—The pink Spaulding Hi-Bouncer ball came off Joey's bat as if it had been fired from a revolver. His "bat" was actually a broomstick. We were kids playing "stickball" in Brooklyn, a game that attempts to imitate baseball under urban conditions. Thus the Spaulding soft rubber ball we insisted on pronouncing "Spauldeen."

On this occasion, the "Spauldeen" was not soft enough. It suddenly hooked foul toward "left field" and arced right into the Walsh's bay window. Our streets were lined with brownstone and red brick, three-story homes. Some had large front windows. Like the Walsh's, for example. Bull's eye. They must have heard the glass falling in Coney Island. Neighbors swarmed onto the street from every direction.

All 12 Walshes were on the scene instantly. They were from Ireland. Then came the Ficarros. They were from Italy. The Gonzales family was out there, too. They were from Puerto Rico. The Nisselsons were from Germany. My mother showed up as if she'd received a telegram. She was from Barbados. In fact, more than half the people crowded around the disaster scene were immigrants or children of immigrants.

They were embracing the American dream of owning a nice home in a good neighborhood. The idea of a bunch of kids breaking a bay window in the American dream was very unpopular. We agreed our work at Mr. Ficarro's grocery would retire our debt and diminish our contrition.

Not long ago, on a gray weekend, I took my three children on a New York City adventure. My daughter, our eldest, escorted her two brothers on a sightseeing tour of museums and shops. Then we had dinner in Greenwich Village near the tiny studio where Dad lived when he ran away from home at 16.

On a drizzly Sunday, we went in search of the old neighborhood, scene of the solid postwar American values for so many thousands of families from all over America and the world. These lovely brownstones had become bombed-out hovels, victims of decades of neglect.

That is the New York story today. The middle class that made the city what it was for so long has deserted an unlivable place. Mostly the desperately poor and the desperately rich remain. The homeless have become the scourge of the city, poking out their grimy hands from dark passages of the subways.

Wall Street, the dream factory of American capitalism, has become the newest icon for greed and reckless pursuit of power for the sake of ego. There they have rewritten the golden rule: Whoever has the gold makes the rules.

No longer thought of as evil, greed has instead become itself a measure of Wall Street success. The more you have, the more you have to have, just to make sure everyone knows you have it all. See New York's leading tabloid luminary of the moment, "The" Donald Trump, as a prime specimen of the new values. Vulgar excess is the only sure evidence of success.

Rich and poor are driven, one by arrogance, the other by despair. The middle class is simply driven out. The schools were the last straw. They can produce only about half of their graduates who are not illiterate, innumerate or both.

Much as I might decry the loss of a neighborhood I wanted to share with my children, the loss of the schools brings real tears. New York City once had the nation's premier public education system. It was created by the Great Depression, in part.

By 1936, New York contained more unemployed Ph.D.s and M.A.s than anyone knew what to do with. New York schools went on a recruiting binge, then locked them in with tenure, generous health benefits and an excellent pension program. They are now almost all retired. For many reasons, successors as talented and dedicated were not, by and large, recruited to replace the class of 1936.

The city and its schools sank in time under the weight of generations of corruption, indifference and blinding self-interest. Once surely America's greatest city, and its largest, the "Big Apple" has become the fulfillment of one of its harshest Depression-era epitaphs. "New York," the saying went, "is a sucked lemon." Its newest mayor, David Dinkins, has my sincere condolences.

My only consolation, as I reflect on the day we mourned Mr. Walsh's window, is that I was fortunate enough to grow up in New York when it was a place of urban eminence. At least I can tell my children I knew it when.

The Life and Death of James Baldwin

December 6, 1987—Louie, one of my neighbors in Greenwich Village, talked incessantly about his idol, a virtually unknown writer named James Baldwin. He lived in Paris at the time, Louie said, but he would return to New York one day. "You must meet him," he repeated often.

We were writers, painters, actors and musicians living in a tenement apartment house, like many others, over small shops and bluesy little nightclubs in the old Village. Our building carried the aura of being the last earthly residence of the great jazz musician Charlie Parker. He must have died a very poor man.

I have always thought of the Village of that era as a great, open university, a beehive of unorganized—to say nothing of disorganized—creative intellectual ferment.

The period was the mid-'50s, the heyday of the silent generation. Save for the Village, there were few such refuges of the unconventional. San Francisco's North Beach, Chicago's Hyde Park and Provincetown, Mass., were among the others.

One evening around a quarter to eight, just as I was fixing a meager meal on my Sterno stove, I heard a pounding on my door. I hoped it wasn't the landlord. The Sterno stove was against house rules. It was also my last stand against starvation.

I peaked through a crack in the door and saw Louie and another figure. I opened the door to find in my hallway a small dark man with large brown eyes standing beside Louie.

As we stood frozen, Louie stepped slightly behind the stranger. Then he lifted behind the visitor's head a copy of a book with the man's picture on the cover. I squinted in the dark and made out the words, *Notes of a Native Son.*

James Baldwin was home from Paris. The year then was 1957. He had already published a novel, *Go Tell It on the Mountain,* and now he had come out with this new book of essays. Still, he was unknown to all but a few Americans. In the peculiar racial irony of those times, Baldwin was better known in France.

We talked that night, and on several others, about the lonely isolation of the black writer in America. He was convinced that if one told the truth, it would be welcome to neither black nor white Americans. Such were the painful hypocrisies of those times as he perceived them.

Within a few short years, as the civil rights movement rose toward its crest, so did the popularity of James Baldwin. It fell to him, as pessimistic as he had been, to provide the great literary bridge between black and white America.

Martin Luther King, Malcolm X and the other celebrated black voices of that era were orators. As such, their words swayed only those of the masses who chose to listen to them. That meant many blacks, but virtually no whites, understood the message of the movement.

Then came Baldwin with *The Fire Next Time* and *Another Country*. In essence, Baldwin became the literary corollary to Martin Luther King. He preached the same basic message in piercing prose to white America: "Why do you need a nigger?"

Where King's message rang in the ear, Baldwin's could be held in the hand, read and reread, taught and discussed in English literature and social studies courses.

Baldwin returned to exile in France, persuaded a black writer could have no effect on the mind of white America. Yet he had a revolutionary effect on the thinking of a generation of his countrymen.

Oddly, perhaps because he remained an exile, Baldwin appears never to have fully realized how profoundly his country had changed in the 30 years since the publication of *Notes of a Native Son*.

Thus the fetching irony that so often accompanies a literary life: James Baldwin died in France the other day at 63 without ever fully knowing how much he had caused his nation to repair toward the goals of his dreams. He was an exile who gave his country a greater gift than either he or we took time to recognize.

All of which is nothing more than another way of saying the life and death of James Baldwin remind us that the conflict over race remains America's most enduring dilemma.

What Was It about the '50s?

January 25, 1987—It was against the rules of our religious household to go to the movies. My parents believed Hollywood perverted the minds of the young. In some ways, looking back, my brothers and sisters and I were lucky. We read more than most of our friends.

All the same, the prohibition against movies was a drag on our social lives. We didn't know what our friends were talking about when the subject of the latest hit films came up. I remember the day my friends tempted me to disobey and slip into the Fox Theater in downtown Brooklyn.

On this occasion, it had been easy to tempt me. The movie was *To Hell and Back*, about the war adventures of Audie Murphy. For a schoolboy in the 1950s, that was worth the risk of being punished. Audie Murphy was the most decorated hero of World War II. To the kids of my neighborhood, he was an almost godlike figure.

The memory of that movie returns because of something else that seems to be happening to us in the waning years of the decade of the 1980s. There is a fervent revival of interest in the artifacts of the 1950s. Soon I'll be able see most of the movies and television hits that I missed 30 years ago.

Nat King Cole's old hits were on the radio the other day. We have already had a television film of the life of President Eisenhower. There are new biographies of two towering figures of the 1950s who became heroes of mine, Edward R. Murrow and Langston Hughes.

Nice as it is to catch up with your own adolescence 30 years later, this sudden revival of interest in the 1950s raises some serious questions for me. What, exactly, are we searching for when we become so enamored of the decade of the 1950s?

It was at once a simple time and a tortured time. The decade began with a terrible war in Korea, one we could neither win nor afford to lose. The Korean stalemate created a bitter frustration in America that helped lead to a dark chapter, McCarthyism.

The '50s was also the era in which we first learned to fear the bomb. We had air-raid shelters, air-raid drills and doleful air-raid sirens, any one of which could be "the real thing."

This pervasive fear of attack from without and of subversion from within brought a grim and pallid patina to our public affairs. No one has developed a full explanation for the reason we became "the silent generation," but I have often wondered about the role of fear.

It was not just the big fears of the bomb and communism. Fear invaded some of our most basic and private concerns. It was fear of parental censure, fear of "fooling around" and getting your girlfriend pregnant. Women were afraid to express themselves, lest men disapprove. Blacks, especially in the South, were afraid to assert their rights.

In other words, to use a term we would use a great deal in the next decade, the '50s was an "uptight" time in many respects.

What the decade had going for it, and the two reasons I suspect it is being revived, were both of profound importance. First, there was a clear moral code that dominated the behavior of my generation.

Family was the center of our universe. Mutual respect was the order of the day. Values meant more than money. The honor code was in place: "I will not lie, cheat or steal, or tolerate those who do."

Having seen what happens to our society and its institutions when those values are discarded, many Americans want to see them revived. I don't think many people hanker for another witch hunt, although some civil libertarians think the drug wars come close.

The search is for a simpler time when behavior was more predictable and our value system had more universal allegiance.

Oddly, the other profound feature of the 1950s was the beginnings of a cultural explosion. Movies exploded in color, even in three dimensions. Television captured the living room. Rhythm and blues set the stage for rock. Jazz came out of the basement onto the concert hall stages.

In many ways, the '50s prepared us for who we are now. Perhaps that is why we go back. Perhaps we are looking in our past in search of our future. That is in part, I suppose, because politically and culturally, the '80s so far stand for nothing in particular.

York, Pa.—An Affair of the Heart

May 27, 1984—York, Pennsylvania, is 50 miles north of Baltimore, 25 miles west of Lancaster and the heart of Pennsylvania Dutch country, 25 miles east of Gettysburg, the great Civil War battlefield, and 25 miles south of Harrisburg, the state capital.

"As you can see," the old local joke goes, "give or take a few miles and York (pop. 50,000) might have been one heck of a town."

Right off, I'll admit my prejudice. I happen to think it is one heck of a town without being any closer than it is to some of its famous neighbors.

But why would a Brooklyn-born-and-raised lover of cities take any time at all to extol the virtues of a small farm town in the middle of the rolling hills of south-central Pennsylvania?

Why, indeed. Therein lies a tale.

The old *York Gazette and Daily* was an unusual newspaper by almost any standard. It was a tabloid newspaper made up in vertical column style that caused it to look like a scaled down version of the *New York Times*.

If it looked unusual, what was in it was even more remarkable. It was the most comprehensive small-town daily you could hope to see. It was filled with local happenings, social events, world news, national news and excellent local sports coverage.

The owner of the newspaper, the late Josiah W. Gitt, was a millionaire lawyer with his own set of rules for publishing a newspaper.

Because J.W. Gitt's father had died from acute alcoholism, he refused to take ads for liquor, wine and beer. Because he believed cigarettes were harmful to health (long before any surgeon general's report), he refused to accept cigarette advertising. Because he believed patent medicines were no good, he refused to take ads for aspirin and bromides.

When the editor of the newspaper, Jim Higgins, was given the assignment of writing the editorials, a chore J.W. kept for himself until his 80th year, Higgins asked how he should approach his new duties.

"Have you ever read the Sermon on the Mount?" J.W. asked his young editor.

Jim said he had.

"Have you ever read the Ten Commandments?" the old man continued.

Jim said he had read them.

"How about the Bill of Rights?" the old man asked.

"Yes," Higgins replied, "I've read that, too."

The old man fixed him with a stern stare and said, "Well, just go write 'em."

Not too long after my 20th birthday, I found myself in the electrifying atmosphere of the newsroom of the *York Gazette*. Jim Higgins read one article I'd written, decided I had "a fair amount of promise" and put me to work covering the police beat in a town that had almost no crime.

During that time, Michael Harrington wrote a book about poverty in the U.S. called *The Other America*. Jim Higgins sent me a copy with a note saying, simply, "How do the poor fare in York?"

Three months later, I presented my editors with a six-part series on poverty in York County, and how it compared with poverty elsewhere in America.

It was printed without fanfare, but the impact was gratifying. Various groups in town began holding seminars on poverty. More important, several influential citizens set about finding ways to remedy some of the conditions described in those articles.

Over the next four years, I was immersed in the question, What makes people poor in America? I was given freedom to explore the impact on poverty of education, housing, transportation, intergroup and family relations and anything else that animated my imagination.

One night I remarked to one of my editors that it was unusual to have the opportunity to study so many urban questions in such a small environment. I'll never forget his response:

"This place is like every other place, just smaller. Here we can examine in microcosm those things you knew and saw in New York City in macrocosm. If you can understand them and write about them here, you will be able to do it anywhere."

All the same, we also had to scramble to cover school board meetings and county zoning board meetings. We sometimes were too busy to examine the distinctions between the microcosm and macrocosm of much of anything.

It was all part of an extraordinary training, one in which the newspaper insisted on a wide scope of thought from its reporters and editors. The publisher gave the stories space and editorial support.

The old man sold the newspaper just before he died in 1970. The successor bears almost no resemblance to the old *York Gazette*.

Twenty years later, the townspeople remember those stories that discovered the poor in their midst. They kindly invited me back last week for a doctorate at the commencement at York College of Pennsylvania. It was an opportunity for them, and for me, to remember those exciting days.

York, Pennsylvania? It's one heck of a town.

The Education of a Young Journalist

May 4, 1986—The Greyhound bus shuddered against the wind and sheets of spring rain. It followed the winding roads across the Pennsylvania Dutch countryside. The rolling hills were rich green, punctuated by broad patches of freshly turned earth.

That bus ride, exactly 25 years ago this week, took me from the uncertain world of a freelance journalist in New York City to my first job on a daily newspaper in the middle of the farm country.

My excitement so took me over that my first act upon arriving on the job in the newsroom was to break out with a huge nosebleed. I'd never had one before, and haven't since.

To say I experienced some culture shock between my native city and Pennsylvania Dutch country would be an understatement. I moved from a city in which people often lived next door to each other for 20 years without speaking, to a town where everybody seemed to know everybody else.

In fact, the first thing I discovered about small-town life is that people often know each other too well. When I rented my first apartment, I owned no furniture. I borrowed a friend's sleeping bag until I could afford to buy a bed.

About a week into my stay, I met one of my new neighbors, an elderly woman with a long memory and keen eyesight. She introduced herself and asked how I liked my new apartment. I said it was just fine, terrific in fact.

"And the floors," she said with a sly smile. "How do you like the floors?"

As I was to learn, the small town has few secrets. That fact turned out to be a blessing for a young journalist. There were stories aplenty to be done because there was always somebody, somewhere, who knew where the body was buried.

That discovery was tempered in a short time by another realization. The small town is where a young journalist learns the impact his words can have on people's lives. In such close quarters, the effects of unpleasant disclosures on people's reputations can be immediate, devastating and irrevocable.

Under such circumstances, you learn how precious a reputation is, and how fragile. We were taught to write with accuracy and sensitivity. One day, as I was working on a "barn-burner" of an investigative story, an editor sat me down.

"You remind me," he said, "of the kid who took apart his toy drum because he just had to know where the noise came from. Be curious, but also be careful."

Sometimes in those beginning days, I was not curious enough. I went to the scene of a fire in which a family was burned out. I had graphic detail, and was sure I had done a bang-up reporting job until I returned to the office.

As I was sputtering various minute detail to my city editor, she rather calmly asked, "And what did you say this family's name was?" I had everything but that. The fire chief proved that day to be part of the journalistic training process.

When I told him of my plight, he added insult to injury. He said with a straight face he had forgotten to obtain the name also. "Reckon you're just going to have to ride back out there and ask them yourself, son."

In 25 years since, I cannot remember failing to ask the names and proper spellings of people's names. More than that, I learned through covering fires to think about the ramifications of the news for others.

After another, even more spectacular fire, I rushed back to the office fairly dancing with excitement. As I bubbled over with details, an editor sat listening with a pensive look on his face. It was a look that said he did not share my enthusiasm.

Finally, he said, "Ever stop to think that great story was some family's home a few hours ago?"

At the end of six years of such lessons and many others, I found myself leaving for larger precincts. Still I cannot imagine anything I would rather have done than to have lived in a small American community and to have felt its pulse and special rhythms.

Odd, just thinking about it, the hardest part is realizing all that happened 25 years ago.

At Home

There was something different about his voice. It had a richer resonance. "Have you met my children?" he asked, drawing the last word out a barely noticeable halfbeat longer then necessary. "Have you met my children?" he repeated, extending his arm to where my brother and I were standing nearby on a Georgetown street in Washington, D.C.

My brother was 3 and I was 16. Our parents had just gotten married. This was the first chance our father had to say it. It was clear he would have been happy to spend the entire afternoon saying "Have you met my children?"

A few years later our younger brother was born. Our father now had even more opportunity to talk about "my children." When all three of us were talking at the same time, he shortened it to "Children!" At those times his voice was not filled with joy. Even then, he wanted his family by his side. Family, Dad once wrote, "is the central nervous system of society." Personally, he always said, it is "essential to my being."

Yet on that crisp fall day in Washington, D.C., it had been a long time since he had a family of his own. Estranged from many members of his childhood family and long divorced from my mother, Dad had concentrated on his career. After more than a decade on the road covering the national scene during the 1960s and early 1970s for the *Washington Post*, Daddy and *New York Times* reporter Nancy Hicks were married. It was time for Dad to create a family of his own.

The change in family life since my father's childhood has been dramatic. My grandmother worked at home. Nancy worked as copublisher of the *Oakland Tribune*. My brothers and cousin also worked at the *Tribune*. My vacations and some of my weekends were devoted to helping my father research and prepare for his speaking engagements and television appearances.

Unlike the stereotypical "Leave It to Beaver" family of the 1950s, ours is one of those new-fangled amalgamated families. We are more like the 1970s "Brady Bunch" but with fewer children, more color and arguments that take longer than a half hour to resolve.

Dad did not fight the changes that took place between the days of his childhood and the days of his parenthood. Instead, as he wrote in an outline for a book on fatherhood: "To preserve the family, we must learn to adjust to those changes and shape those to come as best we can."

That meant we ignored the words that suggest only partial and tentative alliances, such as the "step" word or the "half" word. Instead, we concentrated on the rituals and minutiae that bind a family.

Every year the three of us asked Dad what he wanted for Christmas. Every Christmas, without fail, he would say the same thing, "All I want is my three children home with me." We bought him presents anyway.

We all are political junkies. It is rare any of us miss the Sunday-morning talk shows or "Nightline." When time permitted, and Dad and I had not seen each other in a while, we watched the shows together while we were on the telephone. During commercials we critiqued the various positions advocated on the show.

When Dad's health worsened and I moved back home, neither time nor tradition could ease the tensions sparked by five people in constant contact. Daddy always corrected us in midsentence. Nancy nagged me about what I wear. My older brother liked to poke me in my ribs. My younger brother "borrowed" my older brother's belongings.

One evening after expressing exasperation over too much family fun, I was surprised to hear a familiar note of pride in my father's voice. "But Dori," he said, sounding much as he had more than two decades ago in Washington, D.C., "don't you know that's what a family is all about. They get on your nerves, and you keep them anyway." He laughed his big laugh, and we went back to watching the news.

D.J.M.

It's a Joy to Learn from Your Children

July 12, 1981—This actually happened last April in Chicago. It is the kind of incident that flips back to mind occasionally and demands to be thought about. My wife and I were attending a newspaper publishers' convention. As I was riding down in the elevator one morning with several strangers, an old friend got on the elevator.

"How's the baby?" my friend asked.

"Fine," I said, "He's teething and beginning to talk."

By now we were at the ground floor. One of the publishers on the elevator turned to me as we were emerging and said:

"You mean to say you have a baby, an infant?"

I admitted it.

"I don't think I even want to know you," he said. With those words, he vanished into the crowd. As he departed, he left me for all time with the memory of the look of sheer panic in his eyes at the idea of someone suddenly finding himself as a middle-aged father of an infant. The look in his eyes suggested that if he were given a choice of a coronary or an infant, he would need some time to think it over.

It was too bad, I thought, that he did not give me an opportunity to tell him more about it. I wanted to tell him about breakfast the previous Sunday morning.

The baby and I had come down to the kitchen at about 7:30. We followed our usual routine. As I handed him each item, I would say the name and he would try to repeat, "Toast," "Milk," "Spoon," "Apple," and so forth. Some of the words came out accurately, but since the little dude still did not have all his teeth, some words were less clear than others. He was 17 months old then.

As our one-word game with breakfast was proceeding, his 10-year-old brother came downstairs with his notebook and a pencil. He had a long face and troubled eyes. It was Sunday and he had a problem. He had won the permission of his teacher the previous week to take a two-day trip to Washington, D.C., with his mother. My wife had to deliver a speech and she invited our 10-year-old to make the trip. The problem was teacher, mother and son had made a deal. He could only go if he agreed upon his return to write a report on what he had seen and heard.

Now it was time to pay the piper. He had to finish his report and words were slow in coming. So, in between giving the baby breakfast and helping him learn one word at a time, I began helping the 10-year-old frame a few simple declarative sentences.

Just at that moment, the telephone rang. Our 22-year-old college senior was calling from Vermont. She is working on a senior honors thesis in history, and it happened to be on a subject I once thought I knew something about. She was calling for advice on how to proceed with a particular aspect of her investigation. I tried to give her a few leads and pointers while keeping the toast and the apples flowing for the baby and the sentences about the Washington trip flowing for the 10-year-old.

There was something in that moment that filled me with a sense of pleasure I cannot adequately describe. But if the publisher on the elevator had given me an opportunity, I think I would have told him he need not feel such panic about being middle-aged and having to deal with the young. I think I would have told him that dealing with children is often the most invigorating tonic of youth I know.

The tonic is the challenge my wife and I feel at having to meet the needs of children with such diverse interests and at such different stages of human and intellectual development.

On the day our youngest was born, I called my brother in New York to tell him he had a new nephew. He is a psychoanalyst, so it was quite natural that he would want to know how I was feeling about being a middle-aged father of an infant.

I said it all felt fine except I did have a moment of panic wondering whether I would be up to teaching how to throw a forward pass all over again at about age 50. My brother laughed.

"Don't worry about it," he said. "That's why you have the other guy. He can do the throwing and you can critique. Don't forget the key element of family life is division of labor."

The labor may be divisible, but the joy of watching children learn and grow is indivisible. As on that Sunday morning, I cannot tell which aspect of watching the children grow gives me more pleasure. I remember when the oldest child, now the young woman in college, was the age of our infant. I remember being impatient for her to grow old enough for what I would then call a "real" conversation. One word at a time gave me no particular pleasure then. I remember ruminating over a desire for her to become old enough for us to discuss "abstract concepts."

For whatever reasons, that seems almost unimportant now with the baby. If anything, I find myself favoring his infancy and those simple discoveries so precious to the very young. Each time he lifts his head to the sky and points and squeals, "airpane," I resist the voice within that wants to tell him how to pronounce the word correctly. "Airplane" will come soon enough.

That and more. Soon he will be teaching me. One day last fall, my wife and I took the boys to Candlestick for a 49ers game. The stadium announcer said a particular running back for the visiting team had entered the game. My 10-year-old became excited. Why? I asked. "Oh, Dad," he said, "this guy gained more yards in college than any other running back in the history of his school." I nodded. "Of course," I said. "Never heard of him."

It went that way all season. Whether at the Coliseum watching the Raiders or at Candlestick watching the 49ers, my guide became my 10-year-old. He taught me things about pro football that I might have known when I was 10, but did not know now.

And so it is with the college senior. When she began her honors thesis, I knew more about her chosen topic than she did, but it was only a few weeks before she was calling home with fascinating tidbits of information and genuine insights that were new to me. As she grew into the subject, she soon began to command it and to teach me all manner of things about the subject that I had not known. It made me feel so fortunate to have the pleasure of being taught by my children.

So if the man on the elevator had stopped to think about it, he would have understood why I am not panicked by the thought of a new young child. Every day, he gives my wife and me a new gift of discovery that leaves us again and again in awe of the wonder and the beauty of nature's magical powers.

It is a joy to contemplate having such a continuous education and the rewards and challenges of helping children grow while they help their parents grow.

One evening, we were discussing this with some friends over dinner. One of them said, "Great. Maybe in 10 years or so you guys can have another one." I felt a warm smile forming, but just then I looked over at my wife.

For some reason, she wasn't smiling.

A New Lawyer in the Family

June 14, 1987—This is by way of accuracy in consumer labeling: If you find some ghastly error in syntax or reasoning in this essay, I should explain it in advance.

Ordinarily, the instant I finish a piece, I take it downstairs to the study of my Great Clarifier. She reads each word for its possible other meaning and each sentence in search of ambiguity and potential confusion.

This is something of a first, a piece the Great Clarifier in my life will not have seen before you did. She is in a mad dash to complete law school these days. Graduation is today.

That is one reason, albeit not the best one, for the absence of her rigor on my behalf. Besides, this column is about her. It would not be fair to ask her to search for its flaws. No doubt, though, given the chance, she would find them.

I can imagine few experiences in life quite as remarkable or as inspiring as witnessing the three-year flowering of a legal mind. That is especially so when that mind belongs to your own spouse.

Three years ago, a good friend caught wind of the news my wife was entering law school. He gave me a bit of advice. I should say first that a lot of people had lots of advice, most of it not memorable. His was:

"You had better be prepared. Law school changes the way people think. There's no easy way to explain it, but you will soon see what I mean." I protested that after all our years together, I was pretty sure I knew how my wife thought.

"You just don't understand," he persisted. "They acquire a different way of thinking and a different way of talking. You'll see."

His wife, like mine, had returned to academia years after her undergraduate training and while still raising a family. If I had difficulty grasping his point three years ago, I have none now. A witness to the process must stand in awe of the intellectual undertaking of law school.

Our whole family feels enriched by watching Mom go through law school. Our eldest, a New England journalist, says her mother's accomplishments make her a firm believer that any serious dream is possible if you are willing to put your heart and your head into it. That is not a bad lesson to learn early in a career.

Our teenage son witnessed firsthand the transforming value of learning a discipline such as law. He saw a living example of academic rigor and its reward.

I have no doubts the seven-year-old would be much less argumentative if he had not watched his mother studying the law. At dinner some evenings, it seemed as if he were intuitively challenging her just to see how she would respond.

We managed to maintain dinner as the daily family event throughout. That meal could still be somewhat unsettling. The law student would occasionally hold forth with some doctrine. One evening, she went on at length articulating a rule she was studying in her intellectual property course. It became more and more complicated as she proceeded. At last, she ended with a flourish. Dead silence.

Finally, the teenager looked over at his mom and declared, "Heavy." The littlest guy, not to be outdone, intoned, "Yeah, Mom, heavy!" The table erupted in laughter.

As time went on, I began to understand the point my friend had tried to make three years ago. I experienced it most personally in the Great Clarifier's approach to my column. She began picking up on gaps in the reasoning process neither of us might have noticed before law school.

Moreover, as I listen to her discussing the issues of the day, I can see how legal training helps her spot the pivotal issues. It also helps in examining the obscure as well as the obvious in controversy.

It is easier for me to understand now why lawyers are such a dominant force in our culture. Almost no issue is ever absolutely resolved. Give me a fresh set of facts, says the law, and I'll bring you yet another way to look at the most sacred of doctrines.

I suppose you can get an education on legal education, if nothing else, when you see your spouse go through the rigorous rites of passage into the legal fraternity. I wouldn't have missed it for anything.

Soon again, I hope, I will have the benefit of her eagle, marvelously legal, eye on my work. I just hope I can still afford it.

The Duties of Parents to Children

December 11, 1988—The dining room table at which my brothers and sisters and I alternately studied and frolicked grew tense one evening. My mother had been to see one of my brother's teachers. My mom and dad came into the dining room to say they were not pleased with what she had heard.

Since my mother never made a secret of her displeasure, we were all treated to a meticulous recounting of her visit. She spared us no detail, including how the teacher was attired and the manner of his demeanor.

My brother made the mistake of losing his temper and demanding to know what difference it made to anyone else whether one of his teachers and he got along. "Ain't nobody's business but my own," he said, paraphrasing a popular Billie Holiday song title of the day.

"Ah, there's where you're mistaken," my parents almost sang out in unison. There followed one of the most memorable evenings of our childhood. My father and mother, pushing aside all the textbooks, dictionaries and homework projects, took command of the dining room table.

"You have to understand," my father began, "that we cannot cease our interest in your life from the time you are born until the day you walk out that door to form a family of your own." I remember my mother chiming in, "Until then, everything you do is our business."

In a statement of parental philosophy that might seem old-fashioned today, my parents told us they had an obligation to see to our progress by making sure we had "the tools of success," as they put it.

Those tools, they argued, were first and foremost the correct attitude toward life's challenges. Apparently, one of the reasons my brother and his teacher were not getting along is that my brother was already familiar with the material the teacher was so laboriously reviewing.

"You can always learn more," I remember my father admonishing. He held forth for several minutes on the importance of making every life situation, including boring teachers, into learning opportunities.

At that point, my mother did a hilarious imitation of the fussy attitude and manner of the teacher. As we all howled and doubled over laughing, my brother saw humor in his predicament with his teacher for the first time.

Suddenly, we had a family pet name for that teacher and a challenge to see who could do the best imitation. What had been a potential source of tension became instead a source of great family amusement and moral support for my brother.

That, my mother would later acknowledge with some pride, had been the whole idea. That is what parents are supposed to do, she would say. "You might not always like the medicine, but it's our job to keep all of you on a healthy path if we can."

As we reflect in adulthood on the way my parents ran their household, my siblings and I have to wonder how well mom and pop would have prevailed in an era such as this one. Almost certainly it would have been more difficult to keep track of so many aspects of the lives of six active children.

But the core of their philosophy affected all of us to some degree. Each of us has tried to convey to our children the essence of the message of obligation to help our children find the "tools of success" in the uses of their own minds.

That message seems as valid today as ever. It simply sounds oddly old-fashioned to hear those terms in a time when there are so many messages of a different sort bombarding kids from every direction. The authentic ones endure, I suppose, but only with difficulty. Great difficulty.

A Basic Question about Drug Use

May 8, 1988—My parents played a subtle game at the dinner table with their six children that was designed, I now realize, to embed certain values and principles indelibly in our minds. No student of detective fiction would fail to recognize the technique. It's called "good cop, bad cop." One night Mom would play the toughie; on another occasion it would be Pop.

One memorable evening in the spring of 1950, the subject at the dinner table was drugs, heroin in particular. One of the local papers, the *Daily News*, had a hard-hitting piece on an insidious wave of addiction that was sweeping through the schools of New York City. It painted a terrifying picture of an unfamiliar problem for our cloistered Brooklyn environment.

My dad determined that all of us had read the story and understood its implications. Then the cop show began. "What would you do," my mother asked my father at the other end of the table, "if you discovered one of your children was using heroin?" Given the nature of the question, there was something oddly sweet, almost dulcet in her tone.

My father laid down his knife and fork on his plate and folded his hands on the table before him. He looked first at my mother and then made eye contact with each of us before saying a word. Then, in a low, slow voice, he said, "I would kill him . . . or her."

To this day, almost four decades later, I still feel a creeping chill at the nape of my neck as I recall the steel in my father's voice that night. No one of us doubted he meant what he said, literally. He was a big, strapping man with a temper that rarely showed itself. But we knew what it was like to see him angry. The notion that any of us would use hard drugs was never discussed again in our home. None of us wanted to die.

Over the years, as the drug problem has grown from a relatively isolated big-city phenomenon to a national epidemic, I keep wondering the same thing I wondered that night at dinner. Why do people feel the need to obliterate their brains with powerful, mind-altering substances?

By latest estimates of the law enforcement community, Americans will spend $130 billion this year on cocaine, heroin, pot, speed and a host of other illicit substances. That is a staggering amount of escape.

What on earth has happened to the minds and the wills of the young of our society that drives such an awesome commerce? What are our young people hiding from in clouds of instantly and insidiously addictive crack?

This is no limited phenomenon of the poor in the ghettos and barrios. This is a sickness that has spread to Wall Street, Hollywood, and up and down Main Street USA. Cocaine is everywhere. The drug gangs of Los Angeles now peddle their wares in small towns in Oregon, Washington and other quiet, homogeneous settings.

This great national challenge cannot be met by asking schoolchildren to shout slogans, such as "Just say no." Something deep and dangerous is coursing through our towns and cities. It is clear that our present policies and programs are having no measurable effect on the problem.

Since Jesse Jackson made drugs a priority of his presidential campaign, politicians have been jumping on the bandwagon, inveighing against the dangers of drugs. There is no evidence that any of them has an answer to that most important of questions: Why? For heaven's sake, why?

Neither Congress nor the administration seems to have any idea what is making millions of Americans spend billions of dollars on soul-numbing substances and illicit euphoria. That, it seems to me, is the fatal flaw in any antidrug program. How do we stop something whose cause we do not understand?

The next president and Congress have an obligation, if we are to become serious about this matter, to ask those deeper questions about behavior and choice. That is indispensable before we can map a real assault on the demand side of this disturbing equation.

Meanwhile, I know what made my brothers and sisters and me cross the street when we saw the drug dealers coming. We knew we faced certain death from my father, a point my parents made just once. That was enough.

From Childhood to Parenthood

June 30, 1988—One of our favorite games at home was called "overhearing." My parents and their friends would gather for serious talk in the upstairs parlor. My brothers and sisters and I, supposedly asleep, would take up positions on the stairs above the parlor and "overhear" what the big people said.

The older kids were in a position to know more of the meaning of the old folks' dialogue. Most of the conversation was beyond me, the youngest. My presence was more as solidarity with the five older kids. During one such foray against the privacy of my parents, I was astonished to hear my father talking about us.

"Raising them is wonderful," I remember him saying, "but, unfortunately, they grow up." I recall the tingle of shock I felt at those words. What could he possibly mean?

We played ball that summer in the huge backyard behind the Brooklyn redbrick. I took notice for the first time of how much fun my father had romping and playing with his children.

We played a form of backyard softball that had to weave its way around my mother's "Victory" garden. She started it as a patriotic act during World War II, as did millions, and clung to it for years after. It was a beautiful, lush garden, but it made for a bizarre baseball "diamond." First base was the edge of a clump of radish, as I recall, and third was a cornstalk.

My father grew up playing a mean game of cricket in Barbados. Watching him attempt to swing a baseball bat from that convoluted cricketer's stance was such a hilarious sight one of my brothers considered charging the neighbors admission.

It was much less humorous if you happened to be the pitcher and my father actually got hold of the ball and lined it straight back to the mound. The only thing more terrifying was when Pop attempted to pitch, modifying the cricketer's "bowling" motion. The ball seemed suddenly to appear at the plate from someplace behind second base.

Those cross-cultural softball games with my dad came back to mind the other day and helped me understand better the rueful statement he made about how fast his offspring grew up. It was an evening at the start of summer, when all the balls and gloves and bats emerged, as they do each year, from winter hibernation.

My two older children have long since outgrown either an interest or a desire to be coached in baseball by their dad. The oldest is a journalist in the East, and her once "little" brother is taller than his dad. He's also a better and more knowledgeable athlete than I was at his age.

So there we were, just the smallest one and me, with our own little baseball game. On our lawn, the "diamond" is no less bizarre than my parents' backyard. An agapanthus bush serves dutifully as first base, and a clump of roses is the best we can manage for a left-field foul pole.

I had forgotten there is a special moment for children when they cease to wish to be treated as children when they play ball. They want to emulate the professionals. It happened to me again the other night, for the third and—I guess—last time.

I picked up the baseball, stepped to the mound and began the small child's underhand pitch I have been serving up to my little one now for several seasons. He stepped out of the batter's box, stood to his full height and demanded, "Dad, would you please pitch to me overhand . . . please."

Well, there it is, I thought: Now I have no trouble understanding what my father meant when he said "unfortunately" children grow up. It had been so much a child's game with him before. Suddenly, right there on the front lawn, he made a declaration of manhood at all of eight: Don't pitch to me like a baby, he seemed to say. Pitch to me like a grown-up.

My mind went back to that evening on the stairs. They say that if we live long enough, we become our parents. Maybe so. Maybe not altogether. But I think, in any event, we do come to understand them better.

For a Son, Father's Day
Can Be Every Day

June 20, 1982—The paper is what I remember most vividly. It was a rich onionskin, deep with texture and yet translucent. Years later, when my father's map-tracing exercises began to make more sense to me, I decided to see if I could find some of that onionskin paper, but I never could. I decided I never would. I decided the quality of that paper has been so embellished by time and sentiment that it could never exist in my adult reality and be as rich and fine as it was when I was five.

On Sunday evenings, after a long day of church services, my father would hoist me onto his lap and we would open one of myriad geographical reference books in our library. We would trace the countries of the world on the onionskin. I always thought I was picking the continent and the country we would draw that evening, but now I am not so sure.

The reason I am not sure is this: Of the dozens of countries we drew together, it strikes me now that a remarkable number of them turned out to be on the continent of Africa. In those days, virtually all of that continent was under colonial rule, so the countries bore such names as Anglo Egyptian Sudan and French Equatorial Guinea.

My father would spread the onionskin over the map and use a wooden clothespin with a spring in it to hold the paper steady on the page. Then he would take my tiny hand in his huge, callused palm. Together we would guide the pencil over the page and follow the outlines of the mountain ridges, the rivers and the lakes.

Because of his impeccable attention to detail, it might have taken us two hours sometimes just to make the outline of a topographically challenging country. As we became more deeply absorbed in the work, my father would talk casually about that country, its history and language.

"Let me hear you say Tagalog," he would say as our hands formed the outlines of the Philippine Islands. "Look," he would say, "it says here that almost no outside explorer has ever been among the Tasaday of Mindanao. We know almost nothing about them except that they exist." Soon we would be on to some other place, but a portion of my mind stayed behind to ponder the mysterious Mindanao Tasaday.

One night we traced the Nile its full length and then he read me a poem about rivers before bundling me off to bed. Years later, I discovered Langston Hughes and found the poem my father read in his deep baritone:

My soul has grown deep like the rivers
I bathed in the Euphrates when dawns were young
I built my hut near the Congo and it lulled me to sleep
I looked upon the Nile and raised the pyramids above it . . .
I've known rivers:
Ancient, dusky rivers

The other morning, my two-year-old boy discovered my globe and began spinning it. As he did so, the memories of my father's map-tracing exercises came rushing back. With the recollection came the realization of the powerful impact of those Sunday nights on my life.

I cannot claim to remember much of the evening church services that preceded them, but I can remember portions of those conversations as though they happened yesterday. As my two-year-old and I sat on the floor spinning the globe, I became struck afresh with the impact of fathers on sons.

Looking back, I suppose my father could have been drawing clowns or spaceships. It hardly mattered what the subject was. What mattered was that loving attention, that devotion to detail, the involvement in an intimate search for shared knowledge.

When I was in high school, I made a decision my friends resented. It was the habit of my Brooklyn neighborhood for teenage boys to find themselves under a basketball hoop from the time school let out until dusk. In eighth grade, I broke with the crowd and headed for my room. I had just discovered Langston Hughes and Countee Cullen. My father had given me an old Underwood typewriter.

Exactly how it came out this way, I don't know, but I remember deciding my heroes would be writers instead of basketball stars. My schoolmates missed no opportunity to let me know what they thought of a Brooklyn street dude who would rather read poets than shoot baskets.

It made no difference what they said: I was determined to master those poets and that typewriter. I attribute that determination to many things my mother and father did and said, but I am struck in retrospect by the feeling of warmth and security in my dad's lap. I associated learning with love and strength from then on. Basketball couldn't match it for excitement.

All that set me to wondering how many fathers think about the effects of their every unconscious move on their sons. My wife and I watched our two-year-old on Sunday morning standing with hands on his hips giving his 11-year-old brother Holy Ned. My wife pointed to the way this infant tyrant was standing with his hands on his hips and said, "I wonder where he got that stance." We both burst out laughing.

Lewis Yablonsky, a Southern California sociologist, has written a moving little book called *Fathers and Sons*. He makes a statement early in the book that I found arresting:

"A shift toward a more positive, intelligent enactment of the father role would affect the whole society. More effective fathering could virtually eliminate such social problems as crime, drug abuse and the violence that plagues our society."

That might be a little heavy, but since it is Father's Day perhaps Yablonsky's hyperbole can be forgiven in pursuit of this point: Men who are indifferent toward their sons are creating serious problems for somebody else. Boys will have role models. They will select them from home if there is somebody home to serve in that role. If they find none there, they will find him some place else. I doubt we generally realize how vulnerable boys are in that respect.

Moreover, I doubt we realize how early the process of observation and emulation begins. If adults realized how much more preliterate children understand that they cannot yet express, both the children and the adults would be better off. Children who see love and respect tend to display love and respect. Children who see bickering and disrespect tend to display those tendencies when their turns come to exercise their wills.

When fathers disappear from their children, especially from their sons, they leave more than an economic void. They also leave those boys with no idea of whom to emulate. Later, the first older male to show kindness and leadership is likely to gain their support. If that male happens to be a pastor or a teacher, we are lucky. If it is a pimp or dope dealer, we may get yet another pimp or dope dealer.

All this came clear to me years ago when I was a roving correspondent. As soon as I reached a new place, the first thing I habitually asked for was a map. Upon reflection, it is no wonder why.

Family Values

My father's parents were Christian fundamentalists. They took their children to church several times a week and three times on Sundays. Television and radio were banned for being too worldly. Books, maps and languages were revered for being the keys to understanding and succeeding in life.

Consorting with those outside the religion was forbidden. Believing in the concept of "but for the grace of God, go I" was a fact of life. Christmas and Easter were not celebrated. The Lord's birth and resurrection were to be celebrated every day.

My grandfather was a moving man by profession and a minister by avocation. Dad, the youngest of his six children, was to become a minister. Dad, however, had a plan of his own. By the time he was in his late teens, Daddy fled the confines of the family's fundamentalist life.

In both miles and in mind-set, Daddy traveled far from his parents' restrictive Brooklyn home and he never really went back. From his first stop in Greenwich Village, to his later years at the *Washington Post*, and then his final years in California with the *Oakland Tribune*, Dad spent much of his life learning about the world and those people from whom his parents had tried to shelter him.

He traveled a long way from that childhood, but he always stayed close to his family's values.

My father, in his young adult days, was wary of forcing religion on his children. We didn't go to church for years. As he grew older, he encouraged us to attend church services. Soon it became expected that we all went to church Sunday morning. But long before that, we had been imbued with the values of my grandfather.

My grandfather raised his children with an abiding belief that our first responsibility is to treat our neighbors with respect. It was a truth ingrained so deeply in my father's soul that he never missed an opportunity to pass it on to us, no matter our age. In a letter to be read to me, before I could read, Daddy asked:

"Is there a difference among children? Is there a difference among parents? They might look different sometimes. But when you grow older, much older, you will learn that the only difference among people is how they behave. We never dislike anyone for the way he looks, or speaks, but we might be annoyed at him for the way he behaves sometimes. But we love each other just the same, don't we? We should."

Many years later, I was working in Massachusetts, trying to get a suburban newspaper to care about urban issues. A friend questioned why I cared so much about how other people lived. I was struck by the question. It had never occurred to me that there were those who did not care for the less fortunate. I fumbled around, finally saying, "I guess I was raised that way."

How do you explain a lifetime of dinnertime conversations dominated by talk of social issues and the nightly news. If I were to call my father up and tell him about a new dress, he would say, "Hmm, hmm, hmm." When I called him to talk about welfare reform, he would go on forever.

Much of that mind-set was my grandfather's influence, but the extent of that influence I learned only when I started going through my father's journals. There, in an undated entry, he wrote: "If it seems at times my preoccupation is with life's losers, the underfed, the victims of crime and the victims of the system, that is no accident. That is what I think my life and work are about. I am a son of the disinherited. The urban scene is my scene. The hungry are no strangers. They are my neighbors, not a statistical abstraction. When I speak of the need for wise and humane law enforcement, I am asking for better protection for my wife and children.

"It is the ingrained instinct of my upbringing to think first of those who have no voice of their own. Nothing is more rewarding to me, nothing more in keeping with the character my father tried to help us form than to give our efforts to those in need."

D.J.M.

What Holds a Marriage Together?

August 27, 1987—We never heard them argue, and yet they had many spirited discussions. My parents were married a half-century and went to their graves adoring each other more, they said, than when they first courted.

As children, the thing I suppose we admired—and feared—most about my parents was the way they thought. That is to say, the degree to which they seemed to us to be both emotionally and intellectually inseparable.

Try as we might, we could never maneuver them onto opposite sides of a parental issue. If my mother said no to a request or proposal, chances were excellent my father would say the same, even if he had no idea what my mother's position had been. We used to call their solidarity "the stone wall" long before Watergate.

What started me thinking about that long, loving and impressive relationship was a recent cover story in *Newsweek* magazine about the improving state of marriage. It seems the divorce rate is dipping slightly after years of unremitting increase.

The statistics surrounding this issue are always open to differing interpretations, but it does appear marriages are lasting longer and the divorce option is losing some of its previous appeal. AIDS, it is thought, might be contributing to some sober reflections about the appeal of sexual freedom.

This trend toward less divorce is entirely too new to contribute to many useful conclusions. Why people divorce, or don't, depends on too many variables. But buried in the *Newsweek* piece was something that struck me as an overlooked constant.

It has to do with why some couples stay together through thick and thin. It's also why I believe my parents remained married and devoted to each other despite all the problems you might expect a couple to face raising six children during the Depression and World War II. Those were tough times to be parents.

The special ingredient, I believe, was friendship. My parents were not head-over-heels romantics. In fact, they were rarely demonstrably affectionate around us. But they were friends. Best friends. That, I believe, was the great secret of their devotion.

For a time when I was in high school, my father did some remodeling that required me temporarily to give up my room for an anteroom to my parents' bedroom. That is when I discovered what good friends they were.

Long into the night, especially on weekends, they would talk about the doings of the previous day, the funny things that happened to one or the other of them.

The thing I noticed was the calm, even tone of their voices. They talked almost in a code of their own. They laughed at each other's silly mistakes and foibles. And when they disagreed about something, there was an odd silence. They listened very carefully to each other until each understood the reason for the argument of the other.

Later, I was to learn that most people who argue have ceased listening to what the other person has to say. My parents were the opposite. My father once explained to me why he listened so carefully to my mother's arguments.

"I always learn something by listening to your mother," he said simply. He was by no means a docile person. He often argued back just as vigorously. But they never raised their voices to each other and they clearly respected each other's views on just about everything.

They ran a business together for most of that half century, and there were myriad tough decisions to be made. They had little trouble working those problems out together. It was impressive to see the way they anticipated each other and finished each other's sentences.

Where their true unity of purpose shone was in the manner in which they raised six children together. As we later came to understand, my parents had spent long hours as newlyweds establishing their mutual goals for the family.

They agreed on the code and spirit by which their children would be raised. Above all, they agreed that love was the thing of which their children would have the most. Discipline turned out to hold a solid second place on their agenda. Material things were a distant third.

And when they disagreed, they did it in a friendly fashion that said to the rest of us that they were sure to still love each other at the end of the argument. As I said, it is difficult to know all the reasons people divorce, but one thing I am sure holds couples together. It's friendship.

The Issue of Strength Versus Flexibility

March 19, 1984—My father loved to teach by showing us examples of his lessons. Fortunately for his six children, most of his lessons were touching as well as memorable.

Whenever I witness disputes in which one side or another, or both, take rigid and intractable positions, I think of my dad.

Even though he himself was deeply religious almost to the point of rigidity at times, he disliked arguments in which neither side would back down.

In a household with three boys and three girls, all with an independent view of the world, there were many opportunities for my father to preach compassion for an adversary's point of view.

Often his entreaties were to no avail. While he stood there, we listened and nodded our expressions of agreement. All too often, the moment he turned his back, the argument resumed with its accustomed gusto. Nobody backed down often in our house.

Indeed, one day one of my brothers and I were in such a furious battle that we would not even subside at my father's urging.

Each of us was so certain he was right that at that moment I think each of us would have declared himself ready to die rather than be the one who backed down.

Dad asked each of us if we would apologize to the other for our disrespectful behavior. So angry were we that we spoke almost in unison, and it was the only thing on which we appeared to agree:

"I'd rather die first."

That angry.

My father rubbed his chin, as he always did when perplexed. Without taking his eyes off us, he moved over to a work table and rummaged for a minute or two. He found what he was looking for.

He returned and stood before us holding two rulers, both 18 inches long. One was made of a heavy wood. The other was made of thin, tempered steel. Needless to say, we were instantly nervous as to his plans for those rulers.

My father turned to my older brother first.

"Which of these rulers," he asked, "do you think is the stronger?"

My brother chose the wooden one.

Then it was my turn. I hated myself for having to agree with my brother at the height of our feud, but I had to agree. The wooden ruler looked stronger, I concurred.

"You're both sure?" my father persisted.

We nodded our angry little heads in unison, grimacing all the while.

My father set the thin metal ruler down on the table. He took the wooden ruler into his huge hands, lifted it high into the air and brought it down with a swift crack on his upraised knee. It broke in a sickening flash.

We stood with our mouths agape.

He handed each of us a half of a ruler to see for ourselves that the piece of wood was now two pieces of what once was the thickest ruler in the house, thicker even than the yardstick my mother used for sewing.

"Now," my father said, "try that with this." He handed over the metal ruler to my older brother.

"Break it," my father commanded.

My brother tried to snap it in half over his knee, as he had seen my father do with the wooden ruler. The steel ruler just bent with the force and then snapped back into its previous shape.

Soon it was my turn. I let it dangle over the edge of the table and then pressed down hard and fast. It snapped back up in my face.

After a few more futile attempts, we gave up and handed the ruler back to my father.

"Now, listen," he said as he made us sit down on the couch before him, "I hope you learned this lesson. Rigidity and strength are not always the same thing."

My father's voice was warm and mellow now. He was not scolding but teaching, and he wanted his two sons to take away from their terrible fight a valuable lesson.

Sometimes, he went on, people think that unless they take a strong and rigid position other people won't respect them. For sure, there are times when you must stand firm for what you believe in. But if what you think is right, you need not be so adamant in the face of another point of view.

He spoke of personal experiences he'd had as a boy in the country, and how he had learned that some of the strongest substances in nature gained their true strength from their flexibility.

He told us of the sugarcane in Barbados and the way the hurricanes would come and winds would blow down large and apparently strong structures.

"But those thin stands of sugarcane would survive almost any hurricane because the wind would be so severe it would double them over, and they would snap right back."

People should learn to have some of that quality in their personalities, he went on. They should learn when and how to bend a little rather than assume their only real display of strength is in being rigid and hard.

Through the years, I cannot count the number of times I have covered disputes over ideology, religion, community projects and international affairs, all of them containing some element of that quality of rigidity my brother and I displayed to my dad that day.

On such occasions, I have reflected in my mind's eye on my father standing in front of us, long after that wooden ruler was broken, flexing that thin metal ruler we could not break.

Teaching Children Hope for the Future

February 21, 1982—Sometimes I shudder when I think of the world we are creating for our children. Globally, we are poised on the brink of nuclear extinction one moment and on the edge of involvement in a civil war in Central America the next. At home, we seem incapable of finding the means of working out human relations with each other, whether between the sexes or the races or the classes. Ours is a world in a state of semipeace.

Such cheerless musings are aroused on a day that should be filled with happier thoughts. Our oldest boy and middle child turned 11 years old yesterday, a time when parents begin thinking fondly about the wonderful future awaiting a young man halfway to his majority. Amid the celebrating, I am forced to ask what sort of world we are making for him to inherit. It is not a pleasing question in 1982. The answers are muddled and sometimes frightening.

We are being treated to scenarios of "survivable" nuclear war and trillion dollar–plus defense outlays, none of which promises to make us any more secure. Indeed, one must wonder sometimes whether more massive stocks of arms make us more secure or less secure. Beyond security lies the moral question of whether our society can long justify austerity for the poor and the elderly, the young and the infirm while we bloat our military establishment with virtually every weapons program on its wish list.

Meanwhile, the cities of the nation continue to deteriorate, the children of the poor will have less to eat in school, the streets and highways become increasingly disheveled, and old people who looked forward all their working days to comfortable retirement now face a bleak and uncertain future.

It is not the easiest of times in which to wish a youngster a happy birthday with many happy returns. At a similar point in my own life, I remember the optimism that abounded in our household. The last-born (I am afraid my folks said "the baby") was growing up. The great war to save democracy (the second great war to save democracy) was just over. The economy was beginning to readjust to peacetime, which posed some problems, but on the whole the world was still bright for millions of Americans.

My father cut the cake and my mother made a few observations as she handed me my slice. She reminded me that I had been born during the Depression, and that the family had struggled during those years to make ends meet with six children. She was proud, and reminded us children that we should be too, that my father's "strong back" and the mercy of the Lord pulled us through and then some.

Now, my parents said, it was up to each of us to make the best of what we had been given. It was understood they expected us to exceed their accomplishments. They accepted no notion of limitation. They saw a world of infinite possibilities for their children and would not have thought to enter any caveats or qualifications. They did not say, "You can do well unless, of course, there is a nuclear war." Nor did they say, "You can own a home like the one in which you grew up—if interest rates come down." And they did not say, "Your prospects in the business world will be excellent unless, of course, the economy collapses again."

They readily acknowledged the challenge we could expect from racism but they saw that as a hurdle rather than a permanent burden. They did not expect their children to be slowed for long by hurdles.

Instead, they said the world will be what you children make of it. Today, my son watches pictures on television of nuclear holocaust and listens to our leaders speak of the potential for nuclear war or economic collapse and I wonder what great visionary picture I dare paint for him. Today's children are not likely to sit in wide-eyed wonder eating their ice cream and cake while their parents extol the virtues of the modern world.

They know too much. Television teaches many cynical lessons. They hear talk of war and see too few examples of leadership in pursuit of peace. Anwar Sadat heaves into view one day and speaks of peace. In almost the next instant, the children watch on television as he is gunned down in cold blood. More than that, they see no images of human concern and fellow feeling on that tube. Rarely do they hear a leader suggest the less fortunate are all our concern.

Teaching children the values and ethics of human concern in this age of indifference is hard enough. Impressing them with their possibilities is one of the challenges of our times. And it is not because they are inherently unwilling to embrace the values of caring and concern. It is rather the degree to which such values are contradicted by so much they see around them.

One evening not long ago, I came home to find my 10-year-old watching a prime-time television feature. As I walked into the room, the screen was filled with the image of a man throwing his wife halfway across the room and then pummeling her almost to a bloody pulp. My stomach turned. Calmly as I could, I asked my boy what the story was about. "Oh," he said without taking his eyes off the screen, "it's a story about a family."

It is not just what they see on television that contributes to the new climate of cynicism and insensitivity. It is also what they see and hear on the playground and in other previously innocent settings. If my father could hear the lyrics of some of the songs on the radio today, he would know he was right to have prevented us from listening to the radio, watching television and playing "worldly" music.

So what can you tell a child growing up today? Can one hope credibly to contradict this wasteland of cynicism and dismiss this cloud of potential doom that hovers over humanity? We dare not assume, as our parents did, that the world is what our children make of it. They see too many things too awesome and incomprehensible in their scope.

All the same, it is up to us and them to preserve the planet if it is to be preserved. I am afraid none of us is entitled to say the problems are too big and leave it to the leaders. I am not convinced the leaders know what to do unless we tell them. I am still constrained to tell my son as long as free speech exists he is obligated to work to make the planet safe for his children, and it won't be easy. We are still obligated to respect the rights of others. That and one other thing:

Love is still more powerful than hatred, peace is better than war, and anger is more easily resolved with a hug than a blow.

Jobs Can Teach Youths Responsibility

June 19, 1986—If old Mr. Ficcaro could have seen his grocery cart at that very moment, he would have been fit to be tied. We had a game we played with the "three-legged horse," as we sometimes called it.

Six or so of us would poise the wagon at the crest of a hill. We would jump on, just as the wagon took off. We would scramble off as it hit the bottom of the hill. The last kid off was responsible for pulling the wagon to a halt.

Since it was my job as grocery clerk that got us access to the wagon, I made sure I was the last one off. On this particular summer afternoon, a truck pulled out in front of the wagon just as we were bailing out.

I watched in horror as the wagon headed straight for the path of the truck. If they collided, there would be no more wagon, no more job and no more of my fanny when my parents found out. In a desperate lunge, I pulled the wagon out of the way of the truck at the last possible second.

My friends helped me push the wagon back up the hill. I remember we were dead silent. The only sound was from the iron wheels on the pavement. When I walked back into the grocery store, I must have looked as if I'd seen a ghost.

Mr. Ficcaro questioned me, but I stoically maintained I was all right. I remember that moment as a turning point for me. It was my first summer job, and it was more of a lark than work at first. My main reason for wanting the job was that my big brothers had worked there. It was a family tradition.

As I stood at the counter waiting on a customer, the scene of the near-disaster kept running through my mind. I realized, I suppose, how serious it was to have those responsibilities. I made up my mind to be the best grocery clerk Mr. Ficcaro ever had.

Every year about this time, the nation's high schools disgorge millions of youngsters with little or nothing constructive to do for the summer.

There are few little groceries left, but there are plenty of other chores that young people can do during the summer, and it is important we remain mindful of the value to youngsters of early job development skills.

Kids need not have a hair-raising experience that scares the daylights out of them to discover responsibility. What employers should remember is that summer work experience can be the best education a youngster receives.

My days in the grocery went by in a blur after that experience. I was busy learning the business. I learned how to manage the inventory so the oldest stock moved first, how to balance the cash register and keep the green vegetables looking fresh.

Above all, Mr. Ficcaro preached that the customer is always right. If the customer wants it a certain way, that is the way it should be done if at all possible.

One day, one of the crankiest customers called and demanded I drop everything and rush over to her house with a half dozen eggs. She's crazy, I told him when the customer hung up. "No, she's not crazy," Mr. Ficcaro said, "She's one of our customers."

Lessons such as those last a lifetime. I find myself thinking of that and other summer jobs I had at this time of year especially. What strikes me is that the lessons of responsibility that are learned early eventually become the most meaningful.

More than that, the earlier youngsters are exposed to the rigors of the workplace, the more time they have to prepare for the adjustment. Often, when I meet people who are successful in business, the most common characteristic is that they had some early exposure to business and work.

Three-wheel grocery carts have gone the way of the horse and buggy, of course, but I still think of my close encounter with disaster at the bottom of the hill in Brooklyn.

I think of that day, traumatic as it was, as a signal day in my life. It was a day I learned the difference between work and play. I never offered my buddies a ride in that wagon again, and they somehow had the decency not to ask.

The Color of Justice

May 1, 1992—Sometimes on civilized Sundays, we have breakfast and make a family date or two for the coming week. We might agree to take in a movie together. Other times, we might see a program in the TV book and agree it is something the whole family wants to watch together. Last Sunday, we agreed to gather to watch the final episode of the "Cosby" show on Thursday night. It didn't turn out that way.

By the time Thursday night rolled around, the thought of comedy had turned to bitter irony. We were primed to say farewell to the Huxtable family. They were the first wholesome African-American family on television. We were instead witnessing the return of something ugly and half-forgotten. Urban uprisings, we thought, were a thing of the '60s. Now we were watching Los Angeles burn live on CNN. Cosby turned to ashes before us. The boys decided they did not want to watch the show at all. They were glued to the news on CNN. Their sister called from Detroit. She was on "riot watch" for her newspaper.

"I am afraid for my brothers," she began. "I wonder if this verdict won't set off an open season on young black males. I also fear for the country. The rage is contagious. You cannot guess what will happen next. Is there any way we can just keep the boys in the house for a few years?"

The Rodney King verdict, so surprising and so disconcerting, caught the nation by surprise. Worse, it has revealed us in a light we half forgot. As the flames billowed up over Los Angeles, my mind reeled backward almost three decades. I had covered this story many times before. Not just Watts, but later Newark, Detroit, Cleveland, and cities the names of which I have since forgotten. One city whose fires I will never forget is Washington, D.C.

We have just passed the 24th anniversary of the Washington riots. I have told the family of that awful night of April 4, 1968, when the nation's capital went up in flames. The news of the death of Dr. Martin Luther King Jr. set off an orgy of violence. I remember wondering all that night about the curious logic of riots. How could the death of the apostle of nonviolence result in such unrestrained bedlam?

In some curious way, there was a deep sense of déjà vu the other night. There was that same anger without a constructive channel. The country was going backward, not forward. People were dying in the streets for no good reason. And, as in all those other instances of urban violence, racial polarization was visible everywhere.

On the Larry King show on CNN, one of the Ventura County jurors was describing what made her fellow jurors and her acquit those four police officers. She said many incredible things. None was so bizarre as her statement that "Mr. [Rodney] King was controlling the whole show with his actions." She had persuaded herself that all those police officers raining dozens of baton blows on the head of an unarmed man on the ground were acting in self-defense.

There, in bold relief, is the problem of our times. The gulf of race has not narrowed in the quarter-century since the death of Dr. King. We are still a society divided by skin color and by class.

That fact made the "Cosby" farewell all the more poignant. You could switch channels and choose your America last Thursday night. If you wanted to believe in a hopeful future, you could revel in Theo Huxtable's college graduation. You could envision thousands of young Theos this spring receiving their degrees. Or, you could click the dial and see the madness in the streets. You could reflect on the fact that there are more young black males of Theo's age in the criminal justice system than there are in college.

We have been studiously ignoring this accumulating social dynamite for years now. We have been contenting ourselves with national fantasy. It passed irony that the fantasy of the Huxtables graduated from our national screen on the same night that an old reality revisited our consciousness. The poignant reality in our house is that my wife and I tried to watch "Cosby." Our children were watching the future unfold on CNN.

The High Price of Injustice

March 5, 1993—We have been having this argument—let's call it more of a friendly discussion—for almost 14 years. My friend grew up in a small, close-knit white town in the South. I grew up in the big city of Brooklyn. Our shaping experiences about race could not have been more different. Yet our common agreement about racism was one of the things that made us friends. We both believed from an early age that racism was poison in the well of our society.

The argument started years ago. I told my friend of a theory of mine. The theory was this: Look carefully into any egregious case of racism and you will discover something very interesting. You will discover that the target of the racism, let's say a black victim, is not the only victim. Look carefully, I said, and you will see that even the perpetrators are the victims of their own folly. My friend scoffed.

Over the years, I've offered up what I thought was pretty strong evidence in support of my argument. But the other day, in the little town of Monroeville, Alabama, I hit pay dirt. I found the case that made my friend say, definitively and unequivocally after all these years, "You win."

This is the case of Walter (Johnny D.) McMillian. He is a black man who spent six years on Alabama's death row for a murder he did not commit. He was put there in a willful miscarriage of justice perpetrated by the county prosecutor and a local judge.

There is strong evidence that the real crime for which Johnny D. McMillian was being punished was not murder. He had been keeping company with a white woman. One of his sons married a white woman. The evidence suggests violating the mores of the Deep South was McMillian's real crime.

The case that brought on his troubles was the murder on November 1, 1986, of an 18-year-old white woman, Ronda Morrison, in a dry cleaning store. There was no arrest in the case for eight months. Then the local police arrested Ralph Myers, 30, a man with a long criminal record. His arrest involved another murder in a nearby county.

After a week of grilling by the police, Myers accused Johnny D.

McMillian of killing Ronda Morrison. He said he was there when it happened. McMillian was arrested and, although convicted of nothing, was ordered by the judge to death row at Alabama's Holman State Prison in Atmore. In a one-and-a-half-day trial, McMillian was convicted on the testimony of three witnesses. All their testimony would later turn out to have been perjured or coerced. It also has been recanted.

The CBS News broadcast "60 Minutes" took an interest last fall in the McMillian case because it was such a blatant example of justice gone awry. In the simple parlance of the street, Johnny D. McMillian was railroaded. Had the trial judge not been so bent on vicious vengeance, Johnny D. might have spent his life in an Alabama prison. The judge insisted on overruling the jury's sentence of life in prison and ordered the death penalty. That gave the case the special status that led the other day to the dismissal of the murder charge and McMillian's freedom.

Back now to the old argument and my theory about the hidden cost of racism. The biggest price in this case, of course, has been paid by Johnny D. McMillian. He lost six years of his life, most of his property and no doubt a good deal of his dignity. No one can make him whole for all that, but you can believe he is the likely winner of a whopping big lawsuit against the state of Alabama.

That is where the hidden costs of racism begin to kick in. Alabama will spend hundreds of thousands of dollars defending itself in a blatant wrongful imprisonment case. Eventually, either it will settle for a big hunk of the state treasury or it will bow to a court judgment. One way or another, Alabama will pay. All its citizens will bear the burden.

Consider Ronda Morrison and her family. All this time, her killer presumably has been loose and unpunished. More than six years after the fact, that person seems to have gotten away with murder and may not be found. The costs go on and multiply. They always do in these situations because, as I've been telling my friend all these years, racism has so many victims.

Malcolm and My Children

November 25, 1992—Sunday, February 21, 1965, was a sunny, chilly day in New York City. A group of young journalists was having breakfast in Greenwich Village. The discussion turned to Malcolm X. He would preach within hours at Audubon Ballroom in Harlem. As we talked, a hush, a shudder of foreboding went round the table. We broke up so some could go to Harlem and others to assignments elsewhere.

Mine was elsewhere. It turned out that by the smallest of chances I missed becoming a witness to the murder of Malcolm X. I had listened to him many times before, and he remains one of the most striking figures I ever covered.

Now my children question me closely about Malcolm and his times. They are seized by the fascination created by the Spike Lee film version of Malcolm's life. That they question me so closely about details and possible motivations in the man is a telling point about Lee's film. At first, I thought their questions were as a result of the stimulation of interest the film created. I soon began to sense something deeper.

It finally dawned on me that the reasons for their questions revealed a weakness of the Spike Lee film. It's a serious weakness at that. The problem is this: After watching a three-hour-and-21-minute movie about Malcolm X, the children, one in college and another in junior high, still did not understand him. "In all that time," the oldest son said, "I still didn't understand what motivated him to do what he did in the movie."

As the younger one put it, what made Malcolm turn out to be so different from so many of the other young black "dudes" whose life circumstances were practically the same? The reason this question is important is that it has great bearing on what has become of the black consciousness movement that Malcolm, Martin Luther King Jr. and others spawned in the '60s.

It would take nothing away from the pride of African-Americans if we were to acknowledge that Malcolm X was a giant of extraordinary gift by any standards. Any race or nationality that spawned such a genius would know he was special, that he became who he was by dint of that rare marker that sets a few apart from the many. It is a distinction, regardless of where we see it, that transcends race. It is enough to know that God makes very few in the manner of Malcolm.

Furthermore, his was a time when black intellect was reshaping the American psyche. Miles Davis and Duke Ellington were doing it in music. Lorraine Hansberry and James Baldwin were doing it in letters. Romare Bearden and Jacob Lawrence were stunning the world of the visual arts. Ozzie Davis and Ruby Dee were a new kind of theatrical talent. And, of course, Martin Luther King's ethical crusade would soon transform a nation.

What made Malcolm different from his black street peers? The same mystery of nature made Miles different from every other human who ever blew a horn. The same mystery made Baldwin's typewriter alone achieve the power of *Go Tell It on the Mountain* and gave King alone the power to send shivers up the spine of the whole globe simply by stating, "I have a dream."

I tell my children that to acknowledge the nature of genius they should try to understand Malcolm or Leonardo, Miles or Michelangelo. Genius, I tell them, is so noticeable because it is so rare. We told a generation of African-American children to "be like" Jackie Robinson or Martin Luther King or Malcolm X. In some ways the black consciousness movement may have set them up for failure and frustration. We don't tell white kids they all have to be John F. Kennedy. We made Bill Clinton president because he was the great exception.

In all of Spike Lee's long film, we never hear that special explanation for why a prisoner named Malcolm Little copied out every word in Webster's Third International dictionary. It was not because he was converting to Islam, as Spike Lee would have you believe. How many other Nation of Islam converts read 15 hours a day and could recall years later the placement of a comma on a page? He was special.

Say "genius" when you talk to your children about Malcolm. Say, yes, you can aspire to his exceptional gift for one thing or another. But do not try to become Malcolm X. Be, instead, the best possible Billy or Bob or Kendra or Louise. Take that from Malcolm's life. Seek your own source of satisfaction, tell them. I met a gifted young black theologian in Cleveland years ago. I was covering a march he helped lead. "I only began to grow as a person and a pastor," he said, "the day I decided I was not going to be another Martin Luther King. I was just going to be the best me." Tell that to your children when they ask about Malcolm X.

Why Children Need Fathers

May 13, 1992—She slipped her diminutive hand into mine and we strolled across Harvard Yard. We stood in front of the freshman dorm where John F. Kennedy had lived. We walked to Widener Library and marveled at the thought that we would have free access to the third-largest library in the world.

My daughter was only seven years old the year I became a Nieman Fellow at Harvard University. Yet, she spoke with such a firmness and finality that day in 1965. "When I grow up," she said, "I am going to win a Nieman Fellowship and come here to study. Just like my dad."

At the time, it did not occur to either of us what an improbable proposition that was. We did not know then that only one other person, Hodding Carter III, had ever followed his father to Harvard as a Nieman Fellow. In the intervening years, it would happen only one other time, in 1988, when John Harwood of *The Wall Street Journal* made it. His father, Richard Harwood, is the ombudsman of the *Washington Post*. In 55 years, those were the only two.

Then, on May 4, Dori J. Maynard's 34th birthday, she became the third person, and the only woman, ever to succeed her father at Harvard as a Nieman. All her life, she would later tell me, she had been waiting for that day. The phone rang in our house in California at 6:01 A.M. It was 9:01 back in Detroit, where she lives. She had told me she would be expecting a call from Harvard at around nine o'clock her time.

The instant the phone rang, and before I picked it up, I flashed on that day so many years ago in Cambridge. So, I said to myself with an enormous sense of pride and respect, Dori J. Maynard is a Nieman Fellow. Just as she had been planning since she was only seven.

I had been thinking about fathers and children a lot of late. What had started me thinking about that subject all over again was the decision of the editors of the *Oakland Tribune* to do a major series on gangs. As the events in Los Angeles amply demonstrated once again, gangs play a powerful role in the lives of our urban communities.

The gang is little more than an extended family. More correctly, the gang is the substitute for the family that either does not exist or function effectively for the child. We are fascinated by the gang because of its lore. We are especially transfixed by the violence associated with gangs.

What we miss is the personal pain associated with a feeling of emptiness. The child without adult nurturing, with no channel, guide or structure, is forever angry. Such children are hungry for all the things an adult parent should provide. Especially, they are hungry for someone to be like. Left on their own, they will emulate gangsters, dope dealers and even killers. Above all, they will go around hurting all the time.

My daughter said, "Thanks, Dad," that morning on the phone. I really didn't do much, I said. "You didn't have to do anything," she said. "You just had to be there so I would have my parents to look up to and to try to emulate. That's really all either of you had to do. It's your being there that mattered most."

The other night on the ABC News broadcast "Prime Time Live," there was a painful and poignant story. It was about fathers who just disappear on their kids. Diane Sawyer tracked down one of those fathers. He had run off with another woman. He had not sent a word or a dollar to his two children, a son and a daughter, for years.

You could not help but want to cry at the pain of those kids. To think that scenario is repeated millions of times over simply staggers the senses. How, you ask yourself over and over, could they not know what this abandonment does to their children?

Only a small percentage of those kids join gangs. Many just suffer. A few are lucky enough to find constructive alternatives and make a new life. Almost all will search those empty spaces within themselves, probing their minds, their hearts and souls for what they did wrong to chase away Dad. Most will never understand it was not their fault.

I wish there were more pieces like the one Diane Sawyer did. I wish more dads would have to confront the pain their absence inflicts. I wish something else: I wish they could also know what it feels like to see a child succeed and know they helped. There is no greater reward.

A Path Through Time

Daddy always had an eye to the future. But he loved to tell the stories of his childhood. We children did not spend much time at his childhood home, though at times we felt as if we were right there at 804 Marcy Ave., the Bedford Stuyvesant home in which my father grew up. Daddy would slip into his West Indian accent, introducing us to a cast of characters who died long before we were born.

There was Dad's father, a kind and gentle man with a rigid moral code. Through the stories, my grandfather still manages to admonish his grandchildren to work hard and not to count our chickens until they are hatched.

And there was Dad himself. Dad, the track star. Once, running back to school after lunch, Dad didn't see a car at the intersection until it was almost too late. Without blinking an eye, he simply jumped over the car's hood and sailed into school on time. Or so he said, one day, when he was showing me through the old neighborhood.

Then there was the time he learned to drive. One day in his early teens, Daddy hopped up into the cab of my grandfather's moving truck and took off. Tooling down the streets of New York in the family truck, he taught himself how to drive.

Not all his childhood stories were happy. Though his sisters had successful careers, my father remembered a time when women were urged to marry rather than pursue careers. When I came along, Daddy forbade me from learning to cook, clean or type. "Once it is discovered you can do those three things, you may never be given a chance to do anything else," he would say. He urged me to establish a career first, then worry about marriage. I can only imagine what his parents would have thought.

His parents were strict. By the time I was born, my father had rebelled against the confines of the fundamentalist Plymouth Brethren, and was in contact only with his oldest brother, since that religion frowned on members having contact with anyone outside the faith. My uncle and his family, however, managed to put religion and family in perspective.

After I was an infant, I did not see my grandmother or two of my three aunts again until I was 15. I have yet to meet my third aunt, my father's oldest sister. "I am just trying to live my life as Jesus would want me to," she said, explaining why she could not have contact with members of her family outside the religion.

My father was a spiritual man, but he never got over his suspicion of organized religion. He explained his concern in a 1963 letter to me.

"Many people go to church, saying they are going in Jesus' name. But then, after church they don't act like Jesus would have acted. They call themselves Christian and, I think Christianity might be a pretty good thing. I hope someone really tries it," he wrote.

In his own way, he tried. He did with religion what he did with so many things from his childhood. He used the foundation of his childhood to construct a life that would work in today's world.

"What manner of man was Bob Maynard?" the Reverend Will L. Herzfeld and Reverend J. Alfred Smith Sr. asked at my father's funeral. "As a communicator, his inspiring and informing word was equally challenging as his written word," the Reverend Smith said. "But when he left the tall tower of the *Oakland Tribune* to dialogue with angry and alienated youth of the inner city, his life became the incarnation of the living word.

"And as a sensitive, ethical person whose morality was purified in the streams of prayer, Robert Maynard elected to walk in the dark with Christ rather than walk alone in the light."

There were no Bible studies in our household. There were only stories. There were the stories that taught us the value of hard work. There were the stories that taught us a quick mind can sail over the most daunting obstacles, and there were the stories that taught us God helps those who help themselves.

Life did change between the generations. When it was my turn to learn to drive, my father insisted I take lessons. There would be no jumping into the family car and taking off. Instead, he rented a stick-shift car and showed me how to change gears. Then he left me to negotiate my way home.

D.J.M.

A Deadly Proliferation of Guns

March 3, 1988—The arrest took place shortly after 8:30 in the morning. By noon, the entire student body of Boys High in Brooklyn was crammed into an emergency assembly. "Today has been a tragic day," the principal said in a quavering voice. "A student, one of our fine young men, has been arrested." The charge brought a gasp. "He was found in possession of a revolver."

For the next week or more, little else dominated the atmosphere at school or home. It was impossible to escape stern lectures on the dangers of this new proliferation of pistols on the streets of New York.

Guns showed up in the cities of America in large numbers for the first time right after World War II. Before, only desperate hoods carried guns. Even five years after the war, the arrest of one boy with a gun was momentous.

The world has since turned upside down. What was rare is now common. The schools of some cities are awash in handguns. In part, it has to do with the flourishing drug commerce. Worse, it has become "cool" to have your very own Uzi automatic.

The effect of this phenomenon is best viewed from two vantage points. I speak of the funeral homes and the emergency wards of the hospitals. It is in these places that the import of what we have allowed to happen can be fully appreciated.

In Detroit, one undertaker's business has become principally that of burying juveniles. In Chicago, the problem has set off citywide alarm. In Oakland, some students resort to bulletproof vests. They fear cross fire on campus. The emergency rooms are filled with student gunshot victims, some of whom were "playing" with weapons.

As this grisly business gets worse by the day, a question continues to prey on me. It concerns the gun lobby. As the parade of ambulances relentlessly bears our children to the emergency wards and thence to the morgue, is the gun lobby proud?

After all, it should be congratulated on a significant political victory. Remember "Guns don't kill people, people kill people"? Remember the way the gun lobby stood in the way of even the most tepid measures to give urban police forces some minimal tools to deal with handguns?

Always, common sense has had to combat two false arguments, one emotional and the other constitutional.

The emotional argument is that every homeowner should have the right to a gun for protection. In fact, more family members are killed and maimed by their own handguns than are any criminals trying to rob them.

The constitutional fallacy is that the Second Amendment gives every citizen the right to "keep and bear arms." The Supreme Court has made it clear that that language was meant to protect the right of the states to raise citizen militia. It was not meant to make our communities modern-day versions of Dodge City.

Yet that is what we have, and worse. Gun proliferation is now at the junior high school level. If that trend continues unabated, there is no question guns will soon be common in elementary schools.

Each round of proliferation has brought new levels of senseless killing, fueled by the deadly combination of available weapons and the glut of violence on prime-time television.

A boy was shot in the stomach on a bus in Oakland not long ago. It was a fight over some petty matter. "If you had removed the guns," one police officer said, "it would never have been more than a fistfight on the bus."

That is what the proliferation of handguns over two generations has wrought: Our fistfights are more likely to end as fatal affairs.

E.B. White: A Contagious Spirit

October 13, 1985—The huge moving van lumbering through the streets of New York provided me with my first geography lesson. My father, who often preached by night, operated a moving and storage company during the day. On special occasions, he brought one or another of his six children along for a ride on the truck.

There was no better way to learn the streets and neighborhoods of New York than from the cab of that truck. Our schoolmates were envious and our teachers congratulatory. One of my teachers, knowing of my blossoming love affair with my native city, handed me a copy one day of *The New Yorker* magazine.

She recommended I read an article she had enjoyed about the city. I took it home only to discover another lifetime love, the prose of E.B. White. That particular essay, "Here Is New York," described a great deal of what I also saw in the city. I had hoped one day to put such observations into words myself.

White's essay almost made me wonder if I should continue in my ambition to be a writer. His work, I later learned, had that effect on a lot of people. He has been the quiet idol of at least two generations of American writers.

Upon hearing White died the other day in Brooklin, Maine, at 86, I was reminded of that first essay I read of his about New York. I couldn't have been more than 12, but I remember still how deeply touched I was by such telling prose:

"The island of Manhattan is without any doubt the greatest human concentrate on earth, the poem whose magic is comprehensible to millions . . . but whose full meaning will always remain elusive. At the feet of the tallest and plushiest offices lie the crummiest slums. The genteel mysteries housed in the Riverside Church are only a few blocks from the voodoo charms of Harlem. The merchant princes, riding to Wall Street in their limousines down the East River Drive, pass within a few hundred yards of the gypsy kings; but the princes do not know they are passing kings, and the kings are not up yet anyway . . ."

For me, White connected two compelling inner drives. One was my deep desire to write good prose, and the other was my untiring quest for urban adventure.

This second was constantly fueled by that unfolding city I watched from the cab of the van. One minute we would be in Chinatown, another on the Lower East Side, and not long after that the Upper West Side. In each place there was a story, a history, something to intrigue, some mystery explained. The city, I used to think, was a vast storehouse of human experience. The more you understand the city, I thought, the more you understand life.

That was the kind of thirst I brought to the prose of E.B. White. I did not know then that his work would be, in one way or another, a permanent part of my world.

Years later, after I had read many of White's essays, an editor handed me "the little book," as he called it. Read this, the editor said, before you write anything more. *The Elements of Style* became my bible, as it must be for millions who wish to write with precision.

White's revisions of William Strunk's original work, and his essay on writing style, make "the little book" a most powerful tool for writers of all kinds. Once something of an underground classic, *Elements* is found today virtually every place good writing is taught.

Even so, there was more to White than cities and style. His was a quest for a deeper understanding of personhood through writing. Scott Elledge, at the end of his biography of White, says:

"He once praised Thoreau for believing that 'The big thing was not to create a better mousetrap, or a better lead pencil, or even a better book, but a better man.'"

Because of that contagious spirit, he became a sustaining presence in the minds of his readers. He leaves much to appreciate and remember from days of early discovery. He helped me awaken to the place I lived and the craft I love.

Graffiti: A Very Small Statement

December 18, 1986—It is not clear to me how this occurred, but I have a small son with a big concern. Indeed, his level of moral outrage surprises me in a seven-year-old.

The issue on which you hear such strong opinions from this young crusader is graffiti. Each time he sees a wall on which someone has sprayed a message, he will pipe up. "There they go again," he is likely to say, "and I wish they would get arrested. People who do that should go to jail."

As I said, I cannot explain exactly why graffiti so offends the sense of order of such a young person, but I cannot count the number of times he has demanded to know, "Daddy, why do they do that? It's just not right."

Through all of this, I have not yet had the courage to tell him there is a graffiti story of sorts in his daddy's past. It is one of those incidents I will never forget, and until my son began expressing his outrage, it would never have occurred to me to tell the story.

Probably I was a little older than he is when this happened. I might have been eight or nine years old. I was walking to school alone on a bright spring morning in Brooklyn. At the corner about a block from school, I came upon an irresistible temptation.

A square of broken pavement had been dug up and replaced with a fresh coat of gray concrete. It was so wet that it gleamed in the light of the morning sun. I stopped and looked down at it. The impulse was immediate.

Without more than a second's hesitation, I reached into my book bag and fished out a pencil. I dropped the book bag on the ground as a cushion for my knees and began to etch my initials in the soft concrete.

No sooner had I begun than I felt a sharp pain on my rear end and heard a loud crashing sound at the same time. I looked up with a start to find an angry and menacing mason standing over me. He was holding a galvanized metal trash-can cover. It was easy to deduce it was his weapon of choice for the bottoms of little boys.

Lest he decide to use it again, maybe this time on my head, I began scrambling to my feet, intending to take off as fast as my skinny little legs could carry me. Quick escape was not to be my good fortune that morning.

As I tried to get to my feet, the old man grabbed me in a viselike grip around my upper arm. By then I was truly frightened. My fear reached traumatic proportions when he dropped the trash-can cover with a clatter to the ground and grasped my other arm with his newly freed hand.

"Why are you trying to spoil my work?" he shouted at me. I cannot remember what words I uttered. I only remember being as frightened as I had ever been. "Why?" he shouted again. This time I remember babbling something about just wanting to put my name on the ground.

Then a most remarkable thing occurred, and this is the reason this incident has never left my memory. He released my arms. His voice softened and his eyes lost their fire. Instead there was almost a touch of warmth in them.

"What is your name, son?" he asked in a kind voice. I told him my name, still shaking with fear. "Robert Maynard," he repeated softly. "My boy, this sidewalk is no place for your name. If you want your name on something, you go in that school. You work hard and you become a lawyer and you hang your shingle out for all the world to see."

By now, my fear was transforming to shame, but the old mason was not quite finished with me. "What do you want to be when you grow up?" I was staring at my shoes. I mumbled, "A writer, I think."

This time his voice rang out in the morning air as my school-mates rushed past, unaware of this odd drama. "A writer, a writer," the old man said. "Be a writer. Be a real writer. Have your name on books, not on this sidewalk."

With that, he stepped aside so I could cross the street and complete my journey to school. As I reached the curb, I looked back and he was down on his knees with a trowel, repairing the damage I had done to his work. He saw me looking at him and he only looked up long enough to repeat, "Be a writer."

That night, I told no one at the dinner table what had happened that morning. In fact, I never told anyone. But one day, I think I should tell my son.

The Changing American Family

June 1, 1986—The night before the picnic, I didn't sleep a wink. At the first hint of the red light of dawn, I sprang from my bed and went to the window. The neighborhood was awakening slowly. The grocer was bringing in cases of milk. I watched the vegetable vendor spray down his horse-drawn wagon before starting across the city shouting to the rooftops about fresh this and fresh that.

"Robert!" I sprang from the windowsill at the sound of my mother's voice and headed downstairs to the kitchen, where my mother was already busy at work. She had the kitchen laid out according to the tasks to be performed. My three sisters, all older than my two brothers and me, handled the frying of the chicken and the glazing of the ham.

My brothers were assigned to the potato salad and the sandwiches. I, the littlest one, was assigned to squeeze the lemons for the lemonade. Under the watchful eye of my mother, we worked with a diligent and good-humored fury.

My father was out at the garage getting the big old Buick gassed up and washed for the big day. By the time he returned, we would be ready to load the food and the blankets, the baseball bats and gloves and all the other accoutrements of the outing.

Picnic days always come back to mind with full force at the onset of summer. I remember them so well as the symbol of what big families did in those days. The family picnic was an institution of central importance to our lives.

This particular morning, as I worked the juicer at the kitchen table, I looked up at all the hustle and bustle and felt the excitement and the warmth of family fellowship. I felt a sense of the power of belonging, and I thought I must be the luckiest little boy in the world to be a part of such a large circle of love.

The big family picnic as I knew it then has all but disappeared, mostly because the big family has disappeared. Just the other day, a new poll came out on American attitudes toward family size. Most people said two children sounded like the ideal size for a family.

The world is a different place now, and big families of the sort my parents had are unlikely ever to exist again in any numbers.

The reason, simply stated, is the difference between women such as my mother and women of this generation. My mother never worked a day outside of our home. She threatened only in jest to go out and get a job and leave us to fend for ourselves.

Born at the onset of the 20th century, my mother regarded the rearing of her children as her full-time work, and she expressed no interest in any other career. Her six children were the fortunate beneficiaries of that fact. She lived long enough to see all of us settled in satisfying careers.

At the time I stood at the kitchen table squeezing those lemons, three-quarters of all families were like ours, a father who worked outside the home and a mother who remained in the home. Today, that would describe less than 10 percent of all American households. In a few more years, virtually no such households will exist.

Having been born on the cusp between two different lifestyles, I feel oddly lucky in both respects. There is no question we had a special edge throughout our lives because of the time and attention we received from my mother.

Today's two-career family, however, provides parents and children with many other benefits. The sharing of the responsibilities of parenting and nurturing is one of them. We only took the "big" issues to my father. My children make few, if any, distinctions between the issues they raise with Mom or Dad. It depends primarily on which one of us is handy.

So the big family picnic is gone because the big family is gone. It had obvious benefits, but they are far outweighed by the benefits to all of society of women and men working and sharing the challenges and pleasures of raising children.

The "Long-Playing" Record: RIP

January 7, 1990—We all gathered in the upstairs front parlor of the old house in Brooklyn to witness the miracle. My parents had agreed we could buy one of the new record players, the kind that played "long-playing" 33⅓-rpm records and the new 45-rpm singles.

It was a big day for two reasons. First, my parents had to be convinced that these new devices were not as "devilish" as radio and that new phenomenon known as television. Those were clearly the devil's devices.

My sister persuaded them that this new device would merely make for better listening to records of my parents' favorite hymns. Those we had played for years on the old windup RCA Victrola at 78 rpm. As I remember it, the music sounded as though it originated in a deep well.

The second reason the arrival of the newfangled record player was such a big hit was pride. At last we could go to school and brag that we had something the other kids had. They all had radios. Radios were forbidden in our home, as was television.

Needless to say, my parents' hymns weren't all we listened to. We hid our Nat "King" Cole, Dinah Washington and Frank Sinatra records. Those we played when my mother and father went to church meetings and we supposedly had too much homework.

The new records came to symbolize our liberation, the first chance we had to hear "worldly" music. Over the years, I accumulated a collection of dozens of albums of jazz, classical and pop music on those vinyl discs of magic we came to know as the LP.

At the time I began my collection, I actually imagined this as a lifetime investment, a legacy I would one day hand down to my children. I envisioned telling them the story of how this collection began as a clandestine collaboration of my brothers and sisters.

The other day I was rudely disabused of the notion that my record collection would ever represent anything to my children except quaint rubbish. Without a bang, or even much of a whimper, the LP has vanished. It sank like a stone in the latter days of the '80s. It is just another quiet casualty of the modern era.

My son asked me to stop by one of our favorite neighborhood

record stores. He wanted a couple of tapes. While there, I noticed the place had changed. I couldn't quite put my finger on the difference. Finally, I asked a salesclerk why our favorite record store looked so different. "No records," he replied.

No records? I repeated. "None," the clerk said with a tone of impatient finality. The place is now filled with compact discs, audiotapes and videotapes. There is no floor space devoted to records because hardly anyone listens to them anymore. Those sleek LPs that were a hallmark of my childhood, my first continuous cultural connection to the larger world, are an anachronism.

I shouldn't have been surprised. I have noticed over the last several years that hardly anyone in our house listens to records. Even when the children buy a piece of music on a long-playing record, they immediately transfer it to a tape.

Compact discs and the other digital technologies, including digital audiotape (DAT), deliver such clearer sound, without pops and hisses, that it seemed only a matter of time before the old LP would follow its 78-rpm predecessor into extinction.

The LP swept the market of my childhood in the '50s and had its heyday in the '60s. By the '70s, tape was beginning to encroach. Then in the early '80s, the CD delivered the coup de grace. Now that so many music lovers own a CD player, there are those who believe even the CD's days are numbered. The new DAT technology threatens to combine the quality of the compact disc with the convenience and flexibility of the audiocassette.

There, I suppose, is a small object lesson on the modern era: Form only shallow affections with appliances. The moment you fall in love with one, it is bound to become obsolete.

Reconciliation Struggle

July 9, 1992—The children and I were talking at dinner. The subject was the days of my youth. They always want to know about the world when Dad was their age. What did people wear, eat, think and do in those ancient times? They cannot, of course, imagine a time before hip-hop music, high-top fade hairstyles and color television.

There were deeper differences than those. I tell them of the days of rigid racial segregation, drinking fountains, rest rooms and restaurants for white people only. "That's unreal," the littlest one says. They read of such things in their history books, but it is something else to know someone who can speak of such times from his personal experience.

Outrageous as they find those times, they think about racial issues differently from the way my generation thought of them. My children's generation does not necessarily find that integration is the answer my generation thought it was. For us, the remedy for segregation was to make a world where white people and black people shared everything. We wanted all the schools open to all people. The prevailing doctrine of that time was that if white people and black people were made equal before the law, the problems that came from racial division could eventually be healed.

My children's generation has a different idea. They do not feel that same imperative. They believe they have a right of equal access to those things available to every other American. No question about that. But do they believe the solution to the problem of racism lies in people of all colors living, working and playing together? Well, yes and no. They think that if people can get along and respect each other, that's fine. But if a white person cannot respect them, they do not feel the need to be around that person or, more important, to have that person around them.

As we approach a presidential election, the issue of race will arise again, as it inevitably does in our quadrennial debate about our destiny. In the past, it has been common to discuss the views of the African-American community as if it were a monolith, speaking with a single voice. As I listen to those of my children's generation, I am keenly aware that is not necessarily true. There are growing generational differences in the attitudes of peoples of color toward the matter of race.

Where my generation placed a high premium on the importance of integration, my children's generation cares more about cultural identity and the right to express one's feelings openly and honestly, "whether other people like it or not," as one young man put it to me not so long ago.

In such a circumstance, our political leaders should be very careful this time around. They should be sure about whom they are speaking when they address the important issues of the concerns of the black community. I have become convinced there are deep generational fissures running through this nation today. No place are those divisions more evident than between generations in the black communities.

I think the basic issues of dignity and equal opportunity are still of abiding concern, as they have been for the past half-century. How those issues are expressed, however, is changing with the changing character of a different generation whose experiences are as different as be-bop and hip-hop.

Bridging those differences will be as much of a challenge in some instances as bridging the differences of race that still plague this nation. The danger lies in assuming that race alone determines attitude. Age has a great deal to do with the challenges we face in healing a society that has been riddled with deep divisions over the last few years. In our house, we find ourselves constantly fascinated by the great amount we can learn from each other. We find ourselves constantly referring back to that important bit of wisdom from author Stephen R. Covey: "Seek first to understand, then to be understood."

What's Cooking in the Melting Pot?

June 29, 1986—On Saturdays, when the workload was light, my father delighted in taking us on the moving van. We loved it for many reasons. Chief among them was that the cab was high above the ground, giving a grand view of the cityscape of the 1940s-era New York City.

The other important reason we loved to travel with my father on Saturdays was food. He seemed to know where all the best ethnic restaurants in New York were.

Since he was fluent in Italian and familiar with the culture, he had his favorite Neapolitan restaurant, his favorite from the Genoa region, his favorite from Sicily, and so forth.

Similarly, he adored kosher food, only it was my mother who had picked up a fair smattering of Yiddish. Our all-time family favorite was a place on the Lower East Side that is still there, Katz's Delicatessen.

Katz's produced what my father claimed to be the single best corned beef sandwich in all New York. As much time as he spent traveling the streets of the city, we figured he would know.

Exploring the many ethnic styles of New York, and eventually the country, became a habit of ours. Much of our early education about the diversity of America came through the exploration of food.

Indeed, as we get set for this country's 210th birthday, it is food that comes to mind. If one thing brings America together it is our tummies.

My early explorations with my parents taught me that the nations of the world gave us more than their tempest-tossed yearning to breathe free. Those myriad nations and cultures gave us pizza and bagels, tofu, sushi, Peking Duck, shish kabob and a thousand other unique offerings from distant corners of the globe.

Little by little, the American melting pot embraces these offerings and they slip into the mainstream. Consider, for example, the bagel. It is a round bread first boiled and then baked. It is thought to have come from Poland, where it was first served more than 200 years ago.

When I was a kid, lox, cream cheese and bagels were a treat for which you had to travel across town. Outside of a few neighborhoods, the bagel was unknown.

Things have changed. Eight million bagels are sold daily in the United States. It is a growth product line that now has its own followers among Wall Street stock analysts. One of the biggest bagel factories is in Middle America—Mattoon, Illinois.

Bagel buying has changed in the process. When we were kids we went to the bakery and bought our bread hot out of the oven. Half the bagels sold today are frozen, and they now come in dozens of new and exotic flavors. The bagel has been, in other words, Americanized.

The Americanization of pizza has been even more radical. It came across the ocean as a simple dish. It was a crust, a tasty tomato sauce and mozzarella cheese. It grew in popularity after World War II, and people began adding sausage, pepperoni, anchovies and the like.

In those days you found pizza primarily in Italian neighborhoods in small restaurants of the sort my father loved so much. They were places with names such as John's and Frank's and Joe's.

Then American marketing caught the pizza fancy. Now the names that are common across America are Straw Hat and Round Table. It comes frozen at the supermarket in dozens of varieties and configurations. By now, pizza pie is probably more American than apple pie.

That is what I think we miss in our July 4th celebrations. As we barbecue our hotdogs, really Americanized sausage, we tend to forget the wondrous way in which the rest of the world contributes to the American taste buds. And inevitably, the melting pot makes that unique offering uniquely American.

I heard a commercial the other day for a San Francisco pizza parlor. The offering of the day, unless my ears deceived me, was pineapple pizza. Pineapple? That's pizza? My dad would say, no, that's America.

Government

On the anniversary of the day Fidel Castro started the Cuban revolution, my father wrote me a long letter.

"It was on this day that something happened that was later to very nearly shake the world," Dad wrote, explaining how Castro and Che Guevera stormed a Cuban army base in a foiled attempt to take over the tiny Caribbean nation.

"He was asked at his trial to tell what he was trying to do. He said he wanted shoes for the little children, food for all the hungry people, liberty for those who were enslaved by the mean dictator and freedom for all the people in his country. History, he said, would prove that he was right. In other words, the future would tell the tale," Dad wrote.

I was four. The future did tell the tale and it did not have a happy ending. Later my father would document the despot's disappointing slide from young visionary to aging dictator.

At the time of his letter, though, Dad wanted me to begin to understand the power politics has in shaping a society and the power society has in shaping politics. Without trust, my father told me, both the citizens and politicians faced a shaky future.

It was a relationship he believed to be at the core of our country.

Just before President Johnson was to leave office, Dad took me with him when he was covering the White House. He spent the rest of the day quizzing me on the Vietnam War and the middle-class backlash, making sure I understood the reasons Johnson was leaving office.

"A politician breaks faith with the people at his own folly," my father would say.

Years later, during "Brinkley weekends," my father and I had uninterrupted time to talk about politics and government as he prepared for the roundtable discussion on "This Week with David Brinkley," the Sunday-morning talk show.

They were simple weekends. Friday night we would catch up with each other's news, watch "The ABC Evening News with Peter Jennings" and begin to plot strategy for the show. Saturday, ideas in mind, we would begin to stroll through the city.

We talked as we walked and that's where the predictability ended. Passing the White House we might restart the Watergate debate. Was the country well served by President Nixon's pardon? Or did that pardon lead us to an age of cynicism where people of all groups believed they had a right to break the law because the other guy got away with it?

Bloviation, we called it. The word is hard to find in the dictionary. We first ran into it when reading about former president Warren Harding. It is a word which aptly describes the fine art of holding a long conversation—a Maynard hobby.

Dad did his last Brinkley broadcast in the fall before he died. Clinton had just won the White House. We spent the weekend dissecting the campaign and predicting the future. We walked slowly down M Street, through Lafayette Square, past the White House and over to Fahrney's Pen Inc., Dad's favorite place for fountain pens.

Clinton, he warned, might have trouble as a Washington outsider who did not understand how to get along in the nation's capital. But Bush, a Washington insider, had been ousted because he did not understand the world outside Washington.

It was as he had said a few months earlier, speaking at George Washington University's graduation.

"There were two friends, each 16. They spent much of their time together talking about their dreams for the future. One friend said he wanted to lead a great university. The other said he wanted to become a journalist and grow up one day to own his own newspaper," Dad said.

"One of those two teenagers was your president, Steve Trachtenberg. The other was me. Ordinarily, we would call this a typically American story. These are not ordinary times. These are times of cynicism. Those were times of optimism," he said that May day in 1992, shortly after the Rodney King riots ripped through Los Angeles.

"Most of all, we believed in America and we were certain America believed in us. That, above all, is the covenant our country and its children must renew with each other."

D.J.M.

Conflicts of Freedom

June 12, 1991—She was furious and frustrated, my daughter said, over the debate that is raging over supposedly politically correct speech vs. protected free speech. The debaters, she insisted, were missing the point, "from President Bush on down."

This was to be another of those intergenerational encounters in which my generation always seems to be caught on the silent side of the conversation. My children often take the offensive in setting their parents straight at dinner about some issue of public moment. My parents, I remind the children, wasted no time in laying down the law to my siblings and me.

In both instances, I complained to no avail, I get to listen instead of laying down my version of the law. In this case, it turned out, my daughter and I were not all that far apart on the law.

"The problem is," my daughter the journalist was saying the other day, "that people such as the president confuse the right of political expression with the law against abusive speech, what the Supreme Court calls 'fighting words.'"

This argument is raging on campuses across the nation, but the debate so far has produced more heat than light. Now the U.S. Supreme Court has agreed to hear a Minnesota case involving the question of whether a local law that classifies cross burning as a hate crime might be unconstitutional.

So far I have little hope, and my daughter has less, that the court's decision in this case is going to untangle the muddle in which the nation finds itself over the question of whether direct, personal racist attacks have the same protection as legitimate forms of political expression.

The problem that bothers my daughter is that many people cannot distinguish protected speech from that speech the court has repeatedly said has no constitutional protection. As one justice put it many years ago, "Your freedom to extend your arm ends at the tip of my nose." And in another instance, she reminded me, a justice said that the right of free speech did not permit anyone to "falsely shout 'Fire!' in a crowded theater."

Certain speech, in other words, falls on the other side of the line from that which is protected as political expression. "If a person wants to stand up at a rally and denounce all black people or all homosexuals or people who are left-handed," my daughter was saying, "I regard that as constitutionally protected speech."

On the other hand, she said, "if some fool confronts me as one individual to another and begins to berate me with racial or sexual insults, that is not a free-speech question. Those are fighting words directed at me and calculated to cause a fight. The law has a right to limit his ability to do that, in my opinion."

The St. Paul, Minnesota, ordinance in question might not turn out to be drafted to the taste of this Supreme Court, but its intent was to address the same concern as the one raised by my daughter.

If a man wants to go out into a public park and burn a cross, that is no doubt a form of protected political expression. If, on the other hand, that same man comes onto the private property of an African-American family to burn a cross, as occurred in the Minnesota case the court will decide, that action should not enjoy constitutional protection.

The St. Paul ordinance might be flawed for reasons other than its policy intent. What the court will do with this subject is not easy to guess. It is clear from the speed with which the court agreed to hear the case that at least some are eager to speak to the raging debate over speech coursing through academia.

The Supreme Court has a great opportunity to clarify the issue by harking back to basic principles it has enunciated in the past. They are the same principles about which a daughter took pains to educate her father.

I was grateful for the refresher course, even while wondering how my generation came to be the one to listen to both ends of the generational cycle. "You're just lucky, I guess," she said.

Our Marvelous, Unique Constitution

May 31, 1987—If you can imagine it, the record showed this: One evening 12 delegates at the Constitutional Convention sat down to dinner in the spring of 1787 and consumed 60 bottles of wine. That works out to five bottles a man.

We also know that the summer of 1787 saw the worst heat wave in Philadelphia in 40 years. Maybe that explains all the wine.

More likely, though, it was the pressure of the job. Even now, 200 years after the fact, it is something of a marvel just to think of the obstacles those delegates overcame in the place we now call Independence Hall.

It was not just a great achievement for those times. What is even more amazing is how vast has been the change in the United States in the ensuing two centuries. The document drafted in Philadelphia, imperfect as it was, has managed to accommodate a staggering array of changes. More about that in a minute.

First, the problems that faced Washington, Franklin et al. in May 1787:

The original purpose of the meeting was not to write a new Constitution. It was to repair the old Articles of Confederation.

The states then thought of themselves pretty much as autonomous. The little ones lived in fear of being swallowed up by the big ones. England and Spain were sure the fragile revolution had failed and they hoped to consume the United States in pieces.

The bitter issues of slavery and human rights were ducked, left for future generations to resolve. All the same, lesser men might have failed to achieve even what those delegates did. They created more than a document. They articulated an idea of how free people should live.

The logic of their system was so compelling that future generations, after much agony, had little choice except to see to it that the excluded of 1787 became the included of 1987.

To appreciate the genius of the design of the system, one may look no further than the change in the scale of the country over 200 years.

Philadelphia was the second-largest city in the 13 original colonies. It had all of 30,000 souls in 1787. New York, the biggest town even then, had a population of 50,000. Philadelphia has a population today of 1.6 million and New York is more than seven million.

And so it went across the board. Providence, 6,300 then and 156,000 now. The state of Georgia, 426,000 then and six million now. Connecticut, 142,000 then and more than three million now. It is not just the domestic scale itself, but the diversity that that growth represents.

The men who drafted that document and drank all that wine did not think of themselves as a homogeneous group. True, they all shared an English heritage and were wealthy, but they also thought of themselves as very different. The staunch, stolid New Englanders were not to be mistaken in their own minds with the swashbuckling, free-wheeling Southerners. The feeling was mutual.

By today's standards, they were very much alike. We have seen migrations they would never have dared dream in 1787.

Because the Constitution created such a stable system, the world beat a path to this nation's doorstep. We are still struggling with the challenge of diversity, but the Constitution has proved in 200 years that it can hold up against all those pressures.

The delegates created a system, limited at first, capable of its own renewal and expansion. That remains its principal genius.

Constitutional scholars still marvel that the document ever happened at all. The room was closed and hot. They didn't open the windows out of fear that secrets of their discussion might reach the streets of Philadelphia.

Ultimately, a great deal of credit goes to George Washington. His stature as Revolutionary War hero and military leader kept the often heated debate from degenerating into chaos.

For all his leadership, Washington appears to have said little, proving again that the best leader is sometimes the best listener and not the best talker.

In any event they got it all done by September. It remains a model admired and emulated the world over. They stuck it out over the long, hot summer and brought off a document and a system that remain unique in the history of government. It took lots of smarts, lots of patience, and, apparently, lots of wine.

An Approachable President

May 12, 1993—My niece the philosophy student had us in stitches. She was telling the best Bill Clinton story the family had heard in at least 100 days. As she tells the story, it was a Saturday night. She had set aside her weighty tomes by obscure German sages to give them a well-earned rest. It was time to go out and have some fun.

The next thing she remembers, and her recall is vivid, was Bill Clinton. There she was, in a comfortable Georgetown watering hole, having a couple of beers with the president. "He's such a great conversationalist," she said. Besides, the president speaks a little German and she is bilingual in the language, so they must have had a lot to talk about. "We just hung out and had a really neat time," my niece reported while the rest of us howled.

My niece, of course, was dreaming. She's never met Bill Clinton. She fell asleep in her study and wound up dreaming about a casual conversation with a president. For her, the idea that an African-American graduate student would dream of hanging out with a president was stunning. "Imagine," she said, "someone as distant from the corridors of power as I am even dreaming of such a casual conversation."

My wife and I agreed that was a pretty farfetched dream. Just the same, something pertinent to the president's problems is revealed by that incident. My niece said she has found Clinton to be one of the most accessible political figures she has ever observed. Having lived long periods in Europe, she finds Clinton's remarkably open style to be a departure from anything she has experienced either at home or abroad. She could not imagine dreaming of having a beer with Helmut Kohl, John Major or George Bush. Yet it seemed almost real to have one with Clinton.

That, I feel certain, is one of the reasons Clinton is in the White House. People regard him as a delightful charmer who understands them and would listen to them all evening. You can easily envision him following you into the kitchen after dinner asking which recycling bin takes the paper napkins as he scrapes his own plate.

Therein the Clinton problem: He is too good at charming us and not yet good enough at governing us. He campaigns better than any politician of his generation. In the past, we've had presidents who were smashing on television, but frequently ineffectual in person. Ronald Reagan was that way without three-by-five index cards. Lyndon Johnson was just the opposite. He could charm the skin off a cobra in person. On television and before large audiences he was a disaster.

Clinton is great with crowds and equally terrific in one-on-one meetings. He is the total communicator. That's what came across to my niece. She could easily imagine chatting on about Goethe and Mann with Clinton. That trait, which got him elected, has become part of the criticism of him now. He's too quick to run in search of the crowds instead of bearing down on the execution of a planned agenda.

His critics are telling Clinton to show more personal discipline, to show up on time for scheduled engagements, to stick to the point in conversation and bring meetings to a precise conclusion with a plan of action.

When a president seems to be in trouble, especially a young president, there is a tendency to approach him as though he were a misguided adolescent. The president is provoking the national parental instinct. Everybody has an idea of what he should do to regain that elusive "focus" to which he himself has made several wistful allusions of late.

Time magazine, never shy about giving advice, has all but declared a midnight curfew for the young chief executive. It noted that after a long day, "he went back to the residence and unwound watching the Los Angeles Clippers–Houston Rockets basketball game. He did not get to bed until well after midnight." What if this presidential curfew idea sticks? Even collegians such as my niece are unlikely to dream of drinking with a curfew violator. Clinton still has time, but not much, to emerge as both charmer and leader. He was elected, after all, to govern.

Air Deregulation Was Half Right

July 26, 1987—They were soft raindrops of little significance on a warm Midwestern Sunday night. Off in the distance, a brief, bright bolt of lightning danced across the sky. It looked as much as anything like a leftover Roman candle from the Fourth of July.

If those raindrops and that lightning bolt had been anyplace else, they would have stirred no deep foreboding. What made all the difference is that I was watching them from inside the terminal of O'Hare International Airport, one of the world's busiest. In the instant in which I saw the few raindrops and well before the lightning bolt, I knew one thing for certain. It was going to be a long night getting home to Oakland.

Sure enough, two hours and 25 minutes later, we were still sitting on the runway, awaiting a parting in the clouds and other aircraft to either take off or land. Here we are, I thought, once again on the front lines in the deregulation war. Or is it the cross fire? I'm never sure.

Needless to say, I have had a good deal of time to ponder the subject of deregulation. If anything, I flew more during the days of regulation than I fly now, although sometimes that hardly seems possible. All the same, I have a basis for comparing the two regimes.

The problem of the agony in the sky, it seems to me, is due to a fairly simple affliction. I call it the split equation. A split equation occurs whenever someone develops only half of an argument and forgets to work out the other side.

Deregulation is a good example of a split equation. It basically suffers from being only half an idea. If someone had thought through the other half, we might not spend as many nights as so many Americans now do wondering when we will see our families again.

Back in the 1970s, deregulation fever roared across the land. It was an idea that seemed long overdue. Our markets have too many layers of regulation, went the cry. Free them and let them soar to their real possibilities. In a capitalist democracy, deregulation made a certain harmonious melody.

Indeed, in many instances—banking and financial institutions come readily to mind—the concept made a great deal of sense. Airline deregulation had a basic fallacy built into it that received scant attention then, but which is the crux of the matter now.

When the notion of open competition among airlines was advanced, the idea was that competition would drive prices down and travelers would benefit. What nobody in the planning of this idea appears to have considered is what would happen when those prices fell.

The effect was to bring millions more travelers into the system. They abandoned Greyhound and Trailways and took to the friendly skies. That sounds fine. In a truly open market, the airlines would have gone out and built more airports and runways and put into place the thousands of new air traffic controllers and computers necessary to accommodate all that new business.

That's the rub. Airline companies don't build airports. Indeed, the federal and state governments that have the responsibility for such matters can't get new airports built in crowded metropolitan areas. That's a political hot potato just about everywhere.

Therein lay the fallacy of deregulation of the air. The first half of the equation was dead right. Competition would lower fares.

The second consideration should have been to address the impact on the infrastructure of all that new demand. That question appears to have received little serious consideration. Indeed, the retiring head of the Federal Aviation Administration acknowledged his planners were taken wholly by surprise by the explosion in air travel.

The airlines can add flights, but there are only so many gates at peak hours, only so many runways, and not nearly enough seasoned air traffic controllers. The result? The system is frequently at its limit. Just as often, so is the public's patience.

The infrastructure that serves the air traveler under deregulation is the same basic system that existed before. The difference is that millions more passengers a day now compete to use it.

The net effect of this half-thought-out idea is this: In five years, there will be fewer major carriers than there were before deregulation in 1978. Moreover, the fares will be comparatively higher, service standards will be lower, and the customers will not regard themselves as better off.

As I sat on the rainy runway at O'Hare, I thought: "I have seen the future and it has been delayed."

From Watergate to Anita Hill

June 3, 1992—It was a deeply dispiriting evening. I remember the awkward way we sat, balancing chili bowls on laps, with our eyes glued to the living room TV. The man on the tube was babbling. He was talking about how his father almost struck oil. Almost. In fact, the old man had died broke. "Now, my mother," he was saying, "she was a saint." It went on in that maudlin vein. When we could bear it no more, we turned off the sound and waited for the final picture of the drama. He boarded a helicopter on the south lawn of the White House. Richard Nixon was finally gone. Gone and disgraced, we thought then, forever.

When I was very young, I learned from historians, mostly British scholars, about seminal events. These are moments in history that set the climate for a generation or more. Seminal events make possible changes that could not occur otherwise. They clarify issues by showering them with incandescence, illuminating them with a brilliance that transports their meaning through time and space.

The departure of Richard Milhous Nixon was a moment of signal prominence in our nation's politics. We can see now that it ushered in a new climate, fraught with possibilities for good and evil, so typical of the curious character of the man himself. The events that unfolded in California on Tuesday, indeed even events that unfolded a month ago in South Central Los Angeles, attest to forces that Richard Nixon's breach of the public trust unleashed.

Since we always put the good first when speaking of good and evil, let us begin with the good. Women made history in California on Tuesday. For the first time ever, two women will be running for the U.S. Senate as the nominees of their party. Not only that, both of them stand an excellent chance of winning. If they do—and even if women running for the Senate in Illinois and Pennsylvania should somehow fail—Barbara Boxer and Dianne Feinstein would double the female population of the Senate.

Richard Nixon, who reached the Senate by burying Helen Gahagan Douglas under a heap of anti-Communist hysteria, played a role here last Tuesday. Nixon, before the Watergate break-in exactly 20 years ago, presided over an American consensus. In its most benign rendering, it could be called the "Father Knows Best" motif of leadership. Its roots went deep in American political history. Abigail Adams wrote her husband John Adams in Philadelphia frequently. She always addressed him as "Dearest Friend." She challenged his colleagues and him to think of women as potential cofounders of the new republic. He ridiculed her in response. The next thing you know, John Adams grumbled back to Abigail, you'll be wanting us to include slaves.

That was not an accidental allusion. The two groups studiously ignored in the shaping of the American political ethos were women and people of color. A well-ordered government meant a government of, by and for white males. It remained that way for precisely two centuries.

By the time Nixon was in deep Dutch over Watergate, the benign notion of "Father Knows Best" had been transformed into the "imperial presidency." It wasn't just Nixon, but Johnson before him. And it was not just Watergate. The former slaves were demanding the very freedom John Adams disdained 200 years before.

More, the foundation underlying this concept, that well-ordered meant white male, was shattered by Nixon's breach of trust. In a social cauldron, a generation experienced a shattering crisis of faith. Here a man who had played ugly gender politics against Helen Douglas, and ugly racist politics under the direction of his henchman John Mitchell, was found guilty of high crimes and misdemeanors. He was, despite his oath to the contrary, a crook. A crook in a high place. A crook in the highest place of all. He and his counselors, every one a white male.

There the seed was sown. The genie was out the bottle. The mantle had fallen and been trampled underfoot. Political power need not mean white male only.

Years later, Anita Hill came to town and told her lurid tale of abuse to a panel of white males. The country could see writ bold the evidence that the old way no longer works.

In South Central Los Angeles, angry young men watched power being exercised by the LAPD on the tube, feeling powerless. The lid blew off. It was another ugly example of the power of evil. Another rocket has gone up saying the old arrangements are suspect. New ideas and new blood are needed. That is what the voters said in California. That is what they are saying across the country. More change is on the way, all made speedier by Richard Nixon's seminal breach of faith. It set the stage for a climate change a generation long or more.

A Blossoming of Black Conservatism

November 7, 1985—It was 1968, the year of riot and protest. The letter invited coverage of the first national meeting of black conservative Republicans in Washington, D.C. Intrigued by the potential counterpoint to the activities on the streets and the campus, I requested permission from my editor to cover the event.

"No way," the editor responded. "I would no sooner have you cover that than I would a convention of three-headed calves. It may be a phenomenon, but a representative trend it is not."

Oddity though it might still be to some, the rise of black conservatism is now a decided trend among young blacks.

Deroy Murdock of Los Angeles is 21, black, a senior at Georgetown University and an evangelist of the new right. Sometimes a harsh critic of Ronald Reagan, Murdock accuses the president of abandoning the conservative agenda.

It is startling to many other blacks to hear Murdock refer to affirmative action programs as "covert racism" or to hear him defend the administration's constructive engagement program with respect to South Africa. He is in favor of prayer in the public schools and the entire panoply of the far right agenda. He has attracted a great deal of attention.

In a recent, lengthy profile in the *Washington Post*, congressional conservatives and their supporters were lavish in their praise of Murdock.

"Let me tell you something," said Sen. Orrin Hatch (R-Utah), for whom Murdock worked as a part-time aide. "This young man is going to be a major leader in this country someday. He has that kind of personality . . . I think Deroy is going to be a U.S. senator someday, maybe even more than that. He can go right to the top. He's that good."

To some degree, Murdock is regarded in some quarters as being about as improbable as a three-headed calf. Just the same, the reality is that the number of right-wing blacks in the United States is growing. The group among which it is growing fastest is the young.

In 1980, public opinion polls showed only 10 percent of blacks approved of the job Ronald Reagan was doing as president. In 1985, that number had jumped to 28 percent for blacks of all ages and to 33 percent for those below the age of 30.

Joseph Perkins, 26, an editorial writer for *The Wall Street Journal*, said, "Young blacks like us don't have the baggage of bygone years. We're role models to the extent that we're demonstrating that it's not necessary to benefit from the paternalism of the liberal establishment to be successful."

Two distinct factors help account for the emergence of a new, conservative, middle-class black American:

First, the opening of the doors of opportunity closed during the days of legal segregation. To the extent that blacks are free to pursue the American dream as any other American, inevitably some will choose a conservative ideology. They make that choice, however, while often overlooking the role the liberal coalition played in developing minority opportunity.

Second, conservatism is where all the action is today, and it is natural that some bright, ambitious young black people will gravitate to that action. In doing so, they know the field is wide open because there are still few black conservatives against whom to compete.

It is also important to keep in perspective the fact that the black communities of the United States historically have been more conservative and religious than many of their white allies in the old civil rights coalition. Indeed, until the advent of the New Deal in the 1930s, the overwhelming majority of black voters were Republicans.

For years, many of the legatees of that old black GOP tradition have been arguing that blacks made a strategic political error by becoming so overwhelmingly and predictably Democratic.

Now, to the astonishment of many political observers, highly conservative black people are a lot more common than the three-headed calf.

What Jefferson Wrote
and the Way We Live

July 5, 1981—Most of us have a holiday ritual, a thing we might not think much about until a certain date rolls around on the calendar. The time for one of my favorite rituals is upon us. Sometime during the first week of every July, I like to sit and think about Thomas Jefferson and read once again his (and our) Declaration of Independence.

One thing I cannot do now that I often did when I lived in Washington is to cross the Tidal Basin and enter the Jefferson Memorial and try to hear the voice of the man who could be called the genius of our democracy.

Soon after John F. Kennedy became president, he assembled a group of American scientists to form a council of scientific advisers. Nobel laureates and other great leaders of science and technology gathered in one of Kennedy's favorite rooms at the White House. He began his greeting by saying, "Never has such intellect been assembled in this room, except when Mr. Jefferson dined here alone."

Dumas Malone, the 83-year-old historian who has just completed his sixth volume on Jefferson, was talking about him on television the other day. He reminded Charles Kuralt of CBS News that there was virtually no subject in which Jefferson lacked interest, not mathematics or botany, not history or science. He loved knowledge, Malone said, and he celebrated in the idea of the power of knowledge.

Perhaps he loved one thing more than knowledge itself. He loved the idea of democracy. Aristotle said: "If liberty and equality are to be found in democracy, they be best attained when all persons share in the government to the utmost." That was Jefferson's idea, too.

And, as Malone was saying the other day, when Jefferson put his pen to paper to write the Declaration of Independence, "It was perfect . . . you couldn't touch a word" to improve on what he wrote. To read Jefferson's declaration is to be impressed—impressed to the point where the word "brilliant" would be a trite description of what he accomplished. Perhaps awesome would be more like it.

Yet brilliance, too, has its contradictions and they are readily apparent in any reflection upon the life of Jefferson. I used to stand in the shadow of the statue in the memorial and think of my favorite Jeffersonian sentence:

"We hold these truths to be self-evident that all men are created equal, that they are endowed by their Creator with certain unalienable Rights, that among these are Life, Liberty and the pursuit of Happiness."

How come, I would then ask him, you owned slaves if you could write a sentence of such universal principle as that one? How come? Winthrop Jordan, the University of California historian who wrote *White Over Black*, suggests a partial answer.

He wrote that the reaction of Americans of that day to the "shocks of revolution" was a mixed one. "They hoped for the triumph of liberty in the world but not for a complete one. They delighted to talk of freedom, but they wished their slaves would not. They assumed their slaves yearned for liberty but were determined not to let them have it."

Jefferson, to square his "all men" sentence with the reality of life at Monticello and throughout the South, managed a little logical legerdemain in which he concluded that blacks were not quite yet human, but were someplace above a baboon and below a (white) man.

Still troubled in his conscience, Jefferson resolved that conflict by willing that his slaves be freed upon his death. The matter of Sally Hemmings compounds the contradiction. The late Fawn M. Brodie, a UCLA historian, wrote a compelling narrative of Jefferson's life with Sally Hemmings, a black woman with whom Brodie said Jefferson shared a long, secret love. Other Jefferson historians, most notably Malone, have denouced Brodie's work, but much of her documentation remains essentially unchallenged.

If Brodie is correct, the contradiction is deepened for it suggests that Jefferson's ambivalence about black people and the subject of liberty was deeper than it would appear at first. It is one thing to write that "all men" are created equal and still hold slaves. It is quite another to hold slaves on the basis that they are not quite human and yet have one as a lover and close companion.

Those are the contradictions that are eternally fascinating about Thomas Jefferson. I often wonder if in some sense this contradiction in this one dazzling intellectual does not speak in larger realms about the contradictions of American democracy with which we have been wrestling now for 205 years.

Surely Aristotle was correct when he said liberty and equality are best attained "when all persons share in the government to the utmost." The good sense of that prescription came home to me with brutal force when I was assigned in the 1960s to cover the story of the burning of the American cities. I looked upon the raging mobs and the blazing buildings and I wondered if it were not true that people with a stake in their society would not seek to destroy it.

To recover from the trauma of those days, I often retreated to Jefferson and sought the answer to the imponderable. Suppose he and the other revolutionaries of his day had faced up right then to the contradiction and said that slavery and freedom will not mix? Suppose they made up their minds right then to end slavery and its mockery of democracy?

It is, of course, a fantasy. They did not determine to end slavery. Instead, they mollified their southern compatriots by creating elaborate subterfuges that they hoped would permit the formation of a democratic republic while preserving the South's cherished right to maintain slavery.

It finally became Abraham Lincoln's solemn chore to declare that the United States could not long last "half slave and half free." That was almost 100 years and a civil war after Jefferson's stirring declaration. And more than 100 years after Lincoln, there are those in the South and in the inner cities and barrios of the North who wonder still if our society will ever resolve this profound contradiction over race that has been our painful legacy for all these years.

The question was never better put than by Frederick Douglass in 1852 in a July 4th oration in Rochester, New York. "What to a slave," he demanded, "is your Fourth of July?"

More than a century later, coming from witnessing the destruction of Newark, New Jersey, my ears were ringing with the sounds of angry oaths, the sounds of children chanting death to American society and the smell of tear gas still on my clothes. I asked the taxicab driver at Washington National Airport if we could stop at the Jefferson Memorial on the way to my apartment, and he said yes.

For a long minute, I reflected on the words that conclude Jefferson's awesome declaration: "And for the support of this Declaration, with a firm reliance on the protection of divine Providence, we mutually pledge to each other our Lives, our Fortunes and our sacred Honor."

Fawn Brodie said of Thomas Jefferson:

"Only his conflict over the just treatment of the black people in his life, whose voices, certainly articulate at the time but silent in the documents that have come down to us, remained unresolved, troubling and corrosive."

That is why Thomas Jefferson remains a fascinating contradiction. His life is almost a metaphor for our state of racial relations, still today "troubling and corrosive." And so they will continue to be until that day when we finally find out how to put aside our expensive racial divisions and learn once and for all to pledge to each other, race notwithstanding, "our Lives, our Fortunes and our sacred Honor."

What a Fourth of July that will be.

Hard Times

Every time we went back to the old neighborhood where he grew up, Daddy would point to vacant windows in abandoned buildings and describe what used to be. A law firm, a music school, a friend's home. It's hard now, looking back, to remember all the landmarks we passed. There were so many.

We didn't go often, but when we did go back through Bedford Stuyvesant, we always took a couple of hours to meander while Dad gave his running commentary. Most of the sites depended on the streets we walked, except for one. Almost all streets led to Boys High. There Daddy went to school with David Horowitz, the consumer affairs reporter, and Stephen Joel Trachtenberg, the president of George Washington University. American composer Aaron Copland also went to Boys High, though he was not in Dad's class.

It was at Boys High where Daddy met Mr. Blum, the English teacher, after Daddy was kicked out of Mrs. Pine's English class for pointing out a mistake she had made.

"You just write me an essay every day. I don't care what you write about, you write about what interests you, but you just write," Daddy remembered the teacher telling him. Mr. Blum never gave Dad any of his essays back. He never really commented on them. After Daddy left school and moved to Greenwich Village, he bumped into a friend of Mr. Blum's.

"Eugene Blum," the friend said, "told my father that the best writer he had ever seen in a high school class is a Negro kid named Maynard. Is that you? He said you are an absolutely incredible writer."

And Mr. Blum, said my father years later, was a great teacher.

"He achieved the classic purpose of the teacher," Dad wrote in a journal entry. "He had a lasting effect on his students and through them on society. How important are teachers? Only that important."

By the time I was old enough to hear those stories, the Bedford Stuyvesant of Dad's youth was gone. Mr. Blum had long since retired and Boys High had merged with Girls High. The old Boys High building now houses an alternative school.

I could only imagine the once cozy, integrated neighborhood where parents looked after each other's children. There were no more Mr. Ficcaros to give a kid his first job. Most of the tight-knit West Indian community had moved. The elegant brownstones were boarded up or cut up into apartments. By the mid-1960s, Bedford Stuyvesant had become a symbol of urban blight and poverty.

Walking through Bed-Sty, we talked about Robert Moses, the once-powerful New York City commissioner who built the highways out of New York. Daddy told me about the G.I. Bill and federally approved housing loans which helped many white families build new homes in the suburbs just cropping up.

It nagged at him as he walked through what was left of his childhood neighborhood. None of his children were raised in the old neighborhood. He couldn't even imagine growing up there these days. Yet plenty of children are being raised there, and that nagged at Daddy.

What was his old neighborhood like for the children growing up there now, without Mr. Blum, or the parents who punished you for your misdeeds before you even made it home? What were their lives going to mean in our future? Walking those streets, Daddy would remember his mother's warning that idle hands were the devil's tool. What, he wondered, would his mother make of her neighborhood now?

D.J.M.

Message from the Underclass

December 16, 1990 —This young dude was "just out of the joint" and eager to talk to strangers on line at the airport. He said he did a "trey" in the state's custody for armed robbery. A "trey," I later deduced, is three years. "The joint is OK," he said, "half-decent food and all my friends," but now he wanted to "stay out here." For that he knew he would need training.

He was tall, good-looking and black. As he described his ambitions, I could not help but wonder which of two diametrically opposite statistical possibilities awaited him. His chances of going back to prison are twice as great as those that he will eventually graduate from college.

If . . . I kept thinking as we talked . . . if he stayed the course and graduated into a decent field, he could wind up far away from the life of the street that landed him in the slam. I felt the tension as he described his possibilities.

Talking with this young man made my mind go back to the days of protest in the '60s, before this kid was born. In a way, those protests were supposed to have been for young people yet unborn. They were expected to break the bonds of segregation and poverty and set people free to become equal in America.

Instead, a peculiar thing happened on the way to equality. Some people of color, especially those with good education or some special training, have found their way to the mainstream in increasing numbers. No doubt they encountered racist obstacles and will continue to have to combat them. Mostly, they will overcome, as the song says.

At the same time, a burgeoning underclass threatens the stability of the entire society. Nearly half the nation's black children now live in poverty. Moreover, their life expectancy is no greater than that of a baby born the same day in Bangladesh, one of the poorest nations on Earth. These are circumstances with the power, in time, to destabilize our whole society. These are individual failures that collectively become social dynamite in our midst.

"In some areas of the country," said Dr. Robert Froehlke, "it is now more likely for a black male between his 15th and 25th birthday to die of homicide than it was for a United States soldier to be killed on a tour of duty in Vietnam."

Dr. Froehlke is an epidemiologist at the federal Centers for Disease Control. The epidemic disease he is trying to control at the moment is young, black male homicide. He is losing ground every day. Across the nation, from Oakland to Chicago to New York, the cry is the same: Stop the violence.

That, you may recall, was one of the clarion calls of the anti-Vietnam era of the '60s. Now, physicians, police officers, urban clergy and social workers have raised the cry again. This time, the object of the protest is more amorphous.

The principal reasons for this homicide epidemic, Dr. Froehlke and his colleagues said, were "immediate access to firearms, alcohol and drugs, poverty, racial discrimination . . ." They go on. A spate of studies emerged about this problem just around the time I met the young man who wants to go straight.

All those studies played on the themes of the black man as an endangered species. One inner-city counselor burst forth with a "condor" metaphor. "Young blacks are an endangered species," said Charles Norman of Los Angeles. "They are dying out, like the condor, out there on the streets."

Dr. Froehlke said, "If there were a disease that was causing 40 percent of deaths in a group that should be at the peak of physical health . . . there would be substantial public health efforts trying to address it."

The Joint Center for Political and Economic Studies predicted the other day that urban problems are likely only to worsen, not improve. It said larger and larger numbers of black babies are being born to single mothers with few prospects of jobs or marriage.

"If current trends hold," the Washington think tank said, "these children will be increasingly hard-pressed to overcome the burdens imposed by poverty. Growing numbers of them will not succeed."

Those "burdens" have never been more massive—guns, drugs, rejection, alienation from society and a searing anger at how little value is their social currency.

Which way? I wondered of my airport companion. At first, I hoped he'd make it for his sake. Then I hoped he'd make it for all of our sakes.

The Finicky Face of Justice

March 4, 1990—One of the rare pleasures of balmy winter in California is the opportunity the weather affords for noon-hour strolls. On a lucky day, now and again, time permits me to stroll around downtown Oakland.

Even after 10 years, I still see something I had not noticed before, some architectural detail, or the way the sun strikes a pane of glass or perhaps the breathtaking strides of construction workers walking across steel beams 250 feet in the air.

As I was gazing up in awe at the steel-strolling workers, a young man approached me with a broad smile on his face. He'd heard me speak at his school, he said, and he had always wanted to meet me. That was years ago, he said. He had "been in" for some time.

"Been in" where? I started to ask when it dawned on me not to ask. I knew. He had been to prison. He was just a tall, skinny kid, about the size of my oldest son, the teenager. Now he was out, the young man said, and he wanted a chance to have a job with meaning.

As he talked of his ambitions, my heart went out to the earnest youngster. He was so sure he could make it, he said, if only he had the right opportunity. Finally, I had a suggestion. How would he like to give a call to the head of Human Resources at our newspaper?

He fumbled for a pen and paper. I offered mine. Then the sad thing happened. As I started to give him her name, a look of complete terror and confusion crossed the young man's face. "Would you," he asked politely, "write it out for me?" He was illiterate. Sad to say, there aren't too many jobs on a newspaper for illiterate workers.

That vivid recollection was still fresh in my mind a few days later when the news broke about young black men and the law. It said one-quarter of black men in their 20s were either in jail or under the supervision of the criminal justice system.

On television, the pictures they showed of those young men behind bars looked hauntingly like the young man who stopped me on the street in Oakland. I kept seeing his face among the pictures of the prison bars. I know that a young man who cannot read and write in our society has little chance of staying out of jail.

This massive waste of human resources became much more personal for me as I read the news and the analysis of this "lost generation" of youth without hope. That is what one of the social workers called this group of black youngsters, a lost generation.

Nobody knows what will happen to this group of young Americans. "We don't know what it will mean for the future," said Marc Mauer, author of the report, "because we have never had a situation like this before."

Those words struck me as powerfully ironic. My mind went spinning back 20 years to 1970. One of my responsibilities in those days was to write about the social policies of the Nixon administration.

That year, a Washington think tank came out with a report that spoke of young urban men who were ill-educated and untrained. For the first time, the report said, there existed in America a group of young men and women who might never hold gainful employment.

Before it assumed the usual position of Washington think-tank reports, gathering dust, this one caused a stir. What would it be like, several of us asked, if nothing is done? As I read the latest report, the most significant ramifications of the first report's findings were now obvious.

A second generation of those permanently impaired citizens is now on the streets. In the 20 years since the first report, those about whom it was written are on the verge of becoming grandparents.

The young man I met in downtown Oakland had not been born when that Washington report was written. We are repeating our past mistakes, and the price promises to mount as illiterate, alienated youngsters commute between the inner cities and the prisons.

Our national imagination failed us 20 years ago. Unless somebody in Washington decides to pay attention, history will continue to repeat itself, and we will be the lesser for that fact.

Splitting Generational Seams

June 21, 1992—The young woman was furious at her parents. She didn't know who her father was, she said. As far as she could recall, she had never seen him. Her mother was not at home, possibly "stressed out" someplace on crack cocaine. What right, the young woman asked in a rising voice, did her parents have to be so irresponsible? At 16, she lived with her elderly grandmother, but in truth she was on her own.

The occasion of her comments was one of the series of open hearings we have been holding with the young people of Oakland. In two sessions, we have heard from almost 200 city youngsters, most between 15 and 21, about the quality of their lives. The biggest surprise was the explosion of generational anger. Children need parents. Many of the children who have chosen to come to the youth assemblies to tell their stories speak most vehemently about the disappointments they have experienced because of adult failure.

These disappointments begin with parents. They are also unhappy about ill-staffed, ill-equipped and ill-tempered school environments. The lack of constructive recreational activities is also high on the list of present-day urban adolescent discontent. Needless to say, many of them have other concerns, not the least of them "hassles" with the police over relatively trivial issues.

The school complaints, the lack of recreation and the police hassles were all things one might have predicted before the youth hearings began in early May. How these young people feel about their parents was something else. It is not just that they feel angry at being deprived of something so basic and "normal" as parents. What makes their anger all the more arresting is that it is tinged with genuine outrage.

"What right," the young woman asked, "do these people have to bring children in the world if they don't intend to take care of them?" Grandparents, the young people said, try hard, but they just don't begin to take the place of their flesh-and-blood parents.

Many of the problems of urban America today can be traced to this complaint. The fact that so many parents, fathers and mothers, have abandoned their children has meant that a generation of youngsters has been left to raise itself. When you add to this tragic phenomenon the lack of such resources as education and recreation, you can see the deadly tinder we are storing up.

We learned a new term in our dialogue with Oakland young people. That term is "recreational violence." As one young man put it, "When we don't have nothing better to do, we just go out and find somebody to beat up." This young black man said the targets of his recreational violence tend to be Asian or white. Another described being the victim of recreational violence at the hands of a group of white youths.

These discussions have opened up new horizons for exploration. As we struggle to come to grips with many urban ills, we must face the issue of generations squarely.

The country is coming apart at its seams. The gender seam is clearly rent. So are the racial seams. Those are obvious, as is the class seam. The split in the generational seam is less visible. It is not just about absent fathers and disappearing mothers. Even in homes with both parents, the generational split is more pronounced than it was when I was growing up. The very fact that both parents are likely to work outside the home places stresses on family life. It takes so much more effort to meet the material needs of the family. The children feel neglected, often, by the career demands on their parents.

In larger political terms, the generational split also has a racial and class component. In California, an older, white electorate was the vanguard of a "tax rebellion" in the late '70s. The effect of Proposition 13 was a huge disinvestment in schools and recreational opportunities for a growing population of less well-off children of color. Just the other day, the U.S. Supreme Court upheld Proposition 13. No one here was surprised.

In the last 20 years, we have seen a significant increase in the affluence of the elderly and an increase in the number of children in poverty. There are those who call this "generational warfare." That term seemed abstract to me until I heard about another form of the war, the anger of our young people over the neglect and abuse some of them suffer from an older generation.

This leads me to one of the unfulfilled roles of government, a challenge for the next president. It has to do with generations. We need a leader who can broker the relationships between the generations. The answer cannot be continued generational warfare. As in all other wars, there will be more victims than victors. We need help as a nation to strike the appropriate balances. We need leadership help in establishing our relative responsibilities to each other. Otherwise, we will realize one day how badly we all have lost.

Bad Times, Bad Deeds

January 6, 1991—Because he's been hearing and reading so much about bad economic times lately, our youngest began grilling me on the way to school a few weeks ago about economic history. He wanted especially to know about the Great Depression. How much did I remember? Not much, I told him. It was over by the time I was three or four years old.

What about crime back then? he pressed on. Were Bonnie Parker and Clyde Barrow real? Yes, I said. Would he like to see the movie *Bonnie and Clyde?* It came as a "surprise" in his Christmas stocking. We watched it Christmas night so we could talk about that era.

I recommend a revisit to *Bonnie and Clyde* for all those who speak casually of the notion that we are headed back to the '30s. As my 11-year-old said after the final hail of bullets in the movie, "Dad, that was one mean time." The state of law enforcement was only slightly worse than the condition of the banks.

Before long, my son and I had gone beyond discussing just two kinky desperadoes to a discussion of the history of bad times in America. They tend to bring out the worst in people, I told him.

We need not experience anything like the '30s to know what hard economic times do to the nation as a whole. The other day, we noticed in the morning paper that the incidence of hate crimes is on the rise.

In the Bay Area, as notable for tolerance as for its California sunshine, the number of vicious attacks on synagogues is on the rise. In Oakland the other day, an arsonist attempted to destroy a synagogue.

At first our family did not know what to make of this upsurge in racially motivated criminal activity. Now that we have begun to discuss it, the children see a clearer pattern. As the economy appears to worsen, racial enmity appears to increase.

Going back even before the Depression, the rise of the Ku Klux Klan in the '20s was a function of bad economic times. It has been helpful to our children to understand and have a context for the rising racial tension we see around us. As the economic pie shrinks, the contention over share can become more mean and vicious.

Across the nation, on campuses, in cities and small towns, there is an increasing number of racial incidents with explosive consequences. Some of them are verbal slurs; others are becoming more violent. Racist and anti-Semitic graffiti is escalating. The ordinary forms of civil tolerance are being tested.

In such a climate, government agencies are being asked to try to deal with hate crimes, when few are equipped to do so very well. More police agencies are forming hate crimes units, even as legislatures struggle to define hate crimes. Civil libertarians are arguing in some instances that hate crimes to one group are free speech to another.

I question whether the police can be effective with any other than the actually violent. There is no question, however, that there are two natural allies who should be working together to address this problem on a local and a national level.

The two groups I have in mind are educators and religious leaders. Children are not born hating. They learn hateful words and notions from the adults around them and from other children. I am a great believer in the idea that anything that can be learned can be unlearned.

In the case of hate, there should be some common ground in virtually all communities where the local religious leaders and educators could open a dialogue on how to address a moral issue of this magnitude. Can such discussions take place without running afoul of the prohibition against teaching religion in school?

That's a hard question these days, but if it is addressed, some positive solution will emerge. These times are bringing out some ugly stuff that can do our society and vulnerable citizens long-term harm. The problem should be addressed in both its moral and its educational dimensions. If we don't do something concerted soon, we'll one day wish we had.

The Devil Finds Work for Idle Hands

May 24, 1981—Once, when I had the leisure time for such activities. I had the privilege of reading some translations from Sumerian tablets that dated back to 4000 B.C. They were among the oldest written messages known to exist. The most arresting of them was a message from a father to a teenage son. He was urging the lad to work with diligence and not to associate with those of the village who were idlers and mischief-makers.

The old man did not say so exactly, but the message to his son was no different from the message of my mother to my brothers and myself when we were teenagers: The devil finds work for idle hands. It struck me while reading those ancient writings that the problem of keeping young people out of trouble is probably as old as the human race. And so is the solution: Find ways to keep them busy.

Because of the dismaying crime rate in Oakland, the problem sometimes appears to us in this community to be overwhelming. We have held conferences on the subject. It has been analyzed in the newspapers. We receive letters urging us to call for longer and longer jail sentences.

Last January, this newspaper studied the 1980 crime rate with some care. We have noticed that the violence of last year is likely to be repeated this year, and it might even be worse. We have heard much learned discourse from social scientists and others about the problems of the family and failures of the education system, the problem of crowded housing conditions and the proliferation of drug addiction.

All those are bitter social realities. But after listening to all the expressed concern, the matter comes back to me, first and foremost, as the problem of all those idle hands. In some neighborhoods in Oakland, the rate of teenage unemployment is 40 percent, by conservative estimate. The same condition exists in most major cities with much the same result. Alienated youngsters, full of energy, roam the streets and find outlets for that energy in some antisocial activity.

Worse, the changing nature of the job market suggests that some of those young people may never find a way to earn the self-respect that comes from a decent job. We are on the verge of creating a permanent "under class" of alienated semiliterates for whom society has no use.

More than a generation ago, the former president of Harvard University, James Bryant Conant, looked at this problem and forecast that this country was creating a condition he called "social dynamite." We witnessed the accuracy of his prophecy in the explosions of the 1960s, and we have done nothing about it. Now, we are in the 1980s, and the dynamite is becoming a social cancer eating away at the heart of our great cities, Oakland being a prime example.

The question is whether this condition is reversible or whether we are doomed to relive the lessons of the past because we have not learned from them. Ever an optimist, I live in the belief that we can make the future of our choice, provided we are willing to do what is necessary to build that future. But I am not so foolish as to believe that any community can do this job alone. We need the creative leadership of government at the federal, state and local level.

We also need a partnership between business and the local community, a partnership that involves the schools and the churches, the civic organizations and the police. We need a sense of common purpose and a firm belief that change and progress are possible.

Unfortunately, the problem of crime has about it something that appeals to the worst in politicians. It is a lovely subject on which to spout rhetoric about longer sentences and tougher judges because those are easy things to say. But devising a plan to involve millions of poor children in constructive activity takes work, imagination and m-o-n-e-y. Popularity requires that we champion the reduction of tax burdens and other palliatives that appeal to voters.

Meanwhile, the problem of unemployed youth grows more serious with each passing year. Dynamite or cancer, call it what you please, it is a problem that belongs to all of us and affects all of us. And it takes all of us to solve it.

In the five months that the Reagan administration has been in office, I have heard virtually nothing that suggests there is even an awareness that our cities are still in deep trouble and that they cannot bail themselves out alone. City government in Oakland is about to become the custodian of police and fire services and almost nothing else. The same is true in many other parts of the country.

I am not so naive as to believe that this is a problem whose solutions lie in Washington. The solutions require careful coordination and much hard work at the local level, but some of the money and the support has to come from the central government.

The goal of public policy at the federal and local level must be to make productive citizens of those who now languish outside the mainstream and grow increasingly resentful of those who are in the mainstream, no matter by how narrow a margin.

People with no stake in the public order are not likely to respect it out of anything other than fear. We can become ever more resourceful at locking people up, but it is not a very promising or pretty picture of what we shall soon become as a society. Sooner or later, we have to come to terms with a simple fact: These alienated and antisocial youngsters are our children, too. If ever we face an enemy and need soldiers, we will expect East Oakland to send forth its share.

The founders knew we would only make it as a society if we developed a sense of our common purpose and if we continued to possess a common pride in our unique civilization. They framed a constitution founded on those premises, and it remains as inspiring a set of principles as have been devised by man.

For all that, it is not self-sustaining. The compact between us all as sovereign citizens requires a certain generosity of spirit and a willingness to grapple with our thornier problems.

None of this absolves any of us of our individual responsibility to be good citizens and obey the laws. To be poor is no justification for lawlessness. To be deprived is no excuse to deprive another of his or her property.

To know that as an abstraction is not enough. We must also recognize that rejection is a profound element in antisocial behavior. When people believe they have been declared expendable, they lose their ability sometimes to look kindly upon their neighbors.

To put the matter in the simple terms in which my mother so often put it, those idle hands and minds and bodies are willing prey for the devilish among us.

Somebody knew that in Sumer 6,000 years ago and wrote it on a piece of stone. If anything is more depressing than the crime rate itself, it must be how little we seem to have learned from the simple wisdom of the ages.

New York and Other Cities

It was a long walk, the kind we took when we had time. We had probably meant to take the subway. At dusk we took a detour. Daddy decided to show me his childhood schoolyard. One block led to another in the dim Brooklyn night.

We had been in Crown Heights for a family reunion and were on our way to Manhattan to hear some jazz. It was early yet, so there was nothing to stop us from poking through the stores and exploring the streets in a borough of memories.

The bodegas were still there, their narrow aisles overflowing with green bananas, canned goods and cookies. Now they were joined by other stores, shelves mostly empty, a Plexiglas curtain standing between cashier and customer. My father guessed at their stock in trade: "Drugs."

Crown Heights became Bedford Stuyvesant. We passed Boys High, his alma mater. We did not make our way to Marcy Avenue, the street where Daddy grew up. It was getting dark and there was really no need. We had been before. All that was left was the shell of my father's childhood house. Walking through the burnt-out door, Daddy had taken us on a tour. Soon charred railings became a long banister that needed to be polished each week. Upstairs, standing on boards that showed through to the floor below, he sketched out family bedrooms. By the time we left that afternoon, he'd rebuilt a regal Brooklyn brownstone.

There were no stops in the past this night. We kept walking and talking, and soon, as evening turned to night, Bedford Stuyvesant became Fort Greene, the neighborhood where I had spent a good portion of my childhood.

It was warm. Families talked softly on stoops while teenagers laughed and listened to music on the sidewalk. Children played hopscotch on barely visible lines or chased each other down the street. Some people gave us a friendly nod as we passed. Others, engrossed in their business, ignored us. We could hear a steady murmur tinged with West Indian, Spanish, Southern and Brooklyn accents as we walked toward the end of Brooklyn. The music of steel drums, soulful songs and Latino rhythms, like the accents, blended together.

It was quiet in Brooklyn Heights. The streets were almost empty. We walked over the Promenade, looked at the Manhattan skyline across the river. The red light on the Empire State Building still blinked the way it did when I was a toddler and Daddy took me to the riverfront and pointed out the twinkling light against the dark sky.

We walked for hours that night. In Manhattan we strolled through the noisy streets of the village. We never did get to hear any jazz. Instead we poked around the all-night bookstores, stopping for a quick drink in a crowded, smoky bar before heading on.

We marveled at the many wonders to be found in one city and we wondered. We wondered about the barbed wire blocking some buildings. We wondered about the tension creeping into the city, between the many ethnic groups who had quietly lived there for generations.

It gnawed at my father, a lifelong student of culture, economics and politics. Daddy predicted the urban skirmishes to come. It hurt. He loved the city, its place in our society.

"Good urban life breeds the betterment of the whole society. Just as surely, bad urban life assures the decline of the rest of a society," he wrote in his journal.

Hanging out at the Washington Park fountain with other would-be writers, actors, painters and poets, on his bicycle in Little Italy during a festival, or walking through Harlem, going to the Apollo, all were the backdrops of his education. New York was his classroom.

We used to play a game as we traveled around the country. Pointing at random at a busy block in a new city, Dad would ask me to look closely. Then I had to tell him what I could guess about the neighborhood and its residents.

We didn't play that game that night in New York. There was no need. We just enjoyed the night sights of the city as we walked and talked and hoped it would never end.

D.J.M.

Guns, Politics and Civilization

March 24, 1993—You may have had culture clashes in your life, or you've known of others who have had them. Because we are such a mobile society in the United States, they happen all the time.

I still think this one is in a class by itself: Picture an African-American young man of 22 years old. He was born and raised in Brooklyn. Bedford Stuyvesant no less. He is striving to become a journalist. He finally gets his big break.

He is hired as a reporter on a small newspaper in rural York County, Pennsylvania. He leaves the largest and most diverse urban center in North America to travel to one of its least urban and least diverse communities.

The year was 1961 and York was virtually all white. To this day, most of its population is of German extraction. They are known to the world as the Pennsylvania Dutch, even though their roots are actually in southern Germany.

That young journalist was me. Big adjustment is an understatement.

One day I was bopping through the broad boulevards and narrow alleys of Lower Manhattan. The next I was living in a town whose whole population would have fit on one square block of New York apartments. For weeks I could not sleep for the lack of traffic noise.

But that was not the biggest adjustment. The biggest adjustment was the guns. I'd grown up as a city kid terrified of firearms of all kinds. I moved out to the lovely York County countryside and found my neighbors had enough firepower to hold off a regiment. "It's the way we live," my next-door neighbor said as we were heading into town to buy my first rifle. "A gun is a basic appliance, like your stove or your refrigerator," she went on. "You have to own a gun to live in the country."

Every Saturday, we had target practice and contests. Her kids put me to shame. Even the 10-year-old was a better shot than I was. As for the teenagers, boys and girls, forget it. They were deadly shots with any weapon from almost any distance. My teasing defense of my lousy aim was that people were born with "country genes" and "city genes," and I was richly endowed with the latter.

Nearly 30 years later, the contrasting perspectives of rural Americans and urban American on the subject of guns is no joke. In fact, having spent a good deal of time over the years in the backwoods as well as the back streets, I think the issue of guns and their control is a fundamental dividing line between the city and the country.

As urban gun violence rises, the metropolitan communities are focusing more and more on the role of guns. Because they are so basic to the rural way of life, guns are instantly acquitted by country folk of any culpability in the troubles of the city. The gun lobby, orchestrated by the National Rifle Association, makes certain to keep its base in rural America in high dudgeon over attempts by urban politicians to regulate or limit access to firearms of any kind.

The times are changing. The gun lobby is facing a serious challenge to its previous dominance of public deliberation on this issue. Virginia, despite withering opposition from the NRA and company, recently enacted a measure that limits handgun purchases to one per month per citizen. This after the governor and a U.S. attorney pointed out that 41 percent of New York City's gun deaths occurred with handguns purchased, often wholesale, in Virginia.

New Jersey, principally a suburban state, also turned back the gun lobby, this time on the issue of semiautomatic weapons. Again, a governor took his case to the people and prevailed over the once–all-powerful NRA. One prominent state senator made a public point of returning an anti–gun control contribution of $10,000 to signal that a new day had come to the political dynamic surrounding this issue.

Guns, as I learned in my first sojourn in the country, definitely have their place. That place is not on every urban street corner. Not if we are to have any hope of maintaining a civil society in our cities.

The Genesis of an Underclass

August 9, 1987—On our block in Brooklyn in the 1940s there was a sprinkling of families receiving something then called "home relief." Everyone knew who these families were and why they might need help temporarily. That was the key word. Temporarily.

Someplace between then and now, a vast new population and attendant bureaucracy have been spawned on the idea of permanent poverty. Across the urban landscape, the towers of the housing projects and the low-rise slums speak a different language than their forebears. The first public housing projects in the 1930s were Quonset huts borrowed from the military. Temporary.

The image of poverty of those days was shaped by the experience of the Depression in the '30s. A lot of good, decent and hardworking people had been thrown out of work through no fault of their own. They were down on their luck and needed some help to tide them over until times got better. And surely they would.

How then came we to this pretty pass of permanent pools of poor at the core of our cities? It is one of the largest ironies of modern American history. It began as a search for prosperity. That and patriotism.

Before World War II, most black Americans lived in the rural South. The legatees of slavery stayed close to the land after the Civil War. A few drifted toward the cities in the 1920s and early '30s, but they were pioneers.

When the war began, the defense industries were desperate for new sources of labor. They turned to the South and recruited thousands of workers, black and white, to migrate to Chicago, New York and Oakland to work on assembly lines and in shipyards in a massive defense effort that was unparalleled in history.

The money was good during the war, but when it ended, disaster struck the new urban dwellers. The shift of postwar American prosperity was to the suburbs. The black defense workers were not able to migrate and soon became forgotten people in an alien land.

Those were the grandparents and great-grandparents of the citizens we now call the urban underclass. The majority of welfare recipients remain white Americans. The majority of the permanent poor are black Americans.

Over the ensuing years, cities sagged beneath the weight of this new population that did not make it to the mainstream, only to the sidelines. The infrastructure of the cities, especially the schools, all but collapsed. For a time, it was chic to argue a new social theory that our society did not need cities at all.

Now it is clear we need cities and we must create ways to make them work by finding ways to help the people within them work. That requires a combination of public and private effort. Remarkably, we have heard virtually no discussion of how to stimulate that effort from the presidential candidates of either party.

You would think the exciting possibilities and challenges of the urban renaissance would be high on the agenda of candidates in search of new and attractive ideas. Yet not much seems to come out of their mouths.

In a society in which the top fifth of the population earns 46 percent of the income and the bottom fifth earns 3.8 percent of the income, you might see room for improvement if you sought to be president. Just think of the new consumption potential and therefore tax consequences of getting those citizens into gainful activity.

Ignoring that problem reminds me of a neighbor we had, an auto mechanic, who constantly tossed his soiled and oily rags in the corner of a dark closet. One night we learned the meaning of the term spontaneous combustion as we watched his house burn to the ground.

Permitting a culture of permanent poverty to take root without resistance in our cities would be no wiser than my neighbor was.

An Accidental Neighborhood

September 5, 1991—That winter of 1947–48, my town turned into a winter wonderland. It was a vision so vivid, I am sure it will last a lifetime. I was only 10 at the time. I suppose I had heard the word blizzard before, but I am certain I had no idea what a blizzard really was until about 10 P.M. that Christmas night. Every house across our Brooklyn street disappeared in a swirl of driving snow. It piled so high in our front yard that it buried our front door and crept up toward the second-story windows.

By the time it finally stopped for good, more than a day had passed. Mountains of snow lined the curb, pushed there by the lumbering city snowplows. In the days that followed, those white mountains became a new world of forts and tunnels. We children, unable to go anyplace else, contented ourselves for hours in snow games. We had experienced nothing like it before.

In the pictures from those happy days in Brooklyn, you would see the little boy whose family had moved from Guyana the previous spring. He was seeing snow for the first time. The other kids were of Irish extraction, German, Jewish and West Indian. There were Americans, white and black, from North Carolina, Minnesota and Massachusetts. We knew and understood that our heritages were different. We also knew we shared something special: our neighborhood.

I could not help remembering those days in the snow last week. The reason is that the pictures from Brooklyn lately have been so different. It is more than the difference between summer and winter. It is more like the difference between night and day. The latest pictures showed a Brooklyn seized by anger and alienation. This time, it happened to be between black people and Jews. Not long before, it was Haitians vs. Koreans, and not long before that in Bensonhurst, African-Americans vs. Italian-Americans.

Many of these bitter and violent, sometimes fatal, confrontations are taking place on the same streets where I lived and played in that memorable snowstorm. To see the old neighborhood today through the lens of the network cameras is to see an alien land. Something, it is clear, has gone terribly wrong.

What has gone wrong, some say, is that the American city is dead. The depletion of manufacturing jobs and middle-class tax bases doomed the future of the city. We are left with bitter racial conflict, drugs, crime and violence. Those of that view have difficulty detecting viability. Listen to David Mandelker, a St. Louis urban planner and law professor at Washington University: "The basic problem is that big cities are no longer functional. A handful of cities are redefining their roles. But the rest are losing their place in society. We don't need them anymore."

That judgment calls forth an apocalyptic vision. It is of fire and brimstone raining down on a hundred American metropolitan centers. They vanish in volcanic violence. They are blotted from the map and memory in the manner of Sodom and Gomorrah in the Old Testament.

Lest we permit our imaginations to run wild, there are some facts to be faced. First, cities remain the great nexus of culture and civilization. They have been so since the dawn of commerce, and they still have a great role to play in the evolution of American civilization, fragile as that notion is.

Second, the teeming millions of urban residents cannot be ignored or abandoned, except at our great peril as a nation. Those urban masses are indeed needed. They and their children will be needed to keep this nation's economy in global competition. Show me a society that has abandoned a fifth of its population to the scrap heap and I'll show you a loser.

We cannot afford to abandon our cities or the people in them if we hope to make it into the 21st century. Far from it, we will only be acting in a socially responsible fashion when we have a national urban strategy. It should embrace education, transportation, drugs and crime. A "Look, Ma, no hands" urban policy is a prescription for national catastrophe.

I have friends who grew up in a very different circumstance from mine. They knew only segregated neighborhoods. That, I learned much later, is more the norm. If mine were an accidental neighborhood, it was an accident that worked.

The High Price of Indifference

May 6, 1992—We used to joke as children about my mother's premonitions. They were hunches that turned out so often to be right. "I can feel it in my bones," she would say. A day, a week or a year later, her bones would bear her out. My brother used to say he would bet more on my mother's bones than he would on the stock market. My father never made a business decision my mother's bones advised against. He always regarded that as a major reason for the success of the family business.

We six children always wished we had inherited the sixth sense that gave my mother such skill as a prognosticator. All the same, each of us has had experiences that reminded us of my mother and her hunches. Afterward, we called one sibling or another and related the experience. "Just like mom," one or another of us would say. As the youngest, I always regarded myself as the least likely inheritor of the gift. I always had the fewest such victories of intuition to report.

There was one I will never forget. In 1990, a domestic policy panel at the White House recommended that the Bush administration take an interest in the conditions festering in urban America. It said those conditions should be addressed as part of a larger domestic agenda. The president's closest advisers laughed the group out of the White House. Senior administration officials spoke with great pride about the fact that the president had no domestic agenda and didn't want one.

I remember calling my big brother in New York that night. He is a university professor there. He has a keen interest in cities and their people. I told him this was one I felt in my bones. I had covered all the big urban uprisings of the 1960s. This policy, I told my brother, amounted to almost suicidal recklessness. I feared one day the country would pay a big price for the administration's cavalier attitude. Life in the cities was deteriorating. People were losing hope. All they saw was more homelessness, more violence, more drugs and no future.

I told my brother that night I feared the worst. I had never heard of Rodney King. I just knew about the streets. I had a distinct memory of how each of those major uprisings began. None could have been predicted with any precision. Each had erupted over the most routine of everyday hassles between the local citizens and the police. In Detroit, for example, the police raided a "blind pig," an after-hours joint. It was a Sunday night. By Wednesday, 43 people were dead and Detroit's future was doomed.

So when the president's men so blithely dismissed the call for a serious domestic policy, my bones told me they were making a costly mistake. It is not easy to determine all the things that need to be done in our cities. And surely there are serious questions about how to pay for them. But the idea that our national policy would be to do virtually nothing borders on the insane.

Ask any businessperson in Los Angeles how he or she feels about that today. Since 1981, when the Reagan administration came into office, the federal investment in education has dropped by 82 percent.

Ask the head of any major business in L.A. today how smart that kind of social policy is. Ask any businessperson there who has to cope with the residue of that riot what he would say now about the White House policy of studied indifference. And, of course, it is not just the White House. Congress has its share of the blame to shoulder. So do state and local government. Most of all, the private sector—the news media, business, churches and service clubs—will all admit today that we should have done more.

Whoever thought this nation could permit those inner cities to languish in despair indefinitely guessed wrong. The idea that one day the free market would transform them with no help from the outside was naive at best.

We had a chance to learn all this a quarter of a century ago. We chose to go back to business as usual once the fires cooled. Now we know the price of that indifference. The question is whether we will do anything different this time. I have a feeling in my bones we won't. I can only hope, unlike my mom, that I'll be proved wrong.

A Tale of Three Cities

November 18, 1990—Detroit, my daughter was telling me on the telephone, has been done a bad turn. "Exaggeration," was the word she used. She was reacting to the ABC News feature about the city where she lives and works as a reporter for the *Detroit Free Press*. The network described the "Motor City" as disturbingly close to death. Problems Detroit has, my daughter said, but they were overdrawn by ABC.

"There are some good neighborhoods in Detroit," she said, but "ABC made you feel the place was totally hopeless. I don't think I'd be there if I thought there was no hope for Detroit."

Some things in families seem never to change. In our case, I tell my daughter of the many "urban" discussions that often dominated the dinnertime discussions among my parents, my siblings and me. Those conversations, sometimes heated, concerned the issue of the quality of life in our city, Brooklyn.

The big issue then was this: In our little corner of the world, harmony among the races was a commonplace fact of life. People from all over the world and nearly every region of the United States shared sugar over the back fence, gossip on the front stoop and stickball in the side yard of the church next door.

Yet, when we saw our neighborhood described in the New York papers, it was not a place we recognized. The adjectives were "tough," "rough" and "rowdy."

Our churchgoing community was far from "rough" and "rowdy" as we understood those words. The great debate at dinner was over the reason. Why did the papers insist on descriptions that were false? After all, there were neighborhoods similar to ours all over New York that were not called "rowdy" in the papers.

"It's obvious," one of my brothers said with an air of total self-assurance. "If a certain number of people of color live in a neighborhood, it is by definition a bad neighborhood to the New York papers."

"Not necessarily," one of my sisters shot back. "There are nice neighborhoods on the Lower East Side, too. They are labeled in the press as slums, even though they aren't." The residents there were predominantly Jewish and Italian. Cities, she observed, sometimes get a bad press because they are not well understood.

Now it is my daughter's turn to tell me about media exaggeration of the ills of her city. By now, I can tell her a few more stories of my own about media exaggeration. They are stories about Oakland with which she is familiar. It fascinates me, I tell her, how the newspapers in San Francisco can always find stories about drugs and violence in Oakland and rarely in San Francisco.

The misportrayal of cities, I tell my daughter, has been going on for a long time. The problem it creates is serious. It has to do with that word "hope" she used to describe her positive feelings about some aspects of life in her chosen city of Detroit.

When the news media fail to find anything hopeful in a city, they leave the impression in the community that there is nothing it can do to improve itself. If you ask why only the negative images prevail in stories about certain cities, the answer will always be the same: because that is the way it is.

As my daughter was asking—and as my sister asked many years before her—is that the way it is or, instead, the way a particular journalist chose to see it? If communities are never provided with a balanced view of themselves, they lose the benefit of a healthy perspective about their prospects.

It is not easy for journalists to learn to comprehend this added dimension to their task. Yet it must be taken seriously. There is a difference between the days when the New York papers slammed Brooklyn and the present.

That difference is the power of television to shape images and leave lasting impressions. In the old days, if we didn't like a newspaper's treatment of Brooklyn, we could buy another paper. When television tells the world a major American city is heading hopelessly for the abyss, "it robs people of an accurate mirror," my daughter said. "That is indispensable to any rebuilding."

Life and Death in the City

September 16, 1990—Ever since the death of Brian Watkins, 22, of Provo, Utah, some days ago, I have been thinking about life and death in the city. The city in which Watkins was killed is New York. He and his family, in town for the U.S. Open tennis tournament, were attacked by hoodlums on a subway platform in Manhattan.

As the police tell the story, Brian, his mother, father and others were awaiting a train when the marauders struck. They attacked his father first and took his wallet. They struck Brian's mother; he went to her defense and was stabbed to death.

The attackers, the police say, were on their way to a dance and needed the price of admission to the Roseland Ballroom. Their method of raising money was to rob tourists. This time, the result was also murder.

In Provo the other day, they held Brian's funeral. It was, according to the news accounts, an event of piercing pain: a young tennis star dying a hero defending his mom from a knife-wielding assailant in the subways of far-off New York City. Above everything else, Brian's family, friends and neighbors wanted to know why. In the peaceful precincts of Provo, what happened on that subway platform is beyond imagining.

It might come as a surprise to Brian's friends and relatives, but New York's subways have not always been a cesspool of crime. Moreover, the city that now is being called the "rotting apple" once was as humane and civilized a venue as the nation had to offer. It was once no more a haven of crime than were most other cities, even tranquil Provo.

We used to leave our back door open in Brooklyn so that Brownie, our spitz and fox terrier, could go out during the night. Without giving safety a second thought, we rode those same subways and walked the platform where Brian Watkins was killed. New York City in the '50s was a city of gleaming buildings and millions of budding dreams.

How did such a city turn into a nightmare? How did it become a place where Brian Watkins and 20 other people lost their lives on the same Sunday night? Why do its citizens now cower in such fear behind locked doors that their mayor pleaded with them to come out and reclaim their streets?

It began to change subtly. I was there, and I saw how New York was transformed from a city of dreams to a place of nightmares. Early in the 1950s, when I was in high school, the word heroin crept into the newspapers. None existed at our school, but we began to read daily of this new menace.

As the drug trade grew, gangs grew. Our gangs in those days were territorial social clubs. The worst that ever happened was an occasional "rumble," a fistfight. As the drug traffic grew, gangs gradually were transformed from clubs to businesses. The businesses became more and more aggressive about marketing their wares.

By the end of the decade of the '50s, a new element had entered the drug equation: guns. Little by little, despite one of the oldest and toughest gun-control laws in the nation, the Sullivan Law, the city was awash in guns. Still, the police had a fighting chance until the mid-'60s.

Social turmoil broke out in New York City in the '60s. Poverty, which had been thought of as temporary, became more visibly a permanent part of the city's scene. The system seemed incapable of responding. The education system collapsed under the burden of politics and poverty. Add to those a growing culture of guns and drugs.

By the end of the '70s, social scientists were predicting that without massive intervention there would be masses of illiterate, untrained youth on the streets. They had no access to effective education, but abundant access to drugs and guns. As the '80s became the '90s, this story was to be repeated to greater or lesser degree across the nation. We had created an underclass, a lawless illiterate lot with zero regard for the common decencies of those more fortunate than they.

Brian Watkins and his family had an encounter with our nation's future. Unless we begin to rechannel the energies and reshape the values of the youth of that underclass, none of us is safe in the subway or any other place. In one ghastly moment, the people of Provo discovered they are indeed connected to the distant disarray of our urban failures.

How Hate Can Tarnish a City

May 27, 1990 —She was remembering a time of quiet family pleasure that might never come again. My daughter said the thought
made her sad and angry. We were talking on the telephone the other
night. She was in Detroit, I in New York City.

"Do you remember that walk we took through Brooklyn that
Sunday night?" she began. We must have walked for three hours,
from Flatbush to Brooklyn Heights. "Dad, that was one of the most
enjoyable nights of my life. Now . . ."

Now the tabloids and television are bristling and crackling (and
sometimes screaming) about a city that at times seems to have lost
its head to hate. Those streets my daughter and I walked have been
the scene of ugly racial violence. It seems at times virtually every
ethnic group in the city is at war—the African-Americans and the
Italian-Americans in Bensonhurst, more tension between blacks
and Koreans in Flatbush.

New York has not become Beirut or Belfast . . . yet. That was my
daughter's point. The path from Brooklyn to Beirut or Belfast seems
crystal clear. Fatal violence, the kind that can kill a city, works its
way in increments.

"First it's a single killing," my journalist daughter was saying.
"Then there will be killings in retaliation." It's the oldest lesson of
racial enmity, and the most difficult for communities to learn. We
saw the same syndrome in the West Bank and Gaza over the weekend. Each irrational act justifies an eye for an eye.

"One of the most interesting—and frightening—aspects of this,"
my daughter was saying, "is that soon people forget what the original argument was about. All each side remembers is that there is
always a score to settle with the other guy."

Mayor David Dinkins, aware that the nation's largest city has also
become the nation's largest powder keg, tries to preach racial harmony and media restraint. Neither of those is a bad idea, but New
York will need more than mayoral homilies. Indeed, all our cities
need more than kind words.

What New York and all major cities, including Oakland, need are
three things above all else:

■ First, a human-dignity program. This is a positive reaffirmation by the entire community in its belief in the dignity of every individual. Much of this violence comes from the sense of many, especially underclass youth, that nobody cares if they live or die.

■ Second, cross-community dialogue. The city, the churches, businesses big and small, service clubs, sororities, crime victims and their assailants have to begin facing each other. They have to talk until they get beyond hate and anger and can see other's humanity, vulnerability and pain. Instead of one anti-hate sing-along, such as Mayor Dinkins held the other night, New York needs hundreds of small-setting discussions among its disputing parts. Any city feeling similar tensions should do the same.

■ Third, civic and community leadership and the media, especially media leaders, should be in an ongoing "save the city" dialogue. There is some evidence in New York that journalists are being singled out by all sides as instigators of the confrontations. Reporters on the street are bearing the brunt of community anger for decisions they did not make. That is fundamentally unfair. Those reporters' bosses need to hear what city leaders and ordinary citizens in beleaguered communities have to say about the role of media coverage in perpetuating violence.

Those three things, dignity, dialogue and media education, will go a long way toward countering the hatred and violence that threaten to engulf New York and urban America in general. All the "smart money" is on "a long hot summer" in New York and other tense communities.

The "smart money" can predict rain. Real leaders build arks. Our cities need more real leaders. The media need to listen less to those who thrive on strife. They bask in the glory of the camera, and they will do anything for attention.

On that long walk my daughter and I took through Brooklyn after a family reunion almost a decade ago, we noticed something about our native city. People in every neighborhood, whether rich or poor, were proud to be New Yorkers. "Hate," my daughter was saying the other night, "can ruin the finest of cities."

Uncle Sydney, Daddy and Uncle Edward in 1948
in front of their Marcy Avenue home.

Daddy's sisters Marjorie and Sybil stand in front of their home in 1947.

Dad in his short pants on Marcy Avenue in May of 1948.

Dad on his way to see his sister Sybil get married in 1949.

Uncle Sydney and their mother on Marcy Avenue.

A teenage Dad with the family dog, Brownie.

Dad, who grew to become an avid photographer, shooting scenes of Bedford Stuyvesant at age 16.

Daddy's middle sister, Sybil, and their father in 1953 at a church conference in New Jersey.

Dad holds an eight-month-old Dori.

Dori visits Dad, a young reporter at the *York Gazette and Daily*, in 1963.

Dad as *Washington Post* ombudsman in the early 1970s.

Daddy in the newsroom of the *York Gazette and Daily.*

Dad and Nancy exchange vows, January 1, 1975.

Dad and Nancy enjoy a lovely day in Central Park in 1974 shortly before their wedding.

Daddy does the last of the 1976 presidential debates, moderated by Barbara Walters. Other panelists were columnist Joe Kraft and *Los Angeles Times* Washington bureau chief Jack Nelson.

Dad and David share a quiet moment in Dad's Washington, D.C., studio in the mid-1970s.

Dad in front of the *Tribune* shortly after being named publisher in 1981.

Dad and David in 1980 shortly after the family moved to California.

Aunts Sybil, Eleanor and Mimi upon graduation from Adelphi University.

Family get together at Aunt Sybil's house.

Dad and the boys light the *Tribune* Christmas tree in 1981.

Dad enjoys a good laugh during a lighter moment in his *Oakland Tribune* office in the early 1980s.

Dad and Dori sitting in front of Harvard University Law School during his Nieman reunion in the early 1980s.

Dad makes a point in his *Oakland Tribune* office in 1982.

Dad and Nancy during a break between conference sessions in the early 1980s.

Dad proudly accepts an honorary degree from York College in 1984.

A proud Bob Maynard accompanies his wife Nancy to an awards ceremony where she receives a YWCA tribute in 1984.

Dad and Alex throwing out the opening pitch at an Oakland A's game in the mid-1980s.

In 1991, the Oakland firestorm burned within inches of our house. Dad and Alex survey the damage.

Dad and *Tribune* photo staffers celebrate the paper's 1990 Pulitzer Prize for coverage of the Loma Prieta earthquake.

Dad, the nonconformist, with a group of conform- ists in Japan in 1992.

Dad smiles as he announces in 1991 that the *Tribune* will con- tinue publishing, with financial assistance from the Freedom Forum. To his right is Freedom Forum chairman Allen Neu- harth.

On the March

The family was at a San Francisco Japanese restaurant. As dinner was being served, Daddy asked the waiter for chopsticks. "Why?" the waiter asked. "You don't know how to use them."

My father, a quiet, slow-speaking man by nature, could get even quieter and slower when provoked.

He could have gotten angry at the waiter. He could have pointed out that he and his children learned the foods of the world as toddlers.

Dad did none of those things. He looked the man directly in the eye and simply repeated his request. The family ate dinner with chopsticks that evening.

The summer I discovered racism, the kind of "I don't need to know you to hate you" racism, my father called me and said: "Racism is someone else's sickness. You must never let it infect you. You must not let it change who you are."

That approach came naturally to Daddy. His parents taught their children to have great pride in their race, but they also taught them the reality of racism. When a child came home and complained he or she would never get a decent grade from a racist teacher, my grandparents told them to work harder. "Just be better than they are," my grandparents would admonish.

Even so, in the late 1950s and early 1960s, everyone told Daddy it was time to be practical. He had a young child to support and the white press was virtually closed to people of color. He couldn't give up. It took a couple of years and 200 résumés, but eventually he was hired by a small newspaper in Pennsylvania.

"The truth is that most journalists don't know why they are journalists and that is just as true of me," my father wrote in a 1976 essay. "But when I look back to those early days in Brooklyn, to the death of my neighborhood, I remember a powerful compulsion to know. I wanted to know how my world could have been so sure and snug in wartime and so cold and strange in peacetime. It wasn't in the history of Brooklyn that I looked, or in the history of New York. It was in the history of America. And there I settled on the history of the relationship between Africans and Americans. It seemed to me as I grew and groped that something about the way in which whites regarded blacks shaped far more of their lives and their lifestyle than they could ever guess."

In the 1960s, Daddy started an ongoing, one-sided argument in his head with a nameless white driver he encountered at a stoplight one evening.

According to Daddy, the driver "turned and looked right at me and held my eyes for only a split second, but there was something in his eyes that I will probably never forget. It said something very simple: I hate you." Disgusted, the man turned away from Daddy, leaving him to carry on a solo argument for the next few years. "The first thing I said to him was, 'You don't know me. You don't even know my name. You don't even know what I do.

"'Why am I a threat to you anyway, why should you instantly hate me, huh?'" Dad asked.

Eventually, Daddy answered himself. "Because he doesn't care. He sees, from a distance, four square inches of brown skin roughly, that's all, which he had caught first out of the corner of his eye."

My father spent the early years of his career covering the civil rights movement, the urban unrest and the government's war on poverty—all by-products of our racially fragmented society.

Later, convinced that the nation would not stand a chance to grow and heal unless its newspapers reflected the voices of all citizens, he and Nancy helped to found a nonprofit organization dedicated to increasing minority representation in the nation's newsrooms.

"This country cannot be the country we want it to be if its story is told by only one group of citizens. Our goal is to give all Americans front-door access to the truth," he said in May of 1993 during his last public address to college students at the Freedom Forum.

D.J.M.

Is America a Racist Society?

January 24, 1988—If the definition of news is "when man bites dog," try this sample of our topsy-turvy times: As the nation celebrated the Martin Luther King Jr. holiday, something odd emerged on television.

On several different channels, the scene went this way:

A black civic or political leader is interviewed on the legacy of King. Inevitably, the question, most often from a white journalist: Is America still a racist society? If the answer was no, then the challenge: What about Howard Beach, New York; Forsyth County, Georgia; and Jimmy "the Greek" Snyder?

If the answer was yes, then this challenge: What about Jesse Jackson running for president, Gen. Colin Powell running the National Security Council, and Bill Cosby running first in the ratings as national dad?

In the 20 years since his death, King's dream has become our national riddle: Is the bottle half empty or half full?

Walk down the mean streets of any inner city in America. See the drug dealers, the poverty and—always the hardest to take—children without hope. If the rich cadences of King's dream were to ring in your ear, you would call it a nightmare. Empty bottles everywhere.

Now turn on the tube. The black general is a recruiting-poster artist's dream. This is a general's general, over six feet tall, broad shoulders, exuding confidence and generous doses of charm. He is as effective on television as he is in person.

The word that enters your mind when you meet General Powell is command. He is clearly in command of NSC and of his world in the corridors of military power.

The night King was killed, there was a riot in the nation's capital. It came within 10 blocks of the White House. There was a scramble to defend the city. A high-level planning session was assembled by the federal government.

The black mayor of Washington showed up and was barred. He, by virtue of his color, might have given away the game plan to "the enemy" on the streets. A national security adviser made that decision.

Two decades later, the president's national security adviser is General Powell. In a permanently racist society, do black men ever grow up in New York, graduate from City College, rise through the ranks of the military command structure and emerge as head of the NSC? It certainly couldn't happen in today's South Africa.

So is the bottle half empty or half full? Is America racist? Yes and no. We have made huge progress toward King's dream, but we are still confronted by Howard Beach and the Jimmy "the Greek" Snyders of this world.

Perhaps the better question is this: What does it take to finish fulfilling the dream? Here the issues become more tangled, the assessment of blame more difficult, and a national consensus most elusive.

That last, in my opinion, is the key to our future. If we can develop a no-fault national consensus, we can finish the job. It is in our long-range interest.

A no-fault approach reduces the need to apportion past blame to each group for its part in the mess of the cities, the collapse of public education or the persistence of rural poverty. Let's declare a national moratorium on finger pointing.

Our society will be stronger if we mutually commit to finishing the nation's business. Our economic and political competitors, sharks in the waters of our future, will eat us alive if we continue to burden our society with the pathological legacy of slavery and racism.

Seen that way, King's dream becomes less of a riddle. That is, if each of us assumes a share of the burden for solving the puzzle. We have accomplished mighty things, including winning a world war, thinking and working much that way.

Besides, that approach eliminates one more dumb argument from television over half empty or half full.

Exclusion: A Coward's Game

August 5, 1990—When strangers stop me on the street or at airports, often it is to comment on the essays I write about my family. Those about life in our old home in Brooklyn provoke the most response. "It is obvious," a nun in brown habit said one day, "that yours was a house of joy." I loved the phrase, but it troubled me.

It was not, I started to say to her, always so joyful. In fact, there were times that were painful, as there might be in any family. Some of our dinner-table discussions touched sensitive subjects. For example, our parents often struggled to help us understand and handle racial rejection. It was not always easy for them, proud immigrants in a new land.

One of the heroes of our family in the late 1940s was Dr. Ralph J. Bunche. He was then this nation's highest-ranking black diplomat. He was also a leading academic. His field at Harvard had been international organization, a subject of special interest to our family. It was at the time of the formation of the United Nations. There must have been a dozen pictures of Dr. Bunche around our home. We owned at least one copy of everything published under his name.

The difficult time came the night of Dr. Bunche's public humiliation. He was denied entry to the Forest Hills Tennis Club, then the scene of some of the most prestigious matches in the world of tennis. Quite aside from our appreciation of tennis, Dr. Bunche's rejection became our own.

There were family dinners that are still as vivid in my mind as if they occurred last night. That was one of them, and it was revived with this week's news, 40 years later, about the Shoal Creek Country Club in Birmingham, Alabama. It has been forced to accept a black member to escape pickets over its racially exclusionary practices. The Professional Golfers Association has been economically damaged and embarrassed by its involvement with Shoal Creek.

The Shoal Creek of our time was Forest Hills, no more than 10 miles from our home. The idea that it would reject the hero of our family meant it had rejected each of us. Every morsel of my mother's savory Caribbean cuisine tasted like ashes that evening. Little was said for long stretches. It was as if we had received news of the death of a relative.

As one of my three sisters, a tennis player, began to put her troubled thoughts into words, tears welled up in her eyes and she stopped talking. My mother's eyes met my father's. I could tell they had been discussing this between themselves.

"I want you children to understand what you are seeing here." He pointed across to a side table where the *New York Daily News* lay. The story of Dr. Bunche's rejection was prominently displayed. "I know you feel sorry about Dr. Bunche, but I tell you my prayers tonight are for those men who have humiliated him."

"I hate them," my sister blurted out.

"Do not hate them," my mother cut in. "You must never hate anyone. That is unlike Christ, and we are Christians. Besides, you must understand what your father and I are saying. These men who make rules to reject other people are sick."

My father picked up the theme. "People who create special rules of exclusiveness think they are showing the rest of us what great status they have achieved. In fact, they are really telling us the very opposite . . ."

"The very opposite," my mother repeated my father's last phrase for special emphasis. They often reinforced each other's points by repeating a few of the exact words.

"In fact," my father continued, "when people need racial exclusiveness in their social lives, it is usually to prove to others they have 'arrived.' But that's not how I read such men. I read them as socially insecure. Have you ever noticed that truly confident people walk and work among all with ease? The strong do not need that sort of status; the wealthy but weak do."

"Dr. Bunche," my mother said with a wry smile, "is fortunate he will not to have to associate with such people." At last we laughed.

A Shaper of Dreams

June 30, 1991—One evening in the early 1950s, two lawyers met on a railroad train on their way to Washington, D.C. They had something important in common. Each would appear the following morning to argue in different cases before the United States Supreme Court. One was the attorney for a midwestern state. The other was Thurgood Marshall.

As they reached Washington, the other lawyer invited Marshall, already a celebrated civil rights advocate, to have dinner. If you are planning to argue before the Supreme Court tomorrow, Marshall told the other lawyer, and you have time for dinner tonight, "You are not serious about your case."

That, I was telling the children the other night, was emblematic of the man who helped to reshape the legal landscape of American racial relations. He was gregarious, humorous and totally dedicated to the cause of the clients he represented. Because of that dogged determination, coupled with uncommon courage, Marshall made America a different place.

Just five days short of his 83rd birthday, Justice Marshall announced his intention to retire from the Supreme Court. The great-grandson of a slave, Marshall is the only African-American to serve on the nation's highest court.

Once part of a powerful liberal majority, Marshall ends his 24 years on the court as a lonely dissenter. The conservatives hold the majority now, and Marshall fears the clock is being turned back on the issue about which he cared the most, civil rights.

Despite his pessimism about the direction of the Court, Marshall leaves behind a legacy in the law unlikely to be equaled. He will be remembered as a justice for his unswerving devotion to the cause of the underdog. Indeed, the fact that he was such a force on the Court might eclipse what many scholars believe to be a contribution of equal, perhaps greater, import. That was his role as one the most creative lawyers of his time.

As the general of the army of civil rights lawyers who eventually won the set of cases known as *Brown v. Board of Education*, Marshall made a contribution of unparalleled importance. He persuaded the Court to strike down those laws that held separate education of black children to be equal.

In supporting Marshall's position in those cases, the Court opened the door to a new view of the rights of minorities and women under the Constitution. The country as it existed before the *Brown* cases bears no resemblance to America today.

Richard Kluger, in *Simple Justice*, the best book about the *Brown* cases, reminds us of what this country was like in 1951 at the height of the battle. Texas did not allow interracial boxing matches. Florida did not permit black students and white students to use the same textbooks. Arkansas did not permit black and white voters to enter a polling place together. And 10 states required separate waiting rooms for black and white bus and train travelers.

Above all, in 1951, no fewer than 17 states required the segregation of their public schools. It was those conditions that Marshall and his army of civil rights lawyer-warriors set out to change. Theirs was an uphill, sometimes dangerous, struggle.

It is ironic today that young people of the generation of my children know so little of that legacy. They know Thurgood Marshall is the first of his race to sit on the U.S. Supreme Court. They might even know some of what he has stood for in a generation on the bench.

What they don't as readily know is what led to his great celebrity, the battle to change the course of race relations as a lawyer who was the architect and the embodiment of the greatest change our constitutional law has seen in 200 years.

Marian Wynn Perry, a lawyer who worked with Marshall in the 1940s, said of him that, "He had a terribly deep and real affection for the little people—the people he called the 'Little Joes.'" What Marshall did for those "Little Joes" remains unmatched in our time. And when he argued before the Supreme Court, he always remembered that their cause was more important than dinner.

We Must Make Freedom Ring for All

August 28, 1983—She had the cataracts removed from her eyes that previous April. It was incongruous the way the tortoiseshell-rimmed glasses sat on her nose, two enormous magnifying lenses on her diminutive face.

She told the reporters her age was 89. That was funny because her great-grandson, a strapping lad of 21, stood behind her shaking his head with a big grin on his face.

"She's really 93," he said with a laugh.

"Tyrone," she snapped, "keep your big mouth shut. It makes no difference to these men if I'm 89 or 93. Fact is I am the oldest person on this bus, probably on this march. Now you hush your mouth."

On that sweltering morning of August 28, 1963, she had boarded the bus in York, Pennsylvania, and ridden three hours to be at the Lincoln Memorial. She was one of 250,000 who heard Martin Luther King Jr. deliver one of the most memorable speeches of the 20th century.

And she remains for me, 20 years later, one of the most memorable personages I have ever covered. A young reporter on his first "big" story, I sought out this woman to ask why she chose to make such an arduous journey in her frail condition.

"Freedom," she responded in a flash. "I came for freedom. I've seen our people suffer so much because we aren't free. My momma and poppa was slaves in South Carolina. They died still talking about one day we was going to be really free. I feel it in my bones. I got a hunch we gonna be free one day soon."

Right then, I knew what I wanted to do as a reporter. I wanted to cover this dramatic quest for freedom wherever it went. I wanted to see whether this wonderful old woman's "hunch," as she would call it several times in our conversation, was right.

Martin Luther King's dream and the old woman's hunch took me on a twisted trail that wound through the Deep South and the urban North, to courageous marches on dusty rural trails, to the chaos of burning neighborhoods in big cities and some small ones.

Along the way, I met more solid citizens such as the old woman from York and some wild radicals who claimed the world was divided into those who were either "part of the problem or part of the solution." I met scholars and scoundrels, dreamers and schemers.

Five years after his great speech, Dr. King was killed. That night, April 4, 1968, not very many blocks from the Lincoln Memorial at which he spoke, I watched the nation's capital go up in flames.

It was then that I began to realize a frightening truth. Dr. King's dream and the old woman's hunch were going to come true for some and not for others.

Those in the North and South who were prepared to take advantage of the great opportunities of the early 1960s would go on and live lives that would mirror the hopes of the most ardent social reformer.

Those who were not prepared would not be able to take advantage of those changes. For them, it would be as if none of that remarkable movement had ever occurred.

More than that, the differences between those who would find a path to equality and those who would languish in frustration would be imperceptible to the naked eye.

Next to the burning of the nation's capital, the most devastating urban violence on which I reported was the uprising in Detroit. It was the single largest scene of urban violence in the nation's history. Forty-three citizens lost their lives and acres of urban landscape lay in rubble.

And it began, if you please, at the corner of 12th and Joy.

As the ashes cooled, I decided to make Detroit the site of the most careful study I could conduct on the "why" of an event. The deeper I dug, the clearer one fact became. The intensity of the anger in Detroit had its roots in the fact of the city's large middle-class black population.

It turned out that the anger the poorest residents of Detroit felt was an inner anger that was fed by the realization that some blacks would do well and others would not. True, they blamed "the system," but they could not lay all the blame for their condition on the fact that they were black because right around the corner were blacks living in elegant homes and driving the top of the line Detroit cars.

Indeed, in some instances one member of the family had risen to become an executive or at least a well-paid autoworker and the other was on the skids.

As one woman put it, "The same family can produce a cop and a robber." It was this frightful contradiction that intensified the rage in Detroit and was present wherever urban violence occurred. And that contradiction endures to this day.

The trouble, then, with Dr. King's dream and the old woman's hunch is that freedom turned out to be too simple a term. If it meant the right to vote in Mississippi or eat in a good restaurant in Raleigh, it was possible to attain those things as a result of the movement he launched.

But beneath the surface of the dream there lay a harsh reality. If you cannot read, the vote may mean little. If you cannot afford the price of a meal in that fine restaurant, it makes no difference that it no longer discriminates.

In the euphoria of the moment, that reality was overlooked; the challenge that it poses is too hard to capture in a well-written phrase or well-rounded oratory.

Twenty years later, the legacy of Dr. King is writ large on the landscape of America. Not long ago, I visited those red clay hills of Georgia of which he spoke in that speech. I found just what he dreamed. There were black children and white children playing and going to school together.

Moreover, a black man had just been elected county supervisor. The fact of his race had not come up once in the whole of the campaign. He had, indeed, been elected on the basis of the "content of his character" and not on the basis of the color of his skin.

Ironically, on those mean streets of Detroit and Chicago and a hundred other cities, those who have not had the preparation, mental and otherwise, to tackle the challenges of the society remain as they were 20 years ago, unaffected by all the change that has taken place around them.

The old woman's hunch was half right. Freedom came with a rush and a roar. The other half of the challenge remains for us to do if all of his dream is to be realized.

Indeed, it was not just his dream. He relied in that speech on the dreams of Jefferson and the founders who "hold these truths to be self-evident. . . ."

I think of him, I think of Jefferson, I think of the half-blind woman from York who saw freedom coming. I wonder what it would take for all of them to inspire us afresh to work for the society of which they dreamed. They have given us such a gift, the gift of freedom. So many people on the globe envy us for it, yearn for it, die for it. We have it as our birthright.

I wonder why that doesn't inspire us to make sure we keep it by finding ways for each American to have a stake in it.

The American Road

May 30, 1991—Always, around this time of year, I remember the remarkable old couple in Alabama. I only wish I could recall their names. That piece of information is somewhere in a notebook in a box I have not examined in more than 20 years. We met at a hearing in Montgomery that was called to consider the health conditions of children in the rural South.

To the chagrin of their neighbors, the white couple came to tell the government and the news media that the black children of their community were receiving the worst possible health care, housing, educational opportunities and diet.

In those days in Alabama, that kind of talk tended to arouse a great deal of hostility among the white residents, many of whom relied on a cooperative workforce in a time of racial unrest. The idea of one of their own blowing the whistle to "those people from Washington" took a rare kind of courage. It was rare enough to deserve a longer interview.

"We came down this road," I distinctly remember the husband saying, "only because our consciences would not permit us to remain silent." The wife added an unforgettable sentence. "We could not continue to say we believed in God and live with the way these children are treated here in Alabama."

At that time, I was following Americans traveling down many roads in America in search of equality and justice. It was a deeply moving era in which to be a young American journalist. I met people from so many varied backgrounds for whom the cause had become the central focus of their lives. Some, indeed, lost their lives along that road.

Images of those dedicated souls came rushing through my mind the other day. I was reading several striking stories about the state of race relations these days on the nation's college campuses.

At the University of California at Berkeley, one story said, the percentage of peoples of color exceeds whites for the first time. At the same time, the story said, social self-segregation is rampant among virtually all groups—European-American, African-American, Asian-American and Latin-American.

All American though they may be, they have come to one of the world's greatest institutions of higher learning, only to retreat into isolated social enclaves. Another story was about the lawsuit making its way up to the U.S. Supreme Court. The issue is whether the present laws against segregation necessitate the dismantling of state-supported historically black colleges and universities.

That is when I stopped and reflected on those crusaders I covered on the roads of the rural South a generation ago. They never dreamed that such noble ambitions could produce such painfully exquisite contradictions. They dreamed that by now this would be a nation working on one mutual agenda.

Instead, just when we most need to be a united United States, we are mired in the quagmire of racial politics. The students say the other groups on campus make them uncomfortable in one way or another. The faculties and administrations remain mostly white male, and are therefore not helpful role models for adjustment.

At Southern University in New Orleans and other state-supported black university systems, the African-American community is loathe to part with a structure that assures that black culture and tradition will be maintained. It is still illegal segregation, say the plaintiffs.

The racial cacophony across the American landscape is the modern equivalent of the biblical tower of Babel. Everybody is talking and nobody is listening. This could be a period of healthy dialogue, a transition to a more cohesive society.

Or it could be we are seeing the early signs of the drift into ethnic enmity that threatens now to destroy several countries, from Northern Ireland, across Yugoslavia and on the Baltics, and south through the Caucus Mountains and on to the Indian subcontinent. If we want to see what not to be, there are plenty of places to look these days.

To beat that fate, we need leadership that understands the importance of getting America's people and institutions to recognize their mutual value to each other. We need leaders who know that every child is sacred, who know that the secret to curing cancer could come from any one of 20 million children sitting in class anywhere in the U.S. today.

When I think of that elderly couple, I am forced to recall a more hopeful time in our history. When youngsters at the finest colleges still feel the need for segregation, it is clear we need that hope again.

Prophets and Protesters

August 27, 1989—If Huey Newton and Martin Luther King Jr. ever met, they certainly formed no bond. They are bound nonetheless today by the common threads of how they lived and how each died. In one of history's curious accidents, their deaths help tell the tale of their times.

Dr. King and Huey Newton shared a deep concern for their people and for the plight of the poor. They aroused the passions of their generations. They were charismatic figures whose words were remembered and repeated. In different ways, the movements they led helped change America.

Dr. King was gunned down in Memphis, probably at the instigation of a hate group. Newton was gunned down in West Oakland, probably the victim of criminal street activity. The full extent of his own criminal involvement is not altogether clear.

What is clear in the first half-light of history is how the two men differed. The work of one is revered in much of the nation, yet the activity of the other was reviled by many Americans.

Newton was representative in the '60s and '70s of sharp and chic radical diversion from the mainstream of the civil rights movement. There were others, such as Stokely Carmichael and H. Rap Brown. Their criticism of Dr. King and the nonviolent movement was that it was too passive, even "Uncle Tom." They shouted for "Black Power."

I covered many of those leaders before and after the split in the movement. I found the differences fascinating. So were some of the similarities. All agreed on one basic tenet: Racism was destroying black lives by the millions.

Newton, Carmichael and Brown, though all critics of Dr. King, differed in their styles and approaches. They shared with each other and with Dr. King a great talent at articulating the nature of the inequities in our society.

The radicals differed among themselves and with Dr. King in the solutions they advocated. Newton and the Panthers espoused socialism and allied themselves with fringe groups in the white community. Carmichael and Brown preached black nationalism and racial separation.

Dr. King preached democracy. He resisted those who would change ours to a socialist system. He also had no patience for those who advanced the idea that black people should have a state of their own. Dr. King believed black Americans contributed mightily to the shaping of America and were entitled to their fair share of the American dream.

The struggle of differing views did not die with Dr. King in 1968. Some of those arguments went full force into the decade of the '70s. By then, the Voting Rights Act and other reforms of the non-violent movement began showing tangible results.

The fringe movements died. Their leaders had their 15 minutes of fame. H. Rap Brown took a Muslim lifestyle and name, and leads a very low-profile life. Stokely Carmichael pops up now and again, but he has a small following.

Dr. King, even in death, continues to command the conscience of the nation. This is so because his choice of a remedy was to resort to basic American principles of justice, fairness and equality.

To see the urban underclass is to recognize how much remains to be done. It is also worth noting that the violent streets that spawned the radical movements remain violent streets. It was on those streets that Huey Newton's life ended.

His death is a reminder that the civil rights movement spawned prophets and protesters. Dr. King pronounced a prophecy that remains a challenge to the conscience of our society. And, although Huey Newton and Dr. King differed on solutions, their deaths are joined as reminders of the nation's unfinished business.

A Recollection 17 Novembers Old

November 23, 1980—These are days of universal remembrance. Where were you on that day in 1963 when you heard that President Kennedy had been shot in Dallas? Everyone who remembers at all remembers that day.

For me, it is a dual memory. The first president for whom I voted was killed. But something else happened that day, an event that marks for me the point between two Americas. There had been the old Jim Crow America with the "white" and "colored" signs in the washrooms and other subtler signals of segregation.

As I entered adulthood and the newspaper business, those barriers were falling, but the pace then was slow. One of the problems posed by that slow transition is that some things were open to blacks (we all said Negro then) and some things were not. Often, you only found out by challenging the barrier. That could pose the risk of physical pain sometimes, emotional pain everytime. Being turned away from a restaurant on a hungry night always took a little slice out of your soul.

But I am getting ahead of my story.

Coping with the shock of that day had been difficult for us in the little town of York, Pennsylvania, where I was trained as a journalist. The story coming over the wire would not have been believable if it were not for the television to make it seem somehow more real. Finally, a little after midnight, the newspaper came out. It was confirmed in black and white. We stood around staring at the newspaper. Nobody wanted to go home.

My boss of that time was an adventurer, an editor who played a mean game of tennis every day and who guided his institution on the general theory that the editor edits best who edits least. But he cared passionately about every line in the newspaper and he vented his Irish wrath on more than one hapless soul who forgot the main Higgins rule: "People first. Everything else comes after people."

Higgins simply could not go home that night. (John F. Kennedy had been his Harvard classmate.)

"Listen," he said, "I know this place in Baltimore. It's got great

Greek food and fantastic belly dancers. It's just the thing to pull us out of this mood."

We were on the sidewalk outside the offices of the *York Gazette and Daily*. It was a few minutes past midnight. The chill of the night was nothing compared to the chill that came from thinking of a president shot dead. We walked in silence to the parking lot across the street. "It will do us both good to get our minds off this," said Higgins.

"Jim, do you realize you are inviting me to a nightclub that does not serve Negroes? You're putting me on."

The law on public accommodations was in a peculiar state at that time. In theory, the days when restaurant owners could publicly announce "white only" service was over. The law was shifting toward the position that public accommodation meant just that. But not all establishments obeyed that law in 1963 and many used subterfuges, as Jim Higgins and I would learn on the night of Nov. 22–23, 1963.

The first sign of trouble came when the headwaiter seated 10 people who came in after us and left us standing by the entryway, craning our necks to see the dancers. The dancers were having a good time not remembering, as I remember. Warm and sensuous aromas came from the kitchen. Higgins and I remained by the door.

Perhaps 20 minutes passed. The headwaiter asked us what we wanted. Higgins said we wanted a table. The headwaiter said he had none. We pointed in unison to an empty one not 10 feet away.

"That one is reserved," said the headwaiter.

"For whom?" asked Higgins.

"For a member of the club," said the headwaiter.

"What club?" asked Higgins.

"Oh, didn't you know? This is a private club. Members only," said the headwaiter.

All this was taking place in hoarse whispers by the door. Just then, Higgins spied a man he knew from York. He bolted from our tight little circle and walked up to the table. "Hey, man," said Higgins, "you a member of this club?" The man looked blank. "Club?"

The headwaiter maintained it was a club now, even though it wasn't when Higgins had been there the week before, and even though that man sitting over there did not remember that he joined that night.

"Just tonight? He joined tonight?"

"Yes," said the headwaiter, "just tonight."

"Terrific. We want to join tonight."

"Oh, sorry," said the headwaiter. "You can't. Not tonight."

"Why not tonight? You just said the guy over there joined to-night."

"But it is too late to join tonight."

"But he just joined tonight."

"Yes but you see, the president is gone."

"The president is gone?"

"Yes. Only our president can make you a member and he has gone home for the evening. Sorry."

Higgins exploded. "If you still have a president, you are lucky. We lost ours tonight. So fine, we will wait for your president. We won't leave. Call your president." And before another word was said, we were sitting at that empty table "reserved for a member."

The Baltimore City Police Department arrived in five minutes. As I saw the swarm of blue uniforms coming through the door, I asked Higgins if he wanted to take another minute and review our position as journalists about to make news. He said he didn't give a damn. I said, fine. I was just a reporter.

The owner emptied the joint. The last patron out called over his shoulder in a foreign language that he couldn't wait to compensate us for the inconvenience. One of the belly dancers said she was sorry, that it wasn't fair. Then she left. Soon, it was the two of us, the headwaiter and the policemen. Then all but one of the police-men left. The one who remained said he could do nothing for us or against us. He left. The owner appeared, a short and dapper man who said we had ruined his establishment and we would be called to account shortly. Then he left. The headwaiter said he might as well go and get his topcoat.

We had the joint to ourselves with nothing to eat or drink and no music or dancers.

"I guess we should go," I said to Higgins.

"There's a mob of men out there," he said.

We decided we might as well go and face it. We came to the front door and a roar went up from across the street. There stood perhaps 25 angry patrons. As we moved toward the corner, the mob moved behind us and the curses sounded closer and more sincere.

When we reached the corner, we encountered the last officer to leave the establishment. "I'm sorry you gentlemen didn't have a nicer evening in Baltimore," he said, "but I hope you'll come back some time and give us another chance." With that, he made an odd gesture. He tipped his cap to us.

At the tip of the officer's cap, 50 sets of headlights came on at once. Uniformed police officers appeared from the rooftops and out of cellar windows, or so it seemed at the time. They surrounded us and marched us to my car. They escorted us until we were miles away.

Anyway, said Higgins, it was a nice drive.

In the Classroom

Dad could never pinpoint when the restlessness began. Certainly by the time he was 14, he had grown weary of the weekend trips in my grandfather's Dodge moving van.

On Saturdays my grandfather gave his employees the day off and enlisted my father. They drove, the two of them, side by side, yet inhabiting two different worlds. My grandfather, in the "incredibly bad singing voice" he passed down to us, sang hymns or talked about Jesus. My father looked out of the window, slowly realizing he needed to talk about more than the Bible. He needed to talk about what he was seeing in the world around him.

Dad's favorite early childhood memories all involved his family's dining room table. There, with their parents' tutelage, he and his five brothers and sisters read, exchanged ideas and formed a lifelong love of knowledge.

But as he got older, Dad's siblings began to leave the Brooklyn brownstone for college. Without the constant hubbub of six active, opinionated children, Daddy, the youngest, still had the pleasures of his parent's intellectual vigor, but began to chafe at the confines of a strictly religious world.

Growing up in postdepression Brooklyn, my father went to integrated public schools before busing was a notion.

There, he and his friends learned civics from teachers who believed in their students' ability to participate fully in society. At Boys High, teachers warned students about the folly of prizing athletics over academics.

As Dad recalled later: "We were lucky in those days in Brooklyn. Many of us came from close-knit families, and we had teachers who took pride in a tradition of sharp training," he wrote. There was, for example, Mr. Klein, the math teacher who hammered home the importance of being educated.

"Where so many teachers pointed out the high and lofty benefit of intellect, Mr Klein got our attention by talking bluntly. Wealth vs. poverty, that's what it's all about, he would say," my father wrote. To underscore his points, Mr. Klein warned the inattentive that he could hear their future and it sounded like the click-click of a subway car conductor.

Dad learned math.

And he never forgot the lesson. A solid intellectual foundation was the only sure route to any kind of economic security.

My grandparents also devoted hours to developing their children's intellects, and then told them they could use them only to serve God. It was, my father said, like teaching someone to fly a 747 but never letting the pilot take off.

Slowly Dad began to pull free. He snuck out to a movie. He began listening to jazz.

Then a 10th grade English teacher took his class to New York University to listen to a talk on writing plays.

"He didn't reckon what I'd get out of it. He couldn't possibly guess. But NYU is downtown, in Greenwich Village. I discovered Greenwich Village," my father would later say.

The next Friday night, Dad told his parents he had to go to a school function. He ran back to the Village. Before long, he was spending more time walking the streets of Greenwich Village than in school.

By the time his classmates were graduating, Daddy had abandoned Boys High and his parents' home in Brooklyn for the open classroom in the Village. That, he said, is when his education began in earnest.

Daddy described "wandering through the Village, wandering all the time, with a very private purpose, my own education."

Sitting on the fountain in Washington Square Park, or in a coffeehouse, talking to James Baldwin and other writers, artists, philosophers and historians, Dad taught himself.

Then there were the books. He quickly devoured books by Langston Hughes, Richard Wright, Albert Camus, Leo Tolstoy, historian Arnold J. Toynbee and essayist E.B. White. Many of them still sit in the floor-to-ceiling bookshelves that lined his studio.

Almost a decade later, Dad was at Harvard University, where in 1966 he was one of more than a dozen journalists chosen to be Nieman Fellows.

A year after leaving Harvard he went to the *Washington Post*. It was the late 1960s, a time when it seemed as if everyone in the nation had risen up to scream at each other. Crisscrossing the country, Dad sorted through much of the daily discourse for the *Post*.

When he had time to look back on the cab of his father's moving truck, he began to remember more than the stale air. It was there, while he tuned out his father and watched the world go by, that Dad discovered his mission.

It was, "from that time looking out that truck window, watching New York City and the suburbs, and saying 'You've got something to say about all of this.'"

D.J.M.

Love Is Missing from Learning

May 6, 1990—On some school nights, the big dining room table most closely resembled a library that had been hit by an earth-quake. Books were piled everywhere. Some were textbooks on advanced biology and other life-science subjects. These were close by heavily handled copies of Chaucer, Milton and Dickens.

Add to the disarray on the table the disorder unfolding around it. There were the six children my mother called "rambunctious" doing our homework at the top of our collective lungs. Most of the noise was laughter. The jokes never stopped flowing around the table.

My parents from time to time would bring the decibel level back down to a low roar with a gentle reminder that "this is a home and not a barnyard." That was worth a half-hour's surcease. Spontaneously, we would read aloud to each other from passages or problems we found interesting. The language studies consisted largely of reading aloud to constant and constructive criticism.

The other day, discussing a column about growing up without television, one of my sisters and I had a delightful evening recalling the way we entertained each other. "We never missed it," she told my children and hers. "We were having too much fun most of the time."

I was soon to discover my sister and I are hardly alone in remembering a television-free upbringing as not all bad. The column reaction from friends and strangers all had the same theme. It seemed a loss at the time, but not now.

As one woman told me at a photography exhibit, "I treasure the books I read as a child. I know I would not have spent as much time reading if I could have watched television."

Soon it was clear to me what has happened to hasten the disappearance of literacy. It is the loss of the love of learning. Intense reading provides that. Practically all the letters and comments on the street and in the airport were from people making that point. Those who discovered the challenge of literature early often developed a love for the process of learning itself.

Conversely, a large percentage of those who have become video-dependent for information and mental stimulation never formed a deep emotional attachment to the rewards of written words. Worse, the manner in which reading and literature are taught today all too often suppresses any urge to appreciate them.

John Dewey, the educational philosopher, spoke of three critical stages in the learning process: romanticization, precision and generalization. The first part is where the teacher engages the students in the joy of the subject. In the second, the student learns to appreciate its exacting standards; last, how to apply that knowledge more widely.

It is the first, the romanticization of the art of learning, that seems to be the biggest loss in today's educational realm. Students complain to me of being taught at, instead of being taught. If the only reason to study is to get a job, millions of Americans are deciding they will get that job somehow without enduring the rigors of study.

A deeper basis for learning is lost in today's approach to educational motivation. It has to do with the pleasure of the exercise itself.

My parents knew what they were doing by throwing us all together to study at the dining room table. Just as easily, they could have dispatched us to our rooms to study in solitude. We had many friends whose parents chose that approach. Ours stimulated challenge and companionship. In turn, we associated both of those with learning.

Contemporary education is being asked to do many things at once—perhaps too many—in a desperate effort to rectify a disastrous decline in basic literacy. It is too late to turn off television completely. Instead, parents and educators must learn to compete to counteract its deadly, deadening effects. What appears to be missing from the process is love. We have to find our way back to focusing on joy and fun in learning.

In Search of America

April 12, 1992—My sister and I sat in the yellow sunlight of her new kitchen. She had married a few months before. It had been one of those gargantuan family weddings for which Brooklyn in the '50s was famous. A caravan of cars departed the ceremony blaring their horns. People on the sidewalks waved cheerfully to the bride and groom. We sang "Oh Happy Day." It was.

Now it was a sad day. I had come with news she did not want to hear. I was planning to leave high school and home. I had just turned 16. It had taken a long time that morning to get around to the subject. We drank coffee and talked about every bit of family news we could think of. Finally, there was no avoiding the subject. "You just can't do this," she kept saying over and over.

She talked about the value of formal education. She held two degrees. Ours was a family steeped in book learning, I told her. I wanted to go out and experience life. She tried not to make me feel too guilty about what all this was doing to my parents. They had watched the older five children launch stellar academic careers. Now this.

I had been reading the biographies of writers that summer. The writers I loved then had found their way through journalism. Among them, Langston Hughes and Ernest Hemingway particularly made me want to get on with writing. School, I told my sister, was just delaying me. But to make a difference, she kept saying, you have to have degrees, credentials. My credentials, I remember arguing, would be my work. She shook her head. "Foolish boy," she said, "foolish boy."

There was another reason, and she knew this well. My adolescent rebellion was not just about wanting to write. It had much to do with the religious strictures of our family. Our education at home was rich and deep. The problem was the limits. We were not allowed to go to movies or plays or listen to the radio or watch television. We lived a cloistered, studious life, walled in by my father's faith and my mother's edicts. I was torn by an extraordinary devotion competing with a massive curiosity. I loved our home. Yet I had an insatiable desire to know about America and the world.

I left my sister's house and went down to the Nostrand Avenue station of the Independent subway line. I took the "A" train. I emerged at the West Fourth Street station and walked upstairs to Washington Square in Greenwich Village. I declared myself home. Home and free. But not home free. Not yet. There was work to be done. I promised myself I would read in every subject in which I might have the remotest interest. Some were subjects I might have otherwise studied in a classroom. I also found bright and challenging minds in the coffeehouses of the Village of that time.

Years later, when I was finally a reporter on a daily newspaper in York, Pennsylvania, my editor enjoyed challenging me with vocabulary games. One day, he said he knew he had a stumper I would not get. "What's an autodidact?" he asked with a twinkle of triumph in his merry Irish eyes.

As I searched for the answer, he said, "You're an autodidact. It's a self-teacher. All these years, through your reading and your wandering, you've been educating yourself." With that, he encouraged me to become a Nieman Fellow at Harvard University. I studied art, music, economics and history. I also studied my fellow students, trying to figure out what I had missed. My exam results and grades on papers suggested I had not missed as much by my method as my sister feared.

I came to believe what I missed most was the social aspect of learning. Professors help understanding. Other students stimulate curiosity. My university had been the newsroom until then. I still think the newsroom is the best center of learning ever devised. A good one is, anyway.

By now my sisters and brothers have accepted my choice. My parents did before they died, but never fully. I tell my children what I did would not work if tried today. The world is a very different place. Credentials matter now much more than they did then. I say to young people today that they must stay in school. Autodidacts are of another age, I tell them. School today is imperative. All the same, my adventure suited me, and served me well. My sisters even agree. Grudgingly.

The New Way of the World

March 15, 1992—My children seem never to tire of hearing about life at Grandma and Grandpa's dinner table. Kinship is naturally attractive to children. My brothers and sisters, all of them older than I am, have had the same experiences with their children. Like my own kids, they love to hear about a life they never saw.

Sitting around the big walnut dining room table in the old house in Brooklyn, my parents served more than good food. The dinner table was their seminar setting. They gave us ample opportunities to tell what we had learned. They listened carefully for ideas they did not like. Above all, they pushed the idea of learning as the key to living.

The other day, Alan Greenspan, the chairman of the Federal Reserve, came to San Francisco. He addressed an audience of businesspeople. He said nothing new about interest rates. All the same, he did say something that would have made my mother and father swell with pride. Those two old West Indian immigrants surely would have felt vindicated by no less a personage than the chairman of the august Fed.

The reason is a saying that they repeated often. They wove it into nearly every dinner conversation. "There are only two ways to make a living," one or another of them would say. "Either with your back or your brain." Then the other was almost certain to add, "Your brain is sure to last longer than your back."

Now to the chairman of the Fed. He told the executives in San Francisco an interesting story about the future of the American worker. He said a century ago workers produced goods. Their well-being derived from adding value to raw materials. Now, said Greenspan, the data make clear that a fundamental and irreversible change has occurred. Immutably, he said, "the value now is in conception, ideas, and it is moving away from physical products." Virtually all "the value added comes from the substitution of ideas for physical things."

If my parents had been there, they surely would have said, "We told you so." They held in the utmost scorn those of our friends who decided on physical instead of intellectual pursuits. All physical crafts, they argued, no matter how noble or gratifying, were doomed one day to be "dead-end" pursuits.

Greenspan said essentially the same thing. He said those with college educations are headed toward greater incomes. Those without higher education were headed toward lower incomes. He called it "an extraordinary change in the structure of output." My parents would not have put it that way. Yet their message and his amount to the same thing.

The implications of this change are enormous, Greenspan said. They mean our society runs the risk of a shortage of knowledgeable workers unless we do more to see that a larger number of our young people are trained to "handle this new high-tech infrastructure." He was less clear as to how the government should address this challenge.

We have known this change was coming for a long time. We are not prepared. Japanese students and many from industrialized Europe spend as many as 240 days in school. Our students spend 180 days in school. Even so, the rigor with which American children approach education does not suggest a full appreciation of the ramifications of a world in which the work of the back is valued less each day.

My parents insisted, I tell my kids, on the honing of the brain. They did not insist we pursue any particular endeavor. They insisted only that we understand one thing. The future, they said, belonged to those who think for a living. This was long before computers were in every workplace. They seemed to sense, without knowing exactly why, that we would need our brains more than our backs.

My parents meant no disrespect to hard work of any kind. They believed in it. They just knew, even a half-century ago, what Alan Greenspan said the other day in San Francisco. The world has changed from backs to brains. Too few Americans understand this.

Caring about Children First

November 2, 1989—She does not have quite the robust stride she had when she was my teacher 35 years ago. Although not quite frail, she is smaller now than I remember her. Her mind, though, remains razor sharp. Long since retired, she continues in her passionate concern for children and education.

Theresa Held came to the Tribune Tower in downtown Oakland to see how one of her former pupils was doing. She still lives in the same house in Brooklyn, but she remains vitally interested in her former charges. She checks up on us all over the world.

Former students of Mrs. Held feel blessed because of her. She mentioned another former student with an air of special pride. "She was the first black woman lawyer in Geneva," she said. "I was there to see her."

Now she was in Oakland, and she wasted no time reestablishing our old relationship from high school days. I was still the student, and proud of it, and she was still teacher. The lesson for the day was, of course, children.

"Children cannot learn in a state of anxiety. We are putting too much pressure on children today. We are not giving them a chance to be children. We burden them with the same drives as those of competitive adults. Teaching little kids through rote learning is very bad for children. They suffer anxiety and learn very little."

Without pausing for more than a breath, she went on: "The key to teaching kids is to enhance their sense of self-esteem and show them respect at all times. Showing children you respect them is vital to their development. They cannot learn much if they sense they are not respected by their teachers. It's no mean thing to enhance every child in a classroom, but it can be done."

Mrs. Held told a story of writing to *The New York Times* on the subject of children and respect. "I received a ton of hate mail. I saved one that said, 'You can't teach the children of New York because they are savages.' It was from a teacher."

I had no difficulty as I listened to her remembering why she was one of my favorite adults when I was still a student. No matter the complexity of the subject, she never spoke to her students in a condescending manner. Unlike many of her contemporaries, she worked to make teaching and learning a partnership, a shared interest.

Her special interest was American government and American history. We used to walk together to student government meetings. "Do you know," she might begin as we strolled down a wide boulevard called Eastern Parkway, "the role Tom Paine's writing played in shaping the American Revolution?" I always hated it when we reached our destination.

Eventually, I got to know the whole family. Her late husband was a musician and her son is now a psychiatrist in Oakland. She was always surrounded by books, music and a lively circle of friends. She was often the center of attention because Theresa Held was most likely to have the quickest wit and the most commanding voice in any gathering.

Now she is at the age where many retreat from the world around them. Mrs. Held instead is championing education reform. She is urging that elementary schools become the locus for child advocacy in America.

"The elementary schools have the potential to touch the lives of every child in America. I taught in the university in Zambia after I retired from the New York schools. Those students were struggling because they didn't have basic elementary education. Every child must have that to succeed."

We talked about Oakland schools, and she wondered aloud why a "busy editor" was still interested in education. There is no simple answer to that, but Theresa Held is surely one of the reasons. Few of her former students are unaffected by her role in their lives. To know her is to always remember her. And that, she will tell you with a devilish sort of grin, is exactly how she planned it.

Education Isn't the Same as Learning

April 28, 1988—My brothers and I were squeezed into the cab of the moving van, our little knees bouncing against each other on every wide turn. My father, at the wheel, was impervious to our discomfort.

Steering the van through the streets of New York City with effortless ease, physical discomfort was the last thing on my father's mind.

Instead, his deep baritone voice vibrated in the cab of the truck. "Do you understand," he would say to no one of us in particular, "how our system of justice was influenced by ancient Greece and by the teachings of Jesus Christ?"

There we were, in the middle of the cacophony of traffic trying to cross the Manhattan Bridge. The other motorists might have been listening to the Dodgers game or jazz on the radio. Not us.

In my father's "Green Hornet," as he called the van, lessons on history and theology were in full swing. My parents never missed an opportunity to cram us full of some historical or biblical observation.

Always, it seems now, they were romancing our minds with the idea of the love of learning. I have no idea whether my mother and father read books on the theory of how to hook kids on the life of the mind.

My brothers and sisters, ever an independent lot, agree on one thing a half-century later: My parents deliberately set out to create in each of us a curious and inquiring mind. It is no accident they produced six children who are educators, linguists, journalists and the like.

Even though they came to America as immigrants, my parents never doubted what it took to make it in the United States—hard work and a love of learning.

The strategy of my parents comes regularly to mind of late as I watch the growing debate over public education. It is clear we are about to be inundated with a discussion over the proper role of the federal government in the schools.

As that debate unfolds in the political campaign of 1988, my sense of unease grows. I fear we are about to rush off in the wrong direction.

The present motivation for all this talk by Democrats and Republicans about education concerns the latest political buzzword, "competitiveness."

Because we are in a new global market, competing for jobs with the rising Asian and Latin economies, politicians realize our workforce must be better educated to be competitive in this technological age. Hence the new emphasis among political leaders on education.

Why do I fear they are leading us astray? Only because I think politicians look at education the way they address war—throw massive amounts of money and matériel at the adversary.

More important than money, I would argue, is our attitude toward education. My parents made that point often by speaking with contempt of "educated fools." These, in their lexicon, were people with advanced degrees but without elementary common sense.

For that reason, my folks described people whose intellects they admired as "learned," never educated. That, it seems to me, is a major distinction.

Instead of having "education" as our focus, I think we should aim at "learning" as our goal. The difference is one of attitude, an important aspect of the intellectual process.

This is no mere semantic distinction. It has everything to do with how we approach this "competitive" challenge.

If we think of the national need as being "education," I fear we will think in narrow mechanistic and technocratic terms. Education in that sense is measured in degrees attained and number of hours logged in this subject or that.

By contrast, a lifetime of learning suggests a continuing hunger for new knowledge and new ways of looking at old problems and new ones.

When I think of education, I think of a goal being achieved. When I think of learning, I think of a continuing process of growth and development from infancy to the end of our days.

That is why I hope our political leaders can inspire a national atmosphere where learning is loved for its own sake.

In such an environment, much more than mere "competitiveness" will be attained. That is the atmosphere in which creativity can triumph over the mastery of mechanics.

This is the reason I think we should focus on becoming a learning society as opposed to merely thinking of better education. Learning, if loved, goes on forever.

The Religious Right's Dubious Victory

November 23, 1986—After the teacher read a few pages aloud of Ernest Hemingway, each of us was assigned to choose a Hemingway novel to read over the weekend. Our book reports were due Monday morning.

When I got home with *For Whom the Bell Tolls* that memorable Friday afternoon, I was more interested in running back outside for a pickup game of touch football that was getting under way. I tossed my books on the hall table and scampered back outside, barely saying hello to my mother.

That evening, when I went to pick up my books, the Hemingway was missing. I asked my mother if she had seen it. Instead of answering, she handed me the book. Inside the hard cover was a thick letter from my mother. I'll probably never forget it.

She said she did not mind my reading the book, although she called Hemingway "a heathen author." What she wanted me to bear in mind as I read the book, her letter went on, is that his values and those of "the Communist radicals" were a world away from the Christian values my father and she believed in and wanted us to believe in.

Finally, she said, she hoped my reading the book would help me see that the way of thinking of people such as Hemingway and his hero, Robert Jordan, were antithetical to the teachings of Christ. She hoped I would see that more clearly after reading the book and she was looking forward to our discussion when I finished the book by the heathen.

The other day, I relived that memory after learning of the action of a U.S. District Court judge in an East Tennessee case. Judge Thomas Hull, sitting without a jury, ruled that parents could protect their children from those assigned schoolbooks that offended their religious beliefs.

Judge Hull ruled children may leave the classroom when books to which their parents object are being read or discussed. They can, he said, "opt out" of class if their beliefs are offended by the class texts.

If Judge Hull's ruling is affirmed by the U.S. Supreme Court, the classrooms of America will become more varied in their offerings than the best of cafeterias. Public education, which has been for so long the great common ground for instilling our values, will instead sink to offering the least offensive material.

Imagine the Christian pacifist who believes the teaching of physics is what will lead to nuclear holocaust. Such a parent would then be able to have his or her children "opt out" of physics, not wanting them exposed to "dangerous" scientific thought.

The children of any parent who is offended by any subject will be the losers in the end. At the time my mother commandeered my Hemingway, I was not altogether thrilled at her imposition of her views on my choice of reading. I realize now how much more I could have lost if I had been denied the privilege of discovery.

After reading the Tennessee case, I can see better how fortunate my brothers and sisters and I were. Stern as my parents were in their deep religious beliefs, they were willing for the most part to test their faith against the challenges of the devil in the belief Christ and they would win. Years after their deaths, their track record remains astonishingly good.

That is not to say they were tolerant in everything. Far from it. But they had an abiding faith in the idea that good minds are those minds capable of handling a wide range of information and ideas. Such minds, they believed, would ultimately make the wisest choices.

What Judge Hull ultimately concluded was that if the parents held sincere beliefs that certain books would do harm to their children, then the state had best back off. To do otherwise might well give the schools the color of tyranny in the eyes of the parents.

In truth, such parents would do better to have their children in a Christian academy, and not in a public school. That would be better for all concerned, except for those crusading against "secular humanism." This case was a victory in a war against a sin its opponents cannot define.

All the same, the religious right won, but I think their children, and perhaps many others are the eventual losers. They lose because they are being sheltered from the world of ideas that forms so much of the basis of our common understanding of the world in which we live.

It is hard for anyone to assess what value to place on that loss. I just hope when those sheltered children are adults they are as grateful to their parents as my brothers and sisters and I are to mine.

Prayer in the Classroom:
A History Lesson

August 22, 1982—My mother's jaw was unforgettably firm. She had a way of holding her head at a slight angle when she was listening to something she did not like hearing and planned to reject. If, for example, you were making the case for why you simply had to go out and play before doing your homework, she would hold her head like that and listen before sending you to your room with a crisp no.

On this occasion, it was not one of us children who was getting the "head to one side" treatment, as we called it. It was my fifth-grade teacher.

"Mrs. Maynard," she was saying, "all the other children have taken advantage of the early release for religious instruction on Wednesday except for Robert. I was wondering why. Don't you want your son to have religious education?"

Under this new program, all you had to do to get Wednesday afternoon off was to bring a signed form from home that said you would go to one of the churches in the community on Wednesday. Many of my classmates dropped by the church of their choice, signed in and then disappeared to the nearest basketball court.

"I am not paying you people my hard-earned tax money to send my child to church. I am paying you to educate him," my mother responded. "His religious instruction is not your business. It's ours. My husband and I want him at school Wednesday and every day."

That was that. My teacher and I were often the only two people on the third floor of P.S. 3 on Wednesday afternoon. I can imagine she might have wanted to be other places, but she discovered something we children had known all our lives. There was everyone else's way of doing things and there was Sam and Robertine Maynard's way of doing them.

And when it came to prayer, they had their own ideas of how to pray and when to pray. They were not about to concede that responsibility to anyone. They roused us at the crack of dawn for family prayer hour, they began each meal with prayer and we were instructed not to allow your head to hit that pillow without a final prayer each night.

But, could the public schools of New York City inspire a little prayer here and there? "Not one bit of it," my mother told my teacher. "You teach math. We will teach the prayers."

Years later, I noticed how close the Supreme Court came to echoing my mother's sentiment when it struck down several state school prayer laws in 1963. One justice said: As between a man and his God, the state is bound to remain neutral.

Now I see the newest battle for prayer in the schools is in a terminal state and I remain as mystified as my mother was 35 years ago as to why anyone would want paid state bureaucrats instructing their children in a matter as intimate as prayer.

When I told my wife I was going to pose this question in public, she assured me I would soon have plenty of answers.

This is not to doubt the sincerity of those who have been battling for school prayer. I am certain they do so out of convictions every bit as deep as those of my parents when they argued the opposite position.

My difficulty with their position derives from our unique American heritage of religious freedom. It was a deep desire to escape from religious persecution that brought the first settlers to the New World. That is why religious freedom is first among the principles of American democracy.

Case law is laden with abstractions on this subject. In one of the older cases, Justice Rutledge said for the Supreme Court, the "great condition of religious liberty is that it be maintained free from sustenance, as also from interferences, by the state."

In other words, the same principle that made it possible for my mother to prevent the schools of New York City from sending me off to church every Wednesday afternoon protects everyone's right to worship when, where and how they please.

Unfortunately, what remains painfully clear is that for some people this issue is not an abstraction. They see the moral climate of our society as deteriorating and they feel the injection of a spiritual regime in our public institutions will improve their ability to shape better behavior.

Worthy as that goal might be, such a course is fraught with peril. Today's benign religious regime could become tomorrow's religious tyranny. One of the lawyers arguing against the school prayer law struck down in Massachusetts put it this way:

"Constitutional rights are not made to be broken by majorities. They are for the protection of minorities and of majorities who may one day become minorities."

If you doubt the wisdom of that argument, consider Iran today. Those who fell from the religious favor of the ayotollahs would have been happy to have had the shield of the First Amendment fall between them and the firing squad. Many have died in Iran since the revolution for no better reason than that the wind shifted and they became unprotected minorities where once they might have been in the safe majority.

The theory of the founders in framing the Bill of Rights was that there are some issues that should not be governed by simple majority rule because they are basic to the way our system must work if ordered liberty is to be preserved for majorities and minorities alike. In matters such as religion, it is impossible to predict when today's majority might become tomorrow's minority.

In such a circumstance, what sounded like a good idea to those formerly in the majority might not sound nearly as appealing once the wind shifted. To protect believer and nonbeliever, the founders wisely put religious freedom out of the realm of the state.

When I came home that day from school after my mother and my teacher had their discussion of who was in charge of my religious training, my parents asked at dinner how the rest of the day had gone. I said I did not think my teacher had been pleased but that she appeared ready to make the best of the situation.

My mother asked if I understood why she had taken the stand she took. I said I did. Then she said:

"Now, you remember tonight to say a special prayer of thanksgiving that you live in a free country where we can do what we did today and neither of us was arrested."

It remains impossible for me to hear the pleas for more religion in the public schools without remembering that day when one of the two most devout Christians in my life stood up for the right of her child not to go to church as a matter of first principle.

Not to Value Teachers Is Sheer Folly

February 10, 1985—When I entered first grade at P.S. 44 in Brooklyn, New York, I had the misfortune of being the last of six children in my family to have attended that antiquated institution.

My life was known to practically every member of the relatively small faculty. No place in that school or on its grounds could I hope to do anything without soon hearing from some teacher or administrator, "I know your whole family, and I know your parents would not approve of your doing . . ." whatever.

The effect of that upon my early development, I later discovered, was to merge in my mind the relationship between home and school. They were part and parcel of a close, if not closed, process.

What was initially intimidating became in time reassuring: Home was a little like school and school was a lot like home. Perhaps sometimes too much so, but I grew up to recognize I could have had worse problems than those. When I see the problems school children cope with in today's city, I grow more appreciative of the attention our teachers displayed toward us.

The teachers are what I remember most. I remember them as having enormous stature in our eyes. We thought they were gods and goddesses in their realm. One, we thought, was brutal to children, and we despised her. Part of the reason we hated her so was the very fact of how different she was from the rest.

My favorite of the early grade school teachers was the teacher who helped me overcome a speech impediment and an impenetrable Barbadian accent. Both were so difficult as to cause my parents to worry I might not make it in public school.

Along came this "genius with a wire recorder," as my father would later describe my speech teacher. This was during World War II. She would record at home every evening Edward R. Murrow's "This is London" broadcasts.

Each morning, she would play back a portion of the previous night's broadcast. Then she would ask me to record the same passage on the wire recorder, a primitive precursor to today's tape recorder. We would then listen to my version and go back and listen to Ed Murrow. At the start, it was a laughable exercise. I did not appreciate the humor of my plight.

My vision of the problem was terrifying. I would raise my hand in class, stand up and state what seemed to me to be a perfectly normal answer to a problem on the blackboard, and the teachers and other pupils would stare in bafflement, not comprehending a word I'd said.

At home, where we spoke standard English and Barbadian dialect interchangeably, my speech pattern did not seem all that out of place. But the closer I got to that schoolhouse door each morning, the more aware I became of my inability to communicate with others.

So I looked forward to my sessions with the kind woman with the Webcor wire recorder. She would hold a small mirror in front of my face, and make me watch what I was doing with my tongue and teeth as I pronounced each syllable. It was grueling work for both of us. It went on for hours some days.

Our triumph came at Easter when I was in third grade. I was selected for a principal role in the class Easter play, and my part involved a long speech at the end of the first act. Ed Murrow I was not, but the burst of applause at the end told me all I wanted to know: After two years in an American school, I made myself understood to my peers and teachers.

So special had the triumph been for my whole family that somehow, mysteriously, a Webcor wire recorder of my very own materialized in our household. As my brother said with more than a small touch of envy, "You're a lucky kid; you might have gotten a mirror."

Unique though that story was to me at the time, I was soon to meet dozens and then hundreds of people who had similar or more dramatic stories to tell about how public school teachers had changed their lives for the better. Someplace in the cross fire of the politics of education, the classroom teachers' function and status have disappeared from the debate. Their role has been, and still is, at the core of our greatness as a society.

Today, all we hear from those who study such matters is that teachers are held in about the esteem as trash collectors—which is not altogether accurate, since there are places where the latter group earns more.

This is not meant to be overly simplistic, but I think our society is going deeper into trouble as it lets the importance of teachers, teaching and public education slip under the trash heap of our polity.

Rehabilitating the image of learning as the highest of our capabilities should be close to the top of our societal priorities. How it slipped is a long and complicated story that really needs no great retelling here. A stunning combination of national mood changes has brought us to this place: More than 23 million adult Americans, one-fifth of all adults, are functional illiterates. They cannot follow a bus schedule, fill out a job application or read this newspaper.

Were that a static situation it would be scandalous enough. What is worse is that the number is increasing at a rate of 10 percent a year, according to those who keep track of such depressing news.

What's more, gifted college graduates are avoiding the teaching profession in droves, raising the question of where the potential "geniuses with wire recorders" are likely to want to work today. All too many are choosing medicine, law and engineering.

The salary of the entering teacher is often below that commanded by a good receptionist. In the portions of the system where talent is needed most, the inner cities, the working conditions are often appalling and chaotic. On top of that, teachers have told me of being reluctant at some social functions to admit that they are teachers: To say so can result in being ignored for the evening.

If we stop and think of the importance of this subject to our civilization, it should not take long for us to realize we are on a slippery slope to nowhere unless we grab hold of the issue of teaching, teachers and their status.

Teaching: A Talent to Be Treasured

May 26, 1985—He was a short, slender and balding man whose manner belied the power of his influence over our lives as teenagers. Before 10th grade, I passed him often in the hallways of Boys High. I never knew his name until I landed by random selection in his classroom. His effect from then on was profound.

What made me think about Mr. Blum was the news that the crisis over teaching promises to grow worse. Fewer people want to be teachers, and many of those who wish to teach are among the least well prepared to train the minds of others.

Quite apart from the serious social implications of those developments, the consequences are also personal for many students. Great teachers are great gifts to the personalities of children. It is fair to say those gifts can last a lifetime.

Mr. Blum was an institution in the English department of Brooklyn's Boys High School. He managed to have a program to excite each of his students to love the language and to learn to use it well. He was an evangelist for precision.

When I came to his class, the first lesson was grammar. Most teachers begin that subject with a dreary lecture about the evolution of the English language and a plea for accuracy. He did none of that. He asked each of us to write a page about ourselves and turn it in.

The next day, he called me aside for a "private" chat. I had a sudden fear my grammar was so poor I was about to be dismissed from the course as hopeless. Instead, he offered me a generous opportunity for which I shall always be grateful.

"You really don't need this course," he said. "You need most to write more. Why don't you stay and write me an essay a day? Write about anything you want, just write."

Stunned, I asked what sort of things he wanted me to write. He smiled and said, "You read the *New York Times*, don't you?" I nodded yes. "I want you to read it every morning and all of it on Sunday, especially the magazine. Cover to cover."

Do that religiously, he insisted, "and you will have plenty about which to write. And, by the way, I want a nice long Sunday essay as your weekend assignment."

In those days, for reasons I cannot remember, I wrote in ghastly green ink. I had a Parker fountain pen my parents had given me the previous summer. I used to go through bottles of green ink, churning out essays for Mr. Blum.

He was kind enough to send an essay I wrote for him to one of his neighbors, who was a writer and editor for the *New York Times*. The editor sent me a kind and encouraging note that I carried in my wallet until one day it dissolved from wear and tear.

There is no way to overstate the value to children of being taught to express themselves on paper. Prof. Theodore Sizer, chairman of the department of education at Brown University, was speaking of that the other day.

"It's the only way to catch the student's mind in motion," Sizer said. "You have to get the student to do it. You have to coach the student, critique the work and make sure the student gets lots and lots of practice."

That is what Mr. Blum provided to his students at Boys High. He did it out of love for writing and love for students. His own essays were not published much, but were admired by those who appreciated good writing.

The great poet Louise Bogan, he told us once with swelling pride, did a critique of an essay of his and found a single flaw. He had misused the word "but." Think about that, he exhorted us. "Perfect, but . . ."

It was a rare student of his who used the word "but" in an essay for Mr. Blum after that day. It was not that we feared him. There was nothing fearsome about him except his mind. It was respect and appreciation we felt most toward him.

Mr. Blum, and teachers like him, give children a special gift. By demanding that students write, they open channels of communication that become the pathway to self-analysis and understanding.

A society such as ours needs more of that, not less. Yet, the sad news seems to be there are fewer Mr. Blums blossoming in the world. That is a loss we cannot calculate, but a loss it is.

Reading: The Key to Knowledge

November 30, 1986—We were driving over the Brooklyn Bridge in the old Buick. I was sitting in my big sister's lap counting the cars we passed. Suddenly I looked up as we came off the bridge and saw the sign on a pharmaceutical plant. "Syburb," I blurted out.

"No," my sister said, trying to suppress a giggle. "That says Squibb." I remember peering at the sign again out of the back window. The blur of the arrangement of letters in the English language snapped into focus.

When we got home, I picked up a copy of the *Daily News* and began reeling off the headlines. It was a cause for celebration in our house because reading was regarded as the key to every other aspect of development.

Years later, I was to learn there was a name for what I experienced that day on the Brooklyn Bridge. It's sometimes called the "learning explosion" or the "reading explosion." It does not happen that way for all children, but it happens more often than adults realize.

Just as my parents celebrated the explosion in each of their children, so have I celebrated watching it occur in my children. Indeed what made me recall the bridge experience is a parallel experience in two generations.

When my mother and father stood with pride and watched as I reeled off one word after another, he looked at her and said, "He's the last one we'll see go through this discovery until the grandchildren come."

Here we are, my wife and I, watching our youngest go through the explosion, and it is a wonderful thing to see one last time. It happened with each of the older two children just as it is happening with the little guy. They struggle with words and syllables for months. Then one day, it seems as if they simply cannot find enough to read.

Each one reached a point at which she or he was more interested in the outside of a cereal carton than the contents. At that point, if home and school reinforce the process, the explosion blossoms into the gift of the life of the mind. Once in place, that gift never stops giving.

"There is a vast storehouse in the kingdom of knowledge," I remember my father saying one night after dinner. He used to spin the globe and nearly hypnotize us with the idea of the wonder and the wealth of things to know about the world. But the key, he used to remind us, is being able to read.

Today, many youngsters think my father old-fashioned. After all, with 100 channels of television and counting, many young people think their information needs are being met, and in living color. Why, then, go through the bother of struggling with all those complicated words? they ask.

Sometimes when I watch the sleek videos my boys watch, I can see the nature of the enemy of literacy. The square box imparts so many vivid images to the brain that it would be natural for an impressionable recipient to suppose all those images added up to something from which truth and meaning can be abstracted.

Indeed, some of today's video is such a subtle drug it begins to undermine the intellect and erode any need to think at all. Alarming as that might be, the answer does not lie in banning television from children's lives. Flawed as it may be, it is an information system, one on which their generation relies for some valid reasons.

Rather, I think the best approach is to convert television into a teaching tool. I try to suggest to our children that there is much more to know about subjects that intrigue them on television.

By stimulating a deeper curiosity, parents can help validate the importance of reading. That is best done by carefully observing what interests children on the tube. It's not a bad idea to search for books and other literature on those subjects.

Some parents throw up their hands, others throw out the television set. Neither is necessary. The challenge is to take advantage of children's natural interest in television and use it as a vehicle to advance the cause.

Even as television helps erode literacy, it still enhances sophistication. My children know far more about the world than I did at their various ages, and they learn much of it from television. The assignment parents must accept is to take control of the situation by transforming television from an adversary of literacy to an ally.

As I discovered that day on the bridge, reading is a gift so precious everyone should have it. And almost all can.

Holidays and Outings

My brothers and I loved to go Christmas shopping with our father. Our family never shopped before Christmas week. Sometimes, we didn't make it to the stores until the rush of Christmas Eve. But it still had a luxurious feel, a day with Dad with time to talk as we walked through the shops. No matter what was going on in our lives, at Christmas we all stopped what we were doing to spend time with each other.

It is one of our favorite family holidays, filled with the familiar rituals, traditions and corny jokes.

Dad always said the only gift he wanted was all three of his children home for the holiday. Then he would promise one of us that our only gift was to be a lump of coal in our Christmas stocking.

Ask him a week or so before Christmas if he had finished his shopping and Dad would wince. "Are you kidding? I haven't even begun," he would answer in the aggrieved tone of the unduly put upon.

Finally, around December 22, between news meetings and reviewing the newspaper's budget for the next year, he would write out his Christmas list.

He loved Christmas, but sometimes worried that the meaning of Christmas was being lost.

As soon as I was old enough to understand, he explained Christmas this way in a 1963 letter:

"On this Christmas, when everyone is acting as though this were the birthday of Santa Claus, instead of Jesus, I just wanted you to remember and to know whose birthday this really is—and what He stood for: the love of all men," Daddy wrote. "Many of us love Christ. We love Him for what He stood for, for what He did. He loved children for one thing, and poor people for another. Since you are a child, and your daddy is poor, isn't it a good idea to celebrate Christ's Birthday?"

For Daddy, Christmas was a religious holiday. We went to church Christmas Day. Our pastor and his family came to our house for Christmas dinner.

But with a family came presents, and the crass commercialism Daddy once railed against he came to appreciate as another expression of love. Each gift was really a token of affection, a way of saying I know you, what excites you, what matters to you, and I care enough to be the one to give it to you.

Lingering over a book, or fingering a scarf while shopping, Dad would patiently explain why the subject matter and the author's background combined to make the book a perfect gift for one of our friends. Or the color of the scarf or the content of its fiber might rule it out. If it wasn't a perfect fit, it wasn't a gift for a friend.

D.J.M.

A Day for Whoops of Joy

May 24, 1987—We arose as one at the first red signal of dawn. It was the warm spring morning of a special day in the life of our family. My oldest sister would receive her master of science diploma, the first member of our family to cross that threshold to an advanced degree.

It was a day of pomp and circumstance, and a day on which my mother warned my father several times that if he stuck out his chest any farther he was going to burst every button off his vest.

I remember the ride from Brooklyn to Morningside Heights that morning in 1947 as if it were yesterday. I had never seen a school as vast as Columbia University. The campus was a bewildering sea of black robes. The shared excitement of the graduates and their families created an electricity of love and pride.

Perhaps not on that first occasion, but after many more such, something struck me about spring commencements. Graduation exercises remain all but unique as a shared American ritual. We have few such institutionalized events that cut across so many social sectors.

Graduation is the celebration of success and passage. It is a time of completion that sets the stage for the next phase of life, as commencement speakers everywhere are fond of saying. It is the time for uninhibited expressions of hope and ambition.

It is also a time when people discover they can laugh and cry at the same time. And they need feel no shame. Others are similarly engaged. It is even all right for those who otherwise maintain discreet decorum to let out a whoop of joy when that special name is called and the pride of the family crosses the stage. It's a special day. We all understand.

Every spring, I am privileged to witness a commencement or two. It's always the same for me. I am as moved by the bright eyes of hope in the young as by the glistening eyes of pride in the older generations. On a fine spring Sunday in America, graduation is not a bad place to be. It is this country at its most optimistic.

There is more to graduation than optimism. It is also often the occasion for the leaders and graduates of the institution to reflect for the last time together on the meaning of their common experience. What, after all, are the values and purposes of education?

That is a most important question at this particular time. We celebrate the 200th year of the Constitution in a climate of dramatic moral crisis. A presidential candidate has just self-destructed over a moral issue. Wall Street operatives are being indicted by the day for illegal insider trading. Washington is wallowing in tales of lies and deception at the highest levels of government. Marines are accused of trading secrets for sex.

Alongside those disclosures are accusations against American colleges and universities that they have become little more than glorified trade schools. They are charged of late with turning out mechanical intellectuals, educated cynics said to know the price of everything but the value of nothing.

There are those who see a relationship between those two sets of circumstances. They see the origin of our moral crisis in the failure of our school systems, higher education included, to teach an appreciation for ethics.

Perhaps, finally, that is what I like best about commencements. Odd as it might seem, if it is difficult these days to hear about ethics in the classroom, it is not too hard to hear about such matters from the commencement podium. What the graduates may have heard little of in the previous four years, they won't escape on graduation day.

Almost always, some speaker—usually at unnecessary length, given the heat of the day—will hold forth on the importance of leading a morally informed life. He or she will almost certainly remind the students of the obligations to society that accompany their good fortune.

For whatever reason, the graduation ritual, with most of its values intact, endures and even flourishes in the '80s. Indeed, as I reflect across four decades to my first one, I would say one of the institutions that appears to have remained the most intact in a sea of change is the spring commencement and its attendant rituals.

If someone you love is graduating this season, don't forget: Just this once, it's perfectly all right to whoop for joy.

The Ties That Bind Us to Dad

June 17, 1990 —The silvery thread was what first caught my eye. It was a wide blue necktie, dark and conservative, except for the pattern of silver thread. After Sunday dinner, I slid from my chair, approached my father at the head of the table and handed him the box, kissed his cheek and wished him a happy Father's Day.

"Oh, for me?" he said, sounding like the most surprised man in America. He opened the box and "oohed" and "aahed" over my present. As the youngest of the six children, I had been designated the honored presenter of a gift to dad.

Over the years, the ritual remained the same, even to the time when it was his grandchildren, my nieces and nephews, making the presentation. Always, it was some modest gift, a tie, a shirt, perhaps a new pair of suspenders.

My father was a simple, even pious, man whose interests tended more toward the spiritual than the material. He would not have been comfortable having too much made over him for Father's Day, his birthday or for any occasion. He took his joy from the very existence of his family. He continuously told us he couldn't imagine a gift to match it.

More than that, he rarely ever wore the ties we selected for him with such painstaking care. He had a handful of cravats, all elegant but plain, that he loved to wear. Each attempt my sisters made to "spiff up" his wardrobe lasted about two Sundays. Then he slipped back into his familiar, simple style.

Why, then, I have often wondered, did we go to such lengths each Father's Day to select a gift we doubted he would ever wear? I thought as a child we did it for him. In a way we did. But I also think we had something else in mind.

In the time of our growing up, a father was often a remote figure. That's the way fathers were in those days. All my friends had fathers just like mine. They were stern, strict and not always approachable about the mundane issues of life.

Our ties and other little presents were our way of hoping a part of us would become a part of him. On those rare occasions when he wore one of our gifts our spirits soared.

He made certain we had other ways of knowing he cared about us. He listened to our arguments at dinner, and he engaged us in almost interminable discussions of fine points of theology. My mother and he often told us they had made up their minds on one thing before any of us was ever born: None of us would ever doubt their love or their unequivocal regard.

The parents from the older generation tended to have those values, shaped in the main by a simpler time. Many aspects of those days cannot be reconstructed. Both parents work most of the time now and are very busy even when they are not working. And a growing percentage of children today live with just one parent, mostly mothers.

Since my dad and those of most of my friends worked long hours, seeing them was almost always something of a treat. That also contributed to our sense as children that our father was remote and that our mother ran the home on a daily basis.

So those ties were almost literal. They were a way we tried to tie ourselves to a figure whose presence in our lives was powerful, yet never quite as full as we wished.

One day, as he was leaving on a trip, my father, I noticed, was wearing a different tie from his usual. It was the blue one with the silvery thread I had given him years before. By then I must have been about 10. I remember how I felt. I could only have been happier if I were going with him.

Lugging That Old Green Jug

June 25, 1989 —Summertime. The living was not always easy, but it was almost always fun. We piled into the old Buick and headed out of Brooklyn for Rockaway and Riis Beach, sometimes all the way out Long Island to Jones Beach. For good measure, a couple of times each summer, my parents would load up a moving van and take several dozen kids on a day's outing.

From all those years, one constant presence remains fixed in my memory. It is the old green jug. My mother supervised the making of the punch for every outing. It had to be sweet, but not too sweet. It had to have a certain "tang" to the flavor. Only my mother could say when it was just right.

When the punch finally reached my mother's standards, it was chilled and then poured over ice in the family Thermos. This green, five-gallon jug had been in our family since sometime before the Second World War. I think it was lined with lead and the heaviest glass of its era.

After it was filled, my father and my brothers took turns carrying the jug. From as early as I can remember, I yearned to be thought old enough and big enough to carry the jug. I would pick it up at the beginning of every summer, just to show I was getting there.

Finally, when I was about 10 years old, I picked up the old green jug and it was mine to carry. I was the youngest, and I would be the last, to lug the old green jug. I was surprised at its weight. In time, as we hiked toward the beach, I wondered what made me so eager for this chore, this sign of passage.

I could not help but think of the green jug the other day. The maker, Thermos, has been purchased by a Japanese concern. So Thermos is now on a passage of its own, no doubt to the solid-state digital jug that any kid could carry.

My own passage brought me to a point one summer day when I set the jug down in the sand. My leg had rubbed raw where the jug bumped against me. I rested from the leaden thing and let the rest of the crowd get ahead of me as they hunted for just the right spot on the beach.

Why, I asked myself, had I ever thought it was so important to carry this jug? It didn't take me long to realize that if this had been a prize assignment for my father and my brothers, it would have to be so for me. Little boys, I have since discovered, are often that way.

Needless to say, I went from struggling with the jug to the point where I hardly thought about it. Each summer, each picnic, was an occasion to measure my physical growth until there came a time when the jug meant nothing. It was just another part of the summer equipment.

Summer, it turns out, is for learning. It is a time when children and adults can spend time learning all sorts of things together. In today's busy, two-career world, family time is often hard to come by. Kids go off to summer activities and parents go to work, as usual.

What I remember about those picnics is that they signaled a time of total family relaxation. We ate fried chicken and my mother's memorable potato salad and we crashed against the waves of the Atlantic Ocean. And, of course, we satisfied our thirst from the green jug.

Heavy though it was, one thing I appreciated about that green jug. It was lighter to carry home. It always left the beach on empty. My dad once joked, "We are all helping carry the jug back." Summertime and the old green jug will always go together for me.

I wish you a great, learning summer.

For the True Fourth,
a New Yorker Goes Forth

July 3, 1983—An enormous archway graces the foot of Fifth Avenue in New York City. It takes its inspiration from the Arc de Triomphe in Paris. A fountain sits just beside the Fifth Avenue arch. Both are a few yards away from the Washington Square campus of New York University.

In the 1950s, that fountain was a gathering place for youthful artists, writers, musicians and others of high ambition and few tangible assets. They came from all the boroughs of New York City, some even from nearby towns across the river in New Jersey, to mingle at the fountain for hours and hours at a time.

Almost always, there was someone with a guitar. As the sun began to fall, the singing would begin. A fellow with a harmonica would begin to blow. Once in a while a trumpet player stopped by. A drummer came too, from time to time, but that usually occasioned a visit from the Greenwich Village police precinct, so drumming was discouraged.

Around about midnight, the police cruiser would slowly drive up to the fountain, the ritual signal that the gathering was over for the evening. It was then that we headed for one of the several coffee houses in Greenwich Village to talk the rest of the night away.

On such occasions, it did not fail to happen that someone would mention how fantastically lucky we were to have been born in New York and to be the recipients of such a rich cultural heritage. Almost certainly someone else would add that all good things were found in New York.

Indeed, I remember more than once hearing one New York chauvinist or another declare that there was no reason ever to leave New York. All that was worth experiencing was there. If it was any good, it would one day find its way to New York.

By the same logic, if you were an artist or a writer, you had to "make it" in New York or it didn't count. Because it was regarded as the place with the toughest competition, New York was the only true proving ground of talent to my friends.

An aspiring journalist with no extensive samples of writing to show a prospective employer could not dream of beginning his career on the New York City newspapers of that day. No such thing as internship programs existed then. You either had experience or you could not hope to get much of a start as a writer.

There was, of course, the route of starting as a copyboy. I considered that possibility until I met a fellow 28 years old with a master's degree, who had been a copyboy for the *New York Times* for more than five years. I decided there had to be a better route.

York County is in the middle of those rolling hills in south central Pennsylvania, where the rich soil once fed most of the nation when it was 13 colonies.

I found a small, feisty daily newspaper there that was willing to take in a young fellow with very little daily newspaper experience but a willingness to work hard for little money. (The publisher believed young reporters should receive very small salaries to demonstrate their commitment. I never learned his reason for the pay of more senior staff.)

At any rate, I took a Greyhound bus to York one Sunday night and began working the next morning as a reporter. I was so thrilled to find myself employed on a newspaper that I developed a nosebleed that took the talents of several doctors to fix.

A few weeks after my adventure in rural Pennsylvania began, I took one of my days off, drove four hours to New York City and headed for that fountain, feeling homesick.

My old pals were glad to see me, those that realized I hadn't been around. But when I told them where I had been and what I was doing there, a pall of dismay settled over the usually festive fountain. Friends I had known for years shook their heads in mock mourning. A New Yorker had fallen in with "country" people. Shame. Shame.

When I tried to explain to one of my friends that there was a whole vast country on the other side of the Hudson River, and that I wanted to discover the complexity and variety of America, he looked at me with an expression that denied comprehension.

Deflated by the reactions of my friends, I pointed my Plymouth jalopy west and headed back to York, uncertain if I had made the right choice to go adventuring in America. After all, wasn't it true that all good things were in New York?

Only a few days after I returned to York, my city editor called me over and gave me careful instructions. The following day was the Fourth of July. I can remember him saying, "Now I don't know about you Noo Yawkers, but here we take the Fourth of July seriously. I want you to cover it well."

Eager to do a good job, I rose early and began making the rounds of the picnics and parades, the big swim parties and the myriad barbecues. Every place I went, people were happily giving away food to friends and strangers alike.

Maybe I stayed out among the happy revelers too long. All I know is that when I returned to the office to write my story that evening, I felt a tingle of excitement I had not experienced before. These people were having a genuinely good time celebrating America's birthday, something I could not imagine my friends around the fountain admitting to themselves. That would have been too corny.

By July 5 of that year, my doubts had been resolved. There was something to learn about America that you could not learn by staying in New York all your life. I wrote a letter to one of my friends and told him that, but he never answered.

Confirmed then in my course, I set out to explore even more than I had when I first came to York. I wanted to learn of different lifestyles, different values and different ways of looking at the world.

Years later, I was given the opportunity by the *Washington Post* to crisscross the country at will. Needless to say, I found even more confirmation for my early decision to cut the cord that tied me psychologically to Washington Square Park.

One of the things I noticed is that as July 4 drew near, I would find some reason to be in some small town somewhere in the middle of America. Ours is not culture steeped in a great deal of ritual. There are few things we do consistently the same from region to region, state to state or even town to town.

But there is something about the Fourth of July, especially in the small towns and villages, that is as near to a national ritual as we come. The country has no central character, but it does have a holiday that comes near to being a universal experience.

All enjoy it, except some of those in the big cities, such as New York, for whom admitting to some of the gushy sentiments expressed on the Fourth is just too . . . well . . . country.

Halloween Was Fun
Before They Stole It

October 31, 1982—If he had a name other than Pee Wee, I cannot remember what it was. When you are 10 years old, formal names don't matter. We called him Pee Wee for two reasons. He was the smallest kid in our rowdy little clique at P.S. 3 in Brooklyn, and he could scoop up a hot grounder from the asphalt diamond of our schoolyard with the grace of Pee Wee Reese at Ebbets Field. So Pee Wee he was to us, Pee Wee and nothing else.

Halloween has brought him back vividly to mind. In my memory, Pee Wee was Halloween. You see, Halloween on the streets of New York City in those days was all about children doing scary and dangerous things to hector adults. This Halloween has become a horror of a different magnitude. Some sick adults seem bent this time on doing deadly things to children.

How times have changed.

And just how have they changed? That is what set me to thinking about Pee Wee. Our goal on All Hallows' Eve was to take revenge on all the mean adults in the neighborhood. These would be the people who wouldn't allow us to play stickball or box ball in front of their houses, or the ones who saw you do something and told your parents.

We savored the memories of those slights and insults all year and waited until October 31, the Night of Revenge. There might have been some neighborhoods then that had the tradition of trick or treat, but ours was not one of them. Maybe one or two families would set out some apples for the kids, but we knew their game. Appeasement, conciliation, a gesture of friendship in a time of fear.

But no such gestures deterred us from our mission, which was to ring doorbells with stupifying vigor and run with all our might as soon as we sensed someone inside had had enough and was coming to the door.

Costumes? Yes, we had costumes of sorts and masks, but they served more to protect the identities of the guilty than as part of the ritual of the festivities. Nobody wanted to get caught because that meant the possibility of having to sit on a pillow all of November first.

The ringing of doorbells was not the worst thing we did. That was just the most common. The worst things we did were with chalk. The local candy stores did a brisk business in the days leading up to Halloween in colored chalk. There was green chalk, yellow chalk, orange chalk and, of course, the old standby, white chalk.

The industrious among us made chalk bombs. To accomplish this, we took a whole box of chalk and broke it up into little pieces and put it into the toe of an argyle sock. Then we pulverized it some more so that when you swung that sock and hit a person or object, a good dose of chalk was deposited thereon.

For those adults whose transgressions during the previous year had been particularly offensive, the chalk treatment was in order. The houses were brownstone, so you can imagine that being adorned with green and yellow chalk was not likely to add much to their aesthetic appeal.

The meanest of the mean adults knew to expect us. After all, chances were we had been there last year. So, some adult would have a good vantage point from which to see the front yard. But were mean adults who deserved to have some chalk dust on the fronts of their gates to be spared merely because they had taken precautions to watch out for us vengeance-minded hellions?

Never spare a mean adult was our motto, and that is where Pee Wee became crucial to our operations. Because of his size, Pee Wee could belly-crawl under the windows and get right up to the front door and lay down a good burst of chalk dust before anyone realized the attack was under way.

Ideally, he then was to sprint away from the house and meet the rest of us on the corner so we could cheer and jeer and admire his handiwork from a safe distance. He had done it enough times that we had become confident he could never fail. In other words, we had become too confident.

Until the night he got caught.

Old man Poirer was without a doubt the meanest of the mean adults. He wouldn't allow us to play stickball in front of his house and he was known to have hauled more than one errant youngster home to his parents and demanded that he be disciplined. He had been heard to warn one mother that if she did not lay on a few lashes, he would do the job himself.

This man had to have some chalk every Halloween; no two ways about that. So Pee Wee slipped over the fence, eased past Mr.

Poirer's well-manicured hedges, crawled along under the windows and reached the front door. Just as he was about to haul off and bop that door with his chalk bomb, it opened and out stepped old man Poirer and grabbed little Pee Wee by his upraised arm.

We stood across the street and watched in frozen horror. The impossible had happened. Our best agent had been captured. Pee Wee looked pitiful. Old man Poirer dragged him, kicking and screaming, out the front yard and down toward Pee Wee's house. Freddie Wilson, I remember, made the sign of the cross.

Randy Johnson was the only one who displayed any presence of mind and he saved the day. He ran into the street and shouted:

"Look, look, everybody, old man Poirer wears lady's pajamas."

It was only then that any of us took notice of the fact that Mr. Poirer was wearing a bathrobe and beneath it he wore silk pajamas. We all took up Randy's chant and the poor old man became so startled that he momentarily forgot his mission and loosened his grip on Pee Wee's arm.

The frightened little speed demon took off like a shot and the rest of us with him. We must have run two blocks before we dared stop to rest and realize there was no way on earth old man Poirer could have followed us in his bedroom slippers, pajamas and bathrobe.

We roared with laughter, not knowing which thing we had found most entertaining, the look of poor Pee Wee in the old man's clutches or the look on Mr. Poirer's face when Randy shouted about his silk pajamas. Happy and relieved though we were, I remember that nobody wanted to stain any more houses with chalk that night.

Next day, my parents and all the other adults in the neighborhood had heard one version or another of the story. At dinner that night of November first, my father asked if any of us boys had heard of the terrible events of the night before.

Needless to say, it was news to us.

Well, said my father, it sure is good to know that no child of his would have been involved in such business. My mother said amen to that and looked at me with a look that said, Don't push your luck, kid.

In later Halloweens, I remember, we chalked a door or two, but when we came to old man Poirer's house, we crossed the street without so much as a word or gesture in that direction.

We had learned that mischief has its limits, something some adults have not learned if the dreadful news of this Halloween is any indication.

Thanksgiving Was the Greatest Holiday

November 21, 1982—Thanksgiving. To hear the word when we were children was enough to swell the heart with joy. It might be July, and someone would make some vague reference to Thanksgiving, and we would stop and reflect with pleasure.

Thanksgiving was not a holiday to our household. It was a concept. Much planning went into it, the whole family was involved in all the preparatory chores, and we seemed to celebrate it for about a week.

No holiday bore for us the significance of Thanksgiving. We paid very little attention to Christmas because my father's religious doctrine dismissed as fallacy the idea that anyone knew when Christ was born. Easter suffered similar defects, in my father's way of thinking.

July 4 was always a great deal of fun and so was Labor Day, both of them occasions for fine family picnics. We celebrated birthdays with great family fervor, but with six children, it must have seemed to my parents there was always a birthday celebration going on in our home.

Nothing made us feel the richness of oneness as Thanksgiving did. It must have been the combination of fabulous food and fabulous faith.

Forgive me for talking about the food first. My father and his younger brother migrated to New York toward the end of World War I. Their parents had been able to send them off with a few dollars, but it was assumed they would be earning money soon after they arrived in the big city of dreams.

Instead, it took awhile for them to find work. They lived in a furnished flat and neither of them knew enough about how to cook "to boil an egg," as my father put it so often in telling the tales of his youthful adventures.

Their money ran out quickly because they were eating every meal in restaurants. They nearly starved to death. When my father met my mother and discovered she was a masterly cook, he took it as a sure sign their marriage had been arranged in heaven.

My father was a great believer in the philosophy that no life experience is for naught. Each experience, no matter how painful, held a life lesson for him. So he always taught us. The only problem was that sometimes they were his life experiences but his children were the beneficiaries of the lesson.

That's the way it was with cooking. Even though it was he who almost starved to death, it was we who had to learn to cook. He died not knowing much more about cooking than he knew when he came to New York a half-century before. But he laid down an edict that no son of his would pass his 14th birthday without being able to produce all or most of a major meal.

He might have made the same rule for my sisters but he did not. It was assumed they would learn to cook in the natural course of things. But he was taking no chance on any son of his finding himself in a faraway place unable to fend for himself at a stove.

My mother and sisters were our tutors and tormentors in the kitchen. Each of us boys was oriented to the kitchen first by becoming experts in pot and pan washing. When we displayed due diligence in that department, we moved on to vegetable peeling with a paring knife.

Chickens and turkeys came from the butcher shop in those days with their feathers firmly in place and it fell to us boys to master the art of feather removal. (I never mastered that one.) Little by little, you got a chance to cook something under the watchful eye of my mother and my sisters.

The day you presented a dish to the whole family was the day you passed in our house from useless boy to promising young man. That kitchen was its own form of school, and the great annual celebration of the virtues of the institution of the kitchen was Thanksgiving Day.

We scrubbed vegetables, chopped onions and scurried about from early morning in an atmosphere of family euphoria. The aromas told us "the bird" was nearing readiness and that spurred us to bring it all together in a grand finale orchestrated by my mother.

I remember as if it were yesterday the Thanksgiving I was assigned to make the marshmallow sweet potatoes all by myself. I burned the marshmallows the first time and got it almost right the second time. When the dish reached the table, my father tasted it and declared that he was pleased that his last born might actually learn to cook. No medal could have pleased me more.

My father's faith was simple, but it was the center of his being. He lived to worship God and he lived for his family. He cared for little besides church and home. All this came to fit nicely with Thanksgiving.

In this holiday he found the nexus of his love of God and family. He was a man in a constant state of thanksgiving. He felt richly blessed by the simple rewards of health and a home.

So at Thanksgiving, he encouraged us to share with each other those things for which we felt most thankful from the previous year. Usually, we were most grateful for good grades, but he stretched us and pushed us to think deeper and search for the really important reasons to be thankful.

That turned out to be difficult to do without thinking about some of our disappointments, things we had to admit had not turned out as well as we might have hoped. He always wanted to hear about those because he always wanted to know what we planned to do to make our disappointments eventually become triumphs.

Well, we would always say to that question, we will try harder.

Yes, yes, he would always say, but how? How?

At such times, he would often exhort us to have a bold spirit and an inquiring mind. None of us ever asked him exactly what a bold spirit was. We surmised from the tone of his voice when he said those words that he wanted us to think first of what had to be done and think only after that about the obstacles.

I remember one of my sisters at the Thanksgiving table describing some excruciating challenge she faced as a freshman in college. She seemed truly daunted by all she faced. She finished describing the challenge and there was a long silence. Finally, she asked my father what she should do.

"A little more prayer will take care of it," he said.

In truth, although he exhorted us to prayer and faith, he never allowed us to overlook the benefits of preparation and hard work. That to me is what was so fabulous about his faith. He gave God the credit for all his successes and ours, but he was not about to allow any of us to say we would pray instead of study for an exam.

He believed in rigorous study and the applied use of knowledge. Knowledge that was acquired and not shared was no knowledge at all as far as he was concerned. One of his favorite phrases was "educated fool," a term he often used to describe people with impressive degrees and an unimpressive degree of common sense.

I still awaken excited on Thanksgiving morning. I still love to make marshmallow sweet potatoes and dressing with mushrooms and sausage. But I rarely find myself thinking of those objects purely as food. They have become, for me, much as they were intended to be, symbols of Thanksgiving in its truest sense, a thankfulness for blessings that have no name.

A Christmas of the Heart

December 24, 1989 —The children and I have a standard joke. We dust it off every Christmas. "Dad, what do you want for Christmas?" one of them asks. Oh, says the dad, "as long as I have you three children and your mother, I have all the Christmas presents I need."

My daughter, no less mischievous for being the eldest, was laughing one year about a prank she thought up. She intended to arrive from Boston, gather the boys in her room on Christmas morning, form a procession and present themselves as my only gift. Needless to say, it has been a wildly popular idea ever since.

The reason that joke has an ironic twist is that I grew up in a household that ignored most of the rituals of Christmas. The children have such a hard time fathoming that notion that it has become an outlandish inside joke.

I tell them there are interesting lessons to be learned from that experience. My family of five brothers and sisters got to spend the most time of the year with my parents at Christmas. Once the holidays began, moving and trucking ceased until the first of January.

The kitchen was warmed by a glowing coal stove that gave off heat like an open pizza oven at full blast. The windows were steamed opaque. My mother's kitchen table was the staging area for a five-star food assault. My sisters and she chopped, peeled, scrapped, pared and sliced from morning to late afternoon. We boys were apprentices without portfolios. My sisters had assignments. We went on the high-speed chases.

One Christmas, the year I was 9 or 10, my oldest sister did an odd thing. She had been away at college and came home to an eager family. We were up in her room, when she reached into her bag and produced a small set of screwdrivers. They were made to fit the hand of a boy. "Just enjoy them quietly," she said in a loving whisper.

We never exchanged Christmas gifts because my father and mother, devout fundamentalists, believed gifts, Santa and Christmas tinsel were all signs the Second Coming was long overdue.

That Christmas, with my new screwdrivers in hand, I was old

enough to know a little secret. My brothers and sisters did exchange gifts among themselves. There was no ritual exchange. We just handed each other a nice new pair of gloves, a sweater or a tie.

Since we had a week for these little additional items to surface in front of my parents, we created a euphemism. These were not Christmas presents, nothing of the kind. These were New Year's presents. My parents had no particularly strong feelings about New Year's one way or another.

Because the commercial aspects of the holiday were so suppressed, the family aspect was dramatically enhanced. I remember some of the best times of my youth in that kitchen and the adjacent dining room. I try to get my children to imagine the merry bedlam and the aura of unrestrained affection.

It was in our hearts, I tell them. It was in the conversations, debates, and, yes, a few arguments. My parents leavened our enthusiasm when we seemed on the verge of losing our self-control. To us, behind the frosted kitchen windows, our universe was complete. The phone rarely rang. We had no radio, and no television. No stereo existed then.

Dinners went on for hours. Tons of food disappeared. Most important, a fantastic education occurred. Languages, medical science, religion (of course, religion, lots of religion), sports, business. Everything seemed to interest some one or another of us.

When January rolled around, it was back to a busier life, but we began the year always with a "lift of the heart," as my father would have put it, from that family time.

That, I tell my children, is why I always say I'd rather have them than gifts. (Even though I really don't mean I want no presents.) I try to emphasize that our best times are still found in what we say and do with each other, and not in the material gifts we give. All this is spoken by a man whose Christmas shopping obviously is far from done.

A Small "School" Remembered

December 27, 1981—The house in which I grew up in Brooklyn, New York, was filled with love, laughter and constant challenge. More than most times of year, the Christmas season brings back memories of those days.

It is odd that this season should trigger those memories because my family barely took note of Christmas. My parents did not allow us to celebrate Christmas because my father had strong philosophical objections to the holiday.

He rejected Christmas for two reasons. First, he doubted anyone could say for certain on what day Jesus Christ was born. Second, because of his own deep religious devotion, he believed the birth, life and death of Christ should be observed in all we did and said every day.

If you are getting the idea, therefore, that Christmas was one big bore at our house, nothing could be further from the truth. We gave no gifts and had no tree or other decorations. Instead, we spent a great deal of time together, especially at large family meals. I remember those meals because they were not intended to feed the body. My father always arranged for them to be feasts for the mind.

It is the way in which he caused us to think that I remember at this time of year with so much pleasure. A friend of mine, who is an editor of a national magazine, heard about my father's approach to mealtime and asked me to share it with his two children in a letter. The more I worked on the letter in my mind, the more I felt I wanted to share my father's practice with others.

He drove a truck and hauled furniture by day to feed his family and pay the mortgage. He wanted no more of the material world than that. At night and on weekends, he was either in church debating fine points of theology with his fellow lay preachers or he was in his room with his Bible and his religious reference works.

You might think such a man likely to be narrow-minded, or at least narrow in his focus. He was much the opposite, a man who was curious about every subject under the sun. And that is how our unusual and pleasurable mealtime family tradition came to be.

My father always sat at one end of the table and my mother at the other. The three girls were arranged by age on one side, oldest nearest my father and youngest next to my mother. The three boys were on the other side. I was the youngest child. I sat nearest my mother.

He began the meal with words of grace and thanksgiving and then turned to my oldest sister. His question was always the same, as I remember it: What did you learn today that you did not know yesterday? Each of us in turn would be asked the same question. He would listen often without much more than an occasional and brief question.

After my oldest sister, in graduate school as a social science student at the time, had finished describing some new discovery, my father's usual practice would be to turn to my next-oldest sister and so on down the line until the question got to me.

That sometimes took quite awhile. My brothers and sisters were interested in languages, science, education, philosophy and history, among other subjects. Opportunities for digression presented themselves often. In fact, one assertion or another could turn into a furious debate that my father would have to bring back under control. He did this by thumping the heavy end of his fork on the table, three firm raps. By the third one you could hear a pin drop.

There were no formal rules for these debates. Anyone could jump in at any time. As the younger kids heard the older ones develop a particular viewpoint, it was not uncommon for us to want to revise our position. Nothing pleased him more than to see one of his children discard a bad idea for a better one . . . as then perceived.

The one thing he would not tolerate was so much as 10 seconds of dispute over a fact that could be established. Our house was laden with references, the world atlas, globes, almanacs and several flavors of encyclopedia. The moment the debate seemed to be foundering on a factual difference, the fork would come down three firm times. Quiet.

One disputant or another was dispatched to the appropriate reference to return with a fact. You either returned in triumph or with a sheepish apology to your fellow disputant. Then the debate could flow again.

Often during the holiday season, when we had virtually unlimited time with each other, the arguments begun over dinner would spill from the dinner table to the living room. If a particular place were involved, my father would pull out the globe and help us find the place in question.

He taught us through his questions about more than the physical world. He wanted us to ingest and display certain values, chief among them being respect for the other person's point of view even when it strikes you as totally wrong-headed. And he wanted you to win your argument with facts and skills, never with bombast or intimidation.

Through those evening encounters, he found out how well we were progressing in our studies and how we were getting along with the rest of the world. He used them as his chance to find out what sort of values we were taking into school and onto the streets.

One of my sisters spoke with much pride one autumn evening about how well she had done in her first day in an advanced Italian class. She happened to mention that a young woman sitting next to her had an Italian surname, but had not done as well as my sister on the first quiz. My sister did have the hint of a gloat about her as she told the story.

She should have known better. In one of his gentlest voices, my father asked, "And what did you do to help her along after you found out you knew more than she knew?"

My sister said nothing, but I seem to recall that the young woman with the Italian surname and she became fast friends before the end of that term.

My mother seemed to focus more of her attention on making sure we smaller boys got a word in edgewise. She encouraged us to leap in and have our say. Being the smallest, I was the most shy and the last to speak. Soon after entering first grade, I resolved to find a way to improve my competitive edge.

Each day, right after school, I would go to my room, think of the most important experience of the day and write it. Little by little, my presentations became stories that described the events of the day in third-person narratives. Having my story of the day written out made it easier for me to keep the restless attention of the older children.

One day at recess when I was in second grade, one of my schoolmates ran into the street to chase a ball and was hit by a car. She was not badly hurt, but I wrote an account of the accident, and the fears of my classmates afterward.

I can still recall reading my account that Friday evening slowly, remembering to put in a little emotional touch here and there. When I reached the end, I was not prepared for the total silence that engulfed the room. I wondered if I had said something terribly wrong.

I looked to my mother for some explanation. Her eyes seemed misted with a tear or two. Still no one spoke at the table. Finally my mother did.

She reached over and gave me a hug and said, almost in a whisper, "So you are going to be the writer." Then they all cheered. My oldest sister asked if she could have my little story to save.

Over the years between then and the time I became an adult, I do not remember any other career ever being discussed for me. I was to be a writer. It was understood from that day on, and I have never seriously worked in any other field.

My brothers and sisters went on to various professions, most of them related in some way or another to education. They have attended many prestigious institutions of higher learning and hold various advanced degrees. But often I have thought we all went to the same college, that it was a small school with just six kids, a headmaster and a headmistress.

Both my parents have died, but the love and skill with which they channeled the restless energy of their children has provided us and our children with a gift none of us would trade for the fanciest education on Earth.

Happy holidays.

Idiot Box

D addy hated television. Up in his studio, where the family gathered, surrounded by his books and with jazz playing softly in the background, Dad was almost physically incapable of sitting through even a half-hour sitcom.

He did try. Sitting slightly hunched in his straight-back morris chair, he would peer over the top of his glasses at the television. Soon a gentle rustling sound would mingle with the television dialogue and the sound of Miles Davis on CD. Dad was rubbing his back against the chair, a sure sign he was getting agitated. Next came a deep, gravelly *"Ahhheeemm."* A warning shot. And then, "Are *you* really watching *this?"* The battle was lost. Five minutes into the show and it was clearly easier to turn off the set or change the channel to the news.

There were some exceptions. He loved the savvy, sexy "Civil Wars." Or was it the savvy, sexy Mariel Hemingway? That was one night a week when the TV in Dad's studio was not tuned to the news. The rest of the time it was better not to bring up the "T" word.

It was one of the only topics of which he professed total ignorance. Ask him about almost anything else and he had the answer. He was one of my favorite reference tools, right up there with my dictionary, encyclopedia and thesaurus, and way ahead of most newspaper libraries.

But television—oh he hated that. It just about drove him nuts that he spawned three television-loving children. In the summer of 1977, crossing the country from Washington, D.C., to Berkeley, California, Dad hoped to expose my brother to the vast beauty of this nation.

"The other part of the plan was to keep him away from the damn television drug," he wrote at the time in his journal. "Sure, he's been unable to watch TV in the car, but the minute we get to a hotel or motel with a TV, he is right into it. We'll see how that works out over time, but I think his dependency on the 'plug-in drug' may have been partially reduced by the long stretches away from it."

Nothing doing. Not only did my brother continue to watch TV with undiminished enthusiasm, but our younger brother was soon to join him in front of the tube. Not me. I could never understand their viewing habits. I watched soap operas.

It started when I was five. Dad was working nights in York, Pennsylvania. During my school vacations he would take me to work with him at night. He slept all morning while I amused myself. One morning, Dad woke up early and found me on the living room floor engrossed in a game show. He was not pleased.

"Dori J. Maynard, what do you call yourself doing watching that junk? Don't you know it's bubble gum for the mind? Turn that off immediately," he said, and went right back to bed.

I obeyed instantly, turning the channel to "Days of Our Lives." It took my father 11 years to figure out what had happened. By then it was too late to stop me. After that, walking into his studio and finding me watching one of my "docudramas," Dad needed only to shoot me a quick, baleful glance before I switched to "Inside Politics."

He was only a little better about watching television with us in the kitchen in the evening. He would watch a moment, look up and utter such a devastatingly snide comment, we would switch to "PrimeTime Live" or "48 Hours." Dad would sit, quietly satisfied.

I passed by his studio soon after he died. It was so quiet. I listened to the absence of my father's laugh, deep against Miles Davis's mellow *Sketches of Spain*. But there was something else missing. The sound of television. Dad did hate television. But how else could he see the afternoon "Inside Politics," the Sunday-morning talk shows, the evening news, the prime-time news magazines, "Nightline" and a little CNN in between?

D.J.M.

188   *Idiot Box*

The Television God That Failed

April 26, 1990 —It was one of those usual raucous evenings around our dinner table in Brooklyn. In the midst of it, one of my brothers told a joke. Where, my father asked, had he heard it? Milton Berle, my brother replied.

A hush fell over the table. In an instance we went from boisterous to stone silence. Each of us six children realized simultaneously what a mistake my brother had made. By repeating a Milton Berle joke, he had tacitly admitted he had been watching television at some neighbor's home. We all sat there waiting for my parents to explode. It didn't take long.

"Milton Berle," my father said in a voice that rattled the teacups in their saucers, "is an agent of the devil." He went on to denounce the evils of television as a source of seduction of the innocent. No Christian should watch such a thing, for it was a way of distracting its victims from the path of righteousness, etc., etc., etc. The rest of us were annoyed at my brother for triggering another lecture on a painful subject. We all sneaked off from time to time to friends and neighbors to watch "Uncle Miltie," as Berle was called. But we were mostly ignorant of what was on television. My parents would have it no other way.

In school, we frequently felt disadvantaged when discussions turned to subjects that had been on radio or TV the night before. We were often ignorant of major developments. One of my teachers, noting my unusual reticence one day, asked me after class why I'd been so quiet. I admitted I had neither radio nor TV. "Surely you can afford it," the teacher said with a raised eyebrow. I explained our parents' position. He shrugged in puzzlement. "Never heard of such a thing," he said.

Now the studies show the average American child watches 14,000 hours of television between the ages of 2 and 17. They begin first with cartoons. Then sports and action dramas and eventually music videos, cop shows and more sports. The relationship between all that TV viewing and our social malaise is becoming much clearer than it once was. New evidence suggests that illiteracy and violence owe their origins in some measure to this surfeit of TV images our children are absorbing. Indeed, unless we find a way to tackle the TV dilemma head-on, we are going to be in big trouble.

Many teachers say we already are. The schools are finding it tougher and tougher to compete with powerful video images to teach children reading, math, history and social values. Surely we cannot resort to my parents' methods of exorcising the demon of TV. Far too many Americans have become hooked on the tube as their substitute for religion and many other activities.

Our society is losing in the global marketplace because we can no longer rely on our children, regardless of socioeconomic status, to accept academic rigor. Television viewing is held to be one serious reason for this condition.

At dinner the other evening, my sister and I were telling our children and her grandson what it was like in the days when we had to sneak off to listen to the radio or to watch TV.

Upon reflection, I can find no hint of regret now in our conversation. We had books and each other for conversation as our only major entertainment, my sister and I were telling our children. The amount of TV we were able to sneak in now seems to us to have been just about enough.

Media Violence Begets the Real Thing

February 9, 1989—My sons and I were eating dinner and watching something our family regarded as a news show about entertainment. To all our astonishment, we watched frozen as a woman, described as a "sex groupie," began working her hands up a rock star's thigh. We changed the channel before she reached her target.

As carefully as I could, I tried to explain to my sons that during the "sweeps" period, broadcasters sink to the lowest common denominator to hold on to audiences, thus ratings, thus advertising dollars.

The more I thought about that episode, the more I realized that sweeps season alone does not explain the explosion of explicit sex and graphic violence that now pervades the airwaves. The simple fact is that we are witnessing the downward spiral of values and taste on television.

The competition of cable, VCRs and video games has changed prime-time television from family entertainment to a cesspool of kinky sex, psychotic violence and any other form of depravity that delivers large audiences.

If that fact stood all alone as a new social reality, we might shrug it off. We could hope that as the fascination with raw sewage wore off, the garbage would disappear back into that sinkhole from which it emerged.

Alas, this new phenomenon is not to be shrugged off so lightly. Those who study the relationship of visual violence to actual violence tell a different story. The research suggests we are creating a new climate of deadly violence, spawned in some measure by the "mediamok" we see on the screens of home and movie theater.

Dr. George Gerbner is dean of the Annenberg School of Communication at the University of Pennsylvania. His research persuades him that television is teaching children that violence begets power. If you hurt people, they will do your bidding.

This may be especially true of those children who feel particularly powerless because of family or social circumstance. Thus inner-city children, for example, are likely to believe their ambitions can best be achieved by emulating the brutality they witness on the screen. They are by no means alone in that respect.

It is no coincidence that the magnitude and intensity of urban violence is on the rise. Visual violence begets actual violence. Combine that fact with the phenomenal rise in the availability of high-powered weapons, and you have a socially toxic combination of potentially catastrophic proportions.

Psychologists now are pretty sure that people who watch a great deal of television are more likely to be influenced by what they see than are those who watch only a relatively small amount.

Put another way, the idle of mind and body are likely to watch more television and to be more greatly influenced by what they see. What they see is violence without any real consequences. The combatants pull guns, blow away the opponent and then there is a soft drink commercial.

The scene in the hospital or the funeral home is likely to have very little effect by way of elaborating on the true cost of violence. Besides, even if the moral lesson of violence is pursued in a given show, today's youth would miss it. That is because they are a generation of zappers.

When the scenes of graphic violence are over, the researchers tell us, today's young viewers use the remote control to move on in search of more thrills. They don't hang around for the slow stuff—like the consequences of violence.

Not surprising, then, that there are more and more stories of school yards being sprayed with semiautomatic fire. Not just in Stockton, but in Washington, D.C. and Los Angeles, among other cities large and small. New incidents of mindless actual violence crop up in the news each day.

In fact, the real violence on the news seems to bear an increasing likeness to the fantasy violence in prime time. The more violence against women on the screen, the more violence against women in real life.

Trash-and-bash television does build audiences. Sex and violence still sell briskly. The purveyors are happy television has found a way to hold on to its fragmenting audience share. Society, I suspect, is paying a high price for their success.

Decency's only defense is the off button.

Modern Video: The Blank Blizzard

March 26, 1989—I never know whether to laugh or cry when one of the boys asks Dad at dinner to tell him again what it was like when television was in black and white and there were only five or six working channels. Well, really, I always begin, it was not that long ago. I feel somewhat defensive starting that way.

To a teenager and a nine-year-old, the world of black-and-white television and the era of the horse and carriage were one and the same. This, after all, is a generation with a loose grasp on history at best. Ask some of them who Joan of Arc was and they'll tell you Noah's wife.

All the same, this generation of children is the most visually literate about the contemporary world of any generation in history. They may be ahistorical, illiterate and innumerate, but they know every major sports arena in the world on split-second sight.

When I was a kid, my pals and I knew perhaps a handful of athletes on sight, mostly the stars of the hometown teams. My children know the names, colleges and hometown of third-string pitchers for the Houston Astros and the Cleveland Indians. They are plugged into the worldwide sports community, courtesy of cable television. It teaches them some of the most obscure details.

The way youngsters today use cable television is instructive about the future. They study the various guides carefully every day, and then, in the periods when television viewing is permitted, they traverse the globe.

They might drop in on soccer in Rio, move to boxing in Las Vegas, then to NBA basketball in Dallas. They also will sample the rock and rap videos with a quick ear for identifying the new and skipping the old.

All these are nanosecond visits just to see what's up in the neighborhood. Then they will decide with whom to spend their primary time, while flitting periodically around the globe to check the progress of other things. If a gripping climax appears imminent in any of the contests, they linger until its conclusion. Then it's around the world again.

These footloose and fancy-free viewers of the New Age of Television are driving the networks crazy. How to program for this generation in a consistent, strategic manner is no easy trick. It is no wonder to me that the latest Nielsen data show that cable programming is pulling ahead of the major networks.

All this cable capability is drawing the youth market ever closer to the tube and further away from reading and other activities. If not controlled in the home, this youth-oriented, instant-gratification programming promises to take over.

Beyond sports and the news, New Age Television gets thin very fast. This is especially true if you were not "born yesterday," as *Lear's* magazine puts it. One Saturday evening, my wife and I decided to see how well we would be entertained by our 105-channel cable-ready receiver.

We must have witnessed a half-dozen grisly murders, several dozen acts of wanton mayhem, numerous vivid sexual assaults, enough car chases to keep Goodyear busy a year replacing tires, and some old black-and-white movies to help us recall the good old days for the benefit of our children.

Long before we had intended to, we turned it off. Our search that evening for a halfway decent movie produced a blizzard of rubbish. What might be junk to us is the standard fare of our children's generation. That turns out to be sports, music videos and info-bits from the headline news services.

For those children whose parents are not insisting they read and watch other forms of entertainment, cable helps form larger and larger portions of their global perceptions. Back in the innocent days of three networks, video images were a less pervasive force in our lives.

This generation of Americans, so facile in video, so alien to basic disciplines, promises to challenge the way we live and grow as a society. They seem to know something about everything and nothing much about anything. That, I tell my boys at supper, is not quite the way it was way back in the land of black and white.

Racism

September 29, 1991—Edward R. Murrow, the father of American broadcast journalism, ended his career disheartened at the direction of the new medium. He saw "so many lights in a box" flickering vacuously through our days and nights. That was a pity to him, the waste of what could have been "the biggest classroom in America." It was becoming something much less than that by the time he died in 1965.

Sometimes when a promotion for some lurid tabloid television program comes flickering across our screen, I twitch for Murrow. His worst fears come true daily, his great hope rarely. He was not alone, of course, in prophesying this great video wasteland that now comes through on 105-channel tuners. The medium has become the biggest classroom, all right, but I don't think Murrow would recognize much of what we see as valid education.

Every once in a while, a broadcast comes along that makes you wish Ed Murrow were still alive. I know that if he had seen ABC's "PrimeTime Live" the other night, he would have been proud of helping invent this craft. It was television at its educative best and journalism in one fine hour.

The issue was race. One of the great frustrations about race in America concerns perception. A white person and a person of color can see the same event and come away with distinctly different versions of it.

This is especially true in matters concerning discrimination. Many white Americans, including distinguished commentators, will tell you that race is no longer an issue in America. They say remedial programs are no longer needed. After all, they argue, discrimination is now against the law. But Americans of color will respond that racism is not so easily expunged.

Indeed, there is significant evidence that racism in America is alive and well, living possibly on your street. In a way never before done, ABC's "PrimeTime" demonstrated just how insidious and persistent racism is in America. It was as revealing a piece of journalism on this subject as I have ever seen.

ABC told the story of John and Glenn. They are two young

Americans of average size, looks and demeanor. They were comparably educated and from very similar backgrounds. Only John is white. Glenn is black. Thereby hangs the tale of race in America.

John goes to a store. A salesman rushes to wait on him. Glenn enters the same store a few minutes later. The salesman tails him around the store to make certain he does not steal. John goes to a car dealership. The salesman offers him a no-money-down deal. Glenn waits 10 minutes to be assisted. Then he is told he would have to pay $2,000 down. His offer is $500 higher than John's on a $9,000 car.

John goes to see an apartment. The landlord welcomes him and sends him with a key to look the place over. Minutes later, Glenn is told the apartment was rented hours before either he or John came calling.

Now, about television and Ed Murrow. As Diane Sawyer guided us through this exceptional portrait of America's No. 1 social problem, I kept thinking of Murrow. He believed good journalism required very little embellishment.

The power of the pictures is what makes it news. The power of the images of John's ready acceptance is vivid. The power of the images of the rejection of Glenn, time after time, is also vivid. No one could see those images and declare racism dead.

I asked "PrimeTime" producer Ira Rosen how this piece of journalism came to be. It began, he said, with a young black colleague who knew from personal experience about the power of rejection. That, I think, would make Murrow cheer ever louder. He would know that the telling of the story of America today demands many voices and many minds.

This broadcast is an example of many things done well by the people of ABC News. I have no doubt the country will benefit from seeing this portrait of itself. Thoughtful Americans will know its meaning. They will know what rejection looks like through eyes of color. They will know that it is not true that racism is dead. They might reflect on Glenn.

This is what he said at the conclusion of the broadcast:

"You walk down with a suit and tie and it doesn't matter. Someone will make determinations about you that affect the quality of your life, and the only basis is the one thing that will not change about you. I am not going to take off black skin. I am going to be black forever."

Ed Murrow thought television could help us understand each other. In the matter of race, I have never seen a more telling effort at genuine understanding. This time real journalism transcended the wasteland.

At the Ballpark

Baseball doesn't do a lot for me. Daddy never knew that. Or at least he pretended not to, for those are the compromises family members make with each other. There was, however, little question about how much he loved the sport.

Dad grew up in Brooklyn when the Dodgers' Jackie Robinson broke the color barrier of baseball and Red Barber's voice filled game-time streets. Dad was not allowed to listen to the games on the radio.

Instead, he spent his childhood keeping up with the game at a friend's house on the sly. To hear him tell it, that was just about his only taste of sporting life during his youth. Though he ran track and played a bit of stickball, Dad was rushing to the library while the other boys in his neighborhood were rushing to the baseball diamond.

Later we spent much of our family's free time at baseball games.

"We have tickets to see our local heros," Dad assured me each time I came home during baseball season. Small surprise. We had Oakland A's season tickets.

Sitting in the stands reading a book, a bag full of magazines at my side, I would feel an elbow in my ribs every so often.

"See how the pitcher just psyched out that batter?" Dad would ask. "He just struck out one of the best." "Hmmm," I answered. In what seemed like only moments later there would be another gentle nudge at my side. That same batter was back up and scored a base hit. "You do see, don't you?" Dad would ask. "Hmmm," I would reply.

That year the A's lost the championship. We joined the hot-stove league, a new type of baseball of which I had been previously unaware.

"In the best tradition of the hot-stove league, no question can ever be definitively laid to rest. Since it is baseball of the mind, nothing is ever really settled. There is no final score in the bottom of the ninth," Dad explained in a column. "Finally, the hot-stove league is the place of dreams of what might be next year."

The football season was only marginally better. Since the Raiders left Oakland, there were no local heroes, no season tickets, just millions of games on television.

"You do know," Dad said, as the sound of helmets crunching blared in the background, "that during World War II we had to learn chess and the Germans had to learn football."

I had not known that. Putting down my book, I studiously looked up at the screen just as I remembered I had promised to run out and get Froot Loops for my brother's breakfast.

Dad had better luck with my brothers. Camera on his shoulder, Dad went to just about every one of my younger brother's Little League games. Strolling calmly to the dugout, Dad would quietly counsel the little guy if he struck out or dropped a ball.

"There may be better places in which to watch boys become men, but the Little League field has to be right up there with the very best to witness the unfolding of character," Dad wrote in a column. "They learn to lose with grace and dignity. They learn to hate to lose. They learn that it takes discipline and patience to be a winner."

Dad could no longer get around very well by the time my younger brother traded in his baseball bat for BMX bicycle racing. But when he won a trophy he would bring it to Dad's hospital room.

There my father would muse aloud about the differences between team sports and the challenge of having to race against both your opponent and your last time in a solitary sport such as bicycle racing.

Poking the newspaper in front of my nose, he would lean over and say "You see, each sport has its lessons." Looking up, I would give him a hearty "Ahhhm."

D.J.M.

The Barriers Robinson Broke

April 12, 1987—A hushed excitement fell over our dinner table that spring night in 1947. It was strange and memorable for two reasons. First, despite our excitement, we spoke in a strange hushed tone. Second, my father generally directed our dinner conversation toward issues of morality and learning. Here we were discussing a very different subject, sports.

"No doubt about it," my father was saying, "we are witnessing history." We listened while he noted, still in nearly a whisper, the symbolic significance of what would happen in Brooklyn that year.

Jackie Robinson would put on the uniform of the Brooklyn Dodgers and for the first time ever a black man would do something only white men had done up to that moment. He would play professional baseball.

We know now that Jackie Robinson went through a personal hell for the privilege of breaking that color barrier. Even then we knew it had to be hard. We just didn't know how hard. In his first few seasons, Robinson was the target of intense, racially motivated harassment from his white colleagues and competitors.

In that first dramatic summer of 1947, Robinson's personal hell did not matter as much to us as the thrill we gained from watching his performance on the field. A family in which sports was never important suddenly became bewitched by the phenomenon of Jackie Robinson.

Now, exactly 40 springtimes later, I think I can see better what my parents saw in Jackie Robinson that we as children did not fully grasp. I suspect the same might have been true in other families.

My parents saw opportunity in the Jackie Robinson story. They seized on it as the tool by which to motivate us to excel. They made certain we knew the story of Jackie Robinson. They reminded us constantly of the need to harness discipline to talent.

Once I came home with a dismal midyear report card. I came up with some lame excuse for why I had done poorly. My mother looked at me dolefully and said, "I wonder where Jackie Robinson would be now if he had come up with excuses like that." I remember to this day how stung I felt.

Out on the streets of Brooklyn, it was the rare kid who did not have something with the number 42 on it. Some youngsters had whole Dodger uniforms with 42 on the back. The rest had at least a baseball jersey. Everybody and his brother wanted to play second base.

Even as we children focused on the diamond, our parents focused on the larger ramifications of what was happening. World War II had just ended. That fact ushered in an era of dramatic change.

The postwar era brought a new kind of automobile in a multiple of colors, instead of the traditional basic black. Not only did the automatic transmission change America's driving habits, but automatic washers and dryers and toasters and refrigerators helped set the stage for the liberation of women from the drudgery of housekeeping.

There were dramatic breakthroughs going on all around us in that fascinating period. Miracle drugs such as penicillin became commonplace, and what the war taught us about the separation of blood plasma helped save hundreds of thousands of lives.

On the social front, young black lawyers, back from the war, were determined to make America safe for democracy. So they launched a legal attack in 1947 that eventually led to the crumbling of the Jim Crow legal system in the South.

In all this sea of change, the most dramatic symbol of change in his time was Jackie Robinson. He was important for what he gave us on the field and off. He made it possible for our parents to point to a tangible star and thus make us believe truly the sky was our only limit.

Run, Daddy, Run!

April 11, 1991—In the old house in Brooklyn, the charm was centered in the kitchen. The happiest times, the stories, the jokes, the triumphs all were shared there first. Out through the shed where the dog slept was a big backyard. It seemed bigger to us than it probably was because of the open space of the courtyard of the Episcopal church next door.

We played a mean game of backyard softball out there, sometimes the three girls against the three boys. I don't recall that we boys had any special advantage. The special moments came on those rare afternoons when my father happened to come home early and came out to play.

Actually, he didn't really play. He had a few "at bats," a term that owes its origins to cricket. My father grew up playing that sport in Barbados. He never quite got the hang of baseball, and we didn't press the point. We were just glad to have him on our humble little diamond.

One generation later, the picture of father, son and baseball has undergone some changes. This time, son and father are training son for his first Little League season. This entails early outings on Saturday morning to find empty baseball diamonds on which to train an outfielder. That's easier said than done in Oakland.

We have been playing our own version of one-on-one scrimmage baseball on the front lawn for years. In fact, my smallest son's role in helping dad recover from a major illness was front-lawn baseball. He would hit and run around the bases.

When I finally got up to hit, I smacked the ball into home-run country and stood at home plate admiring my shot until I heard a pleading little voice command, "Run, Daddy, run!" "Son," I started to say, "I'm not quite up to running the bases." Instead of protesting, I dropped the bat and began to run. As I trotted around our tiny base path, I began feeling my physical self again. It was the first time I'd run in a year. The little boy smiled.

Now he has me doing infield drills, throwing drills and batting drills. Getting ready for Little League has been the biggest event in his life since his first day at school. He loves the sport, and he loves having to make dad run and catch and work out ancient kinks.

Fortunately, because he is an outfielder, we have to spend a certain amount of time on fly balls. Thank goodness. After he has run me ragged on the infield, I find myself suggesting it's time for some outfield work. That way, I can hit the first few over his head and watch him run while the old man rests.

Finally, opening day arrived. There he was in his red-and-white uniform out there in right field. He has learned the outfielder's trick of plucking up a few strands of grass and tossing them in the wind. He knows then which way the wind will carry the ball.

My wife and I watched him from the bleachers with the other parents and grandparents. This was the moment for which he had been working and waiting. He was plucking grass and then leaning on his knees watching home plate intently.

The high fly ball was not too deep when it came. He adjusted quickly and settled under a ball hit by one of the popular kids on the other team. "Miss it, miss it," one of the other team's partisans shouted toward right.

"Forget it, pal," I said under my breath. "That's my boy and he is not about to miss this ball." It dropped into his glove with a satisfying thud perhaps only a father can appreciate on opening day of the Oakland Babe Ruth League. Unfortunately, his team lost, and we had to have a talk on the way home about bouncing back from adversity.

This time, Mother Nature intervened to underscore the point. The very next morning, the school called the office around 11 o'clock. The boy had the chicken pox. There would be no school for him for the entire week. Worse, there would be no baseball practice with dad or with the team. He was a grounded outfielder.

Kid, I told him, that's life. There will be more chances to play ball, more chances to practice and more chances to keep your daddy running on the ball field.

When Baseball Gets in Your Genes

September 8, 1988—Before I tell this story about a boy, baseball and a hometown pennant race, I must make a small confession. The national pastime and I had a falling out that lasted 20 years. In fact, there were times when I doubted we would ever get together again.

I grew up with the pangs and palpitations familiar to anyone who followed the Brooklyn Dodgers in the 1950s. When they finally won the World Series, we danced in the streets.

Our joy turned to ashes soon afterward when the team was snatched away to Los Angeles. I vowed then never to watch another baseball game, a promise I kept until we moved to Oakland nearly a decade ago and I warmed to the Oakland A's and baseball again.

Even so, baseball was still an abstract experience. The old emotions weren't there as they were when Jackie Robinson, Duke Snider, Carl Erskine and Pee Wee Reese romped the diamond of my youth.

In truth, I doubted they would ever be rekindled again until the remarkable season of 1988, the best baseball season I have enjoyed since that fateful day 30 years ago when we awakened to the anguish of the Dodgers departing Brooklyn.

Two things turned this season into a magical reunion between baseball and me. The first one must be obvious. Our local heroes here in Oakland have the best percentage record in baseball.

That fact should be enough to rekindle the heart of any previously disenchanted baseball fan. But that is just half the story. The other half is watching an eight-year-old become a true fan, as in fanatic, of the game of baseball.

My wife is sure his baseball mania is genetically acquired. She and her mom tried never to miss a Giants home game in the Polo Grounds in the glory days of the "Say Hey Kid," Willie Mays.

Ever since he was capable of walking, our youngest child showed an affinity for baseball. The year Rickey Henderson set his stolen-base record on the A's, our little guy, then not quite three years old, went sliding all over the house. Our friends and neighbors called him "Little Rickey" so often that some people thought it was his real name. He still has a pair of blue jeans with Henderson's autograph on the knee.

He continued to show a certain imprecise enthusiasm for the game until this summer. A sudden and unexpected learning explosion erupted in July. The kid caught baseball fever. He began collecting cards with a passion. He dropped the comics page and now heads straight for the sports section religiously.

He recites batting averages and earned run averages at the dinner table. When a batter comes up, he can tell you his history in the major leagues and a mind-numbing litany of other information that he acquires with spongelike zeal.

The other day, I was describing this remarkable metamorphosis of our last-born into a baseball fan to a friend of mine. "Does he remind you of anyone you know?" my friend asked with a grin. I thought way back and acknowledged I had been that way once, long ago.

But then I thought about that and realized this kid is even more of a fan than I was. He has two favorite teams, one in each league. Because he lives in Oakland, he is devoted to our awesome A's. But he reminds us he was actually born in a San Francisco hospital and didn't come home to Oakland until he was all of five days old. The Giants, therefore, have his equal loyalty. Maybe my wife is right, and some of this is genetic.

If he has a long look on his face when I go in to put him to bed, I never have to guess this summer what the reason is. "Did your beloved Giants lose?" I ask. He gives me a sad nod. I remind him he still has the A's, who tend to lose considerably less often this season. It's usually the bright reminder he needs to put his smile back on.

So baseball, which had become a distant affair, is once again a big part of our family life. I am rediscovering in a direct and immediate way what a thrill the game can be, and why it really is worthy of its exalted place as the national pastime.

And just think, it might turn out we take our revenge on the Dodgers come October.

A Question of Educational Priority

April 13, 1986—Rodney and Dana were two of my best friends in high school. We shared the excitement and terror of crossing the bridge from boyhood to manhood. Our voices changed within weeks of each other.

Our other great mutual interest was sports. Rodney played basketball, Dana was a running back, and I was a sprinter. We worked out together so often the coaches and other students called us The Three Musketeers.

All that changed with a dramatic incident in our sophomore year. Rodney and I had no academic problems, but Dana flunked math and science.

The football coach called him in and broke the news. He would be dropped from the athletic program and encouraged to seek enrollment elsewhere. The school was for scholarship first and sports second.

Besides ruining a friendship, that incident taught me a lesson and it was lost on none of us. The purpose of school is education.

Rodney and Dana and the whole painful incident were buried in my memory until the other day.

A committee appointed by the regents of the University of Georgia issued a report on that very subject of schools, education and sports. It was courageous and disturbing.

What the report says about the University of Georgia could be said to a greater or lesser degree about many major schools. It says simply that the university harbored athletes, especially football players, who could not meet the school's academic standards.

It describes in vivid detail the manner in which the school corrupted its own standards in pursuit of winning football.

One young man was described in the Georgia regents' report as FFFF. He was failing in everything. When his teachers warned him he was in danger of expulsion, he laughed them off. He knew better. He knew the football coach had the power to keep any student in good standing academically as long as he was of value to the team.

Faculty members are incensed at the way of life at Georgia. When faculty members wanted to fail nonperforming students, they usually lost. The tough cases wound up in the office of an academic dean who knew the ropes. Faced with the choice of failing a football player or going along with the system, the academic enforcers virtually always backed down. This appears to have been true of everyone in academic leadership right up to the president of the university.

There appears to have been no one in the leadership of the University of Georgia like the coach of my old high school, someone who cared more about the development of young people than about winning at sports.

In one way or another, the practices revealed at Georgia go on all across the country wherever revenue-producing sports are a major feature of university life. The schools that do a good job of academic training of athletes are the exceptions.

Georgia is therefore no worse probably than many other schools with top contending teams. What brought Georgia's story to national attention was a lawsuit.

Jan Kemp, an English teacher, got fed up with the academic corruption at the school. After confronting the system, she was fired.

After hearing her story, a jury awarded Kemp $2.6 million in damages for wrongful dismissal. The jury believed Kemp, and not the heated denials of university officials.

In the wake of the Kemp verdict, the regents appointed their own committee. Before the committee's findings were made public, the university president resigned.

Even though some university officials are denying the regents' report, others welcome it. This may be a time when Georgia takes a hard look at itself and institutes reforms. In that sense, it may come out ahead of those schools still ignoring corruption in their midst.

The moral issue universities have been avoiding up to now concerns their obligations to their students. As a faculty member at Georgia said, "The football program should exist to serve the university, not the other way around."

Granted many collegiate athletes arrive unprepared to meet college academic standards. The reason for that is too few high school coaches with academic standards of their own.

Universities can create strong remedial programs, as some have already done. Georgia has something called the Development Studies Program, intended to help athletes. As it turned out, the program merely sheltered the athletes from the normal standards of the university.

The tragedy of this situation falls on the young athletes. They attend college for four years, play ball and leave with no education and no skills. The tiny fraction lucky enough to end up in the professional leagues is too small to measure.

It passes irony that the institution responsible for helping young people prepare for life sends its athletes away prepared only for failure.

My friend who was kicked off the football team went to another high school and eventually college. He played ball but was never a star. He has gone on to a decent life.

None of us knew 30 years ago our coach was doing Dana a favor. Now it is clear that favor is not done often enough in a society obsessed with winning at any price.

Today's Choice of Heroes

September 13, 1990 —Heroes are a subject about which my children and I speak often. They have many, mostly figures on the tube whose character and execution seize their fancy at any fleeting moment. I had few, having been born in an age before television and nourished more on scripture and the lore of antiquity than on sport and entertainment.

Jackie Robinson, I tell them. Now there was a great one. He burst upon our bucolic scene when I was 10 years old, the same age as our youngest. And I was the youngest. Somehow, and I have not understood this now for two generations, the newest hero belongs to the youngest member of the family. Jackie Robinson was somehow my hero because I was still at an age when heroes really count.

Brooklyn Dodger uniforms, never a particularly hot seller in our neighborhood, became an overnight sensation in 1947. They came in all sizes and could be made to fit all shapes, as long as the number 42 was on the back. With that number, you needed little more to tell the world your hero was Jackie Robinson, the first black man to play in major league baseball.

Things have become much more complicated since then. Try keeping a 10-year-old today in one simple uniform. The kids are decked out in heroes' garb from Michael Jordan hats to Rickey Henderson T-shirts, from NFL shorts to Bo Jackson Nike shoes. And that's just for Monday.

All this brings me, by embarrassing indirection, to the Andre Agassi shorts. Not his. Mine. The Day-Glo kind you see at center court. Dad in Agassi shorts? Give me a break, dude. That's tight. (Tight is today's preteen talk for awful, terrible and downright disgusting.)

We had not played tennis until late spring, around the French Open. Someplace in that mysterious time period, yet another hero crept into the house. I looked up at breakfast one morning to discover the 10-year-old's nose buried in Andre Agassi news. He wanted to know all about the American tennis star with the formidable ground stroke.

Suddenly, we were back into family tennis. The littlest guy was winner of the first family trophy, a proud moment. He led me into the pro shop one day to show me something he wanted for me, not for himself. "You want me to wear these?" I heard myself exclaiming. He looked at me with a smile someplace between adoration and exhortation. "Dad, you would look so cool. Please. At least try them on."

That, I suppose, was my first mistake. If I were to avoid going out in public looking like a 20-year-old goony bird, I should never have put them on. The shorts were exceptionally comfortable. The little fan was bubbling so that his pleasure was not diminished much when he learned that none to fit him was in stock.

There I was a few days later on one of the lower courts. We were back where I hoped none of the adults in the club would notice me. I was decked out in my super-cool Agassi tennis shoes with the pink trim and my denim shorts with neon pink inner lining. In the locker room, I did briefly consider adding a disguise.

Before our hour on the court was over, I wished I had given more thought to the disguise idea. Along came an old acquaintance, a college professor. We had once served on the same faculty and had thus known each other for 20 years. As he strolled past our court, he took one look at me and nearly dropped his expensive racket.

I couldn't figure out why he was staring at me until I looked down and remembered the last image of myself I had seen up in the locker room. That's when I thought again about the disguise. Or, I said to myself, I could address him in the language of the 10-year-old's generation: Yo, listen up, dude! This is my kid's idea. My kid is in love with Andre Agassi's formidable forehand and backhand ground strokes. Can you dig, dude?

Great athletic performance, the psychologists tell us, begins with mental modeling. You see your hero execute an act in a certain manner and style, then you begin to emulate those moves. If my 10-year-old ever grew up to hit a tennis ball like Andre Agassi, dad won't mind that the kid once urged him onto the tennis court looking like a commercial for Day-Glo spray paint.

A footnote: Agassi was defeated in the U.S. Open Sunday in straight sets. Pete Sampras had 13 service aces. He wears plain white, a fact not lost on my 10-year-old son—or his dad.

Growing Up, Not Old

Jogging around Oakland's Lake Merritt, Daddy stared up at the Tribune Tower. The newspaper was a mess. Riddled with typos and out of step with its community, it was ridiculed throughout the industry. Back in Berkeley, doing his yoga and meditating, Dad quietly envisioned the day he would own the *Oakland Tribune*.

It was the summer of 1978. Daddy and Nancy had left their jobs at the *Washington Post* and *New York Times* a year earlier. In a spare room of our Washington, D.C., home, they helped found the Institute for Journalism Education. Tired of hearing editors say they could not find qualified people of color to hire for professional newsroom jobs, Daddy, Nancy, Earl Caldwell, John Dotson, Frank Sotomayor, Walter Stovall, Dorothy Gilliam, Roy Aarons and Steve Montiel founded the institute, which included a journalistic boot camp to train about a dozen reporters each summer.

That summer, Nancy and Steve Montiel directed the summer program, housed at the University of California, Berkeley. Dad spent the summer at the Berkeley home we rented, writing and crafting a business plan for the Institute.

Back in Washington, D.C., a few months later, the Gannett company's vice president of news, John Quinn, made one of his regular calls to Dad. John mentioned that the newspaper group was considering a corporate acquisition that included the *Oakland Tribune*. John wondered if Dad had any suggestions for possible *Tribune* editors. Dad did indeed.

There was little reason to have faith in the paper. By the time Gannett bought it in the summer of 1979, the *Tribune* had had three owners in as many years. Its readers were confused by the continual changes. The staff was demoralized. Dad had underestimated his undertaking, something he realized soon after he entered the newsroom.

"The date was August 30. It was a Thursday. I can remember as if it were yesterday. . . . It turned out there was a lot more to mastery of the *Oakland Tribune* than I guessed in 1979," Dad wrote 12 years later.

There was the urban/suburban dilemma. Should the paper pour its resources into the suburbs? Or, should the *Oakland Tribune* concentrate on Oakland? Then there was what my father called the "cost structure."

Four years after buying the paper, Gannett opted to sell it, and in 1983 my family purchased the *Tribune*. Without corporate backing, the paper's finances became even more important. The *Tribune* executives cut expense after expense. Still, the paper found itself on the brink of closure in August of 1991—ready to become another of the country's 1,000 daily newspapers to close in this century.

By then, it had been four years since the doctors had told Dad he had inoperable prostate cancer. His health always in question, his paper's survival always in question, Dad's optimism and faith were tested.

"So much needs to be turned around that at times even I fall into a depression at the thought of it all," Dad wrote in his journal.

Yet, a few days later he would write, "Only 10 days ago, I was at sea on the subject of my health and my spirit," vowing that if he could restore yoga and journal writing "to their rightful place and keep them there, no obstacle can really keep me from my goals, personal, family, business and community."

He and Nancy searched for solutions to keep the struggling paper publishing. At the last minute, the Freedom Forum stepped in with a much-needed loan. Still, a year later, Dad's failing health forced the family to sell the paper. That, Dad was fond of saying, was life. You had to acknowledge the negatives, concentrate on looking for solutions and keep the faith.

"We came to see the welcome light of dawn because we never gave up believing it was possible. Many was the night we sat here going through one difficult scenario after another, never sure what would work or when. The edge was never far away, but neither was our faith that we were right and that right would prevail," Dad wrote on August 19, 1991, only days after the *Oakland Tribune* was saved.

He didn't grow old, and I used to tease him that he never grew up, a charge he did not deny. He would simply remind me of his old Aunt Maude, who taught him you are as young as you feel, and your life is what you make of it.

D.J.M.

Fifty Years Filled with Changes

June 21, 1987—The jokes people tell when they find out you have turned 50 are terrible. My least favorite is this wisecrack: "Actually, 50 is middle age only if you expect to live to be 100." To which I reply: "Thanks loads. I just might."

Truth to tell, I find no fault with 50. It's a nice round number and you have little trouble remembering your age. I am told such matters become harder to recall as the springtime of life advances toward autumn.

Actually, there is much to be said for those of us born in the same year as the opening of the Golden Gate Bridge and the first McDonald's restaurant (in Pasadena).

The year 1937 also saw the establishment of the first blood bank. Nylon was patented. Those who may not even know what a stick shift is might like to know that General Motors introduced the first automatic transmission in that same golden year.

What we who turn 50 this year can say with little risk of contradiction is that we grew up in as turbulent and fascinating an epoch as this nation has seen. We who are now a little less than one-quarter the age of the republic witnessed some remarkable historical events.

When we were born, the population of the United States was 128 million. It is 240 million today. More important, that population explosion began right after World War II.

That war was the shaping experience of our generation. We were just old enough to know something momentous was happening. We were also too young to grasp its full significance. All the same, we came to understand the profound manner in which World War II set the stage for the reshaping of the American social, political and demographic landscape.

The war itself was the occasion for profound scientific and technological breakthroughs. In medicine, the development of penicillin. In physics, nuclear fission and rocket propulsion. In manufacturing, plastics. There were many, many more.

The war changed America from a rural to an urban/suburban society. All across the nation, people streamed off the farm and headed to the cities and to the defense plants. They earned wages unheard-of back in Iowa or Alabama.

For many, there was no returning home once the war was over. Federal legislation provided new highway and housing subsidies right after the war. They helped create new suburbs across the nation.

Most serious students of contemporary history attribute much of the postwar transformation to the GI bill, especially the educational opportunities it provided. Millions of veterans, many with little previous training, had the chance to obtain college educations and professional degrees, profoundly changing their lives and the country. White-collar and high-tech opportunities proliferated, along with an expanded middle class.

Young though we were, we who were born in 1937 were witnesses to all the profound change in this country in those years immediately after the war. In fact, those changes helped set the stage for the sweeping social movements of the 1960s.

Those movements took root among the baby boomers who were born, so to speak, on the GI bill. When they reached adolescence, they brought to the American value system a very different notion of themselves and their rights. Their parents were much more accepting of the status quo. The protest movements were most appealing to women and people of color.

President Kennedy once said we were all "generational chauvinists" to some extent. We tend to think the era in which we live has to be the best. All the same, I would be hard-pressed to name another 50-year period the equal in excitement and discovery of the period between 1937 and now.

Amelia Earhart, the aviator, was lost at sea in 1937. It was the dawn of modern aviation. In a sense, Earhart's loss was a metaphor of that era. She was groping on the frontier of the new technology we now take for granted. It came of age in that half-century.

We pay many prices for our progress, not the least of them at the grocery store. A loaf of bread in 1937 cost a dime, one-seventh its cost today. Similarly a half-gallon of milk cost 50 cents then and more than a dollar now.

You could have picked up a brand-new Ford that year for less than $600. A new Ford today fetches nearly $10,000. But the average American wage was about $2,000 a year then and about $18,000 now. You can see why an average three-bedroom house cost $4,000 then and $80,000 now.

It has been quite an era, but profound change didn't necessarily make everything better. All the same, joke about us if you will, but remember: We who turn 50 were born in a year when one of the hottest songs was "Never in a Million Years." There is no telling what we will do and see in our next 50 years.

How Aunt Maude Lasted So Long

May 19, 1988—It was one of those hot June nights so memorable in my parents' household because somebody was always graduating, getting engaged or married. With six children in the house, my parents always seemed to be celebrating the landmarks of their offspring, and June was always the month of such family fanfare.

June was also the month of Aunt Maude. I don't know why, but Aunt Maude's visits in June made a deep impression on our household. She came to all major family functions. My mother's aunt, our great aunt, was both beloved and feared throughout all our childhoods. Already in her 80s when I was a teenager, she lived past 100, proud to have "buried" most of her enemies.

On this occasion, after complimenting my mother on her skills as a parent, she held forth before all assembled on how she would have raised each of us differently, and with even more superior results.

The family mystery, often debated in whispers in one or another of our rooms after bedtime, was what kept that wiry, brilliant woman going so strong for so long. Her own answer was simple. She never smoked, drank "or let a man so much as touch me."

My mother's explanation was also simple and tinged with the tolerant humor necessary to life with Aunt Maude. "It's the devil in her," my mother would say with a slight twist to her lower lip. "She wouldn't die out of spite."

All my life, I've observed older people with the question of Aunt Maude lingering in the back of my mind. It is so obvious that state of mind and life attitude have a great deal to do with longevity.

Aunt Maude was a shining example of the scientist who said those who tend to live longest are those who continue "to use the old bean." Those who cease mental activity at retirement, studies show, do not tend to live as long as those who continue to pursue some form of challenging mental activity.

Atrophy of the brain seems to be the precursor to atrophy of the body. Yet, in truth, we know very little about what accounts for a longer life. Indeed, we are constantly being surprised by odd discoveries about life and age.

What, for example, are we to make of the latest study of the life spans of retired baseball players? It turns out, according to a team at the University of Alabama School of Public Health, that those retired pitchers with the lowest earned-run averages tend to live longer than pitchers with high earned-run averages.

And, you guessed it, batters with high batting averages tended to live longer than those with low batting averages. Moreover, say the findings in the current issue of the respected *New England Journal of Medicine*, infielders as a rule lived longer than players of other positions—especially catchers.

Has anyone an explanation for all this? Not really. Longevity certainly seems to have a great deal to do with how those retired professional athletes took care of themselves in their later years. But no one can say why infielders, good batters and the better pitchers lived longer than other men in a control group and longer than less-successful ballplayers.

The 985 men in the study were active in the major leagues between 1911 and 1915 and died between 1925 and 1985. Babe Ruth, who died at age 52 of throat cancer, and Casey Stengel, who lived until 85, were among those studied.

Needless to say, the intriguing Alabama study raises more questions than it answers. All the same, there is that all-important issue of attitude lurking beneath the surface of the data, begging to be explored.

We know, or think we know, that successful athletes have a more positive outlook on life than mediocre ones. We don't always know whether talent feeds confidence or confidence helps bring out ability. If the attitude theory has any applicability off the field, could that explain the correlation between a low ERA and a longer life?

Those intriguing questions await further exploration. But the little we are learning does help my brothers and sisters and me with the puzzle of Aunt Maude. I have to believe a tough pitcher, a batter with a high average, and even a good infielder have something in common. They have to be aggressive. That was my dear Aunt Maude all right. She gave aggression special meaning.

We Are Only As Old As
We Think We Are

July 10, 1983—When she was well past 90, my Aunt Maude took the Eighth Avenue subway we called the A Train from upper Manhattan to Brooklyn on a regular basis, too regular for some members of our family. I was not one of those who dreaded her visits.

In fact, I often found a comfortable spot beneath the dining room table so I could listen to her endless stories. What sent my brothers and sisters scattering to the nether reaches of the house was that they had heard all of Aunt Maude's stories more times than they could count.

To me, as the youngest, it was all fresh and fascinating stuff. She might on occasion forget where she left her glasses or her ever-present umbrella, but she could tell you the color of the gown in which you came from the hospital after birth. She had more family history at her command than any of her younger relatives.

If you wrote her a poem for her birthday years before and she liked it, she could quote its entirety at will. Her ability to recall was so intimidating that once she asserted something as a fact, most sensible family members conceded her the point out of icy fear that a 90-year-old woman could prove any one of us wrong by reeling off detail we could not match.

Often, after she left to take the A Train home again, we would all sit down and shake our heads in unison at this amazing and tenacious woman, whose body was frail and slight, but whose mind was ever expanding with age.

Over the greater part of my adult life, one of my dearest friends has been a gerontologist with whom I have shared many Aunt Maude stories. Unlike my family and other friends with whom I have discussed her, Dr. Robert Butler never found anything the least bit amazing about my Aunt Maude. He thought she was delightful, for sure, but amazing? Not really.

Dr. Bob, as our family calls him, has a theory about aging. First of all, he rarely calls it aging. He prefers the term "human development." The reason for his preference coincides with his theory. The theory is called compensation.

Stated perhaps too simply, it says that as we grow older, we lose some of our physical agility, true. But our beings are compensated, rewarded, by the benefits of greater mental capacity. This capacity comes about through two primary elements. The first is simply experience.

The line, "I'm not getting older, I'm getting better," has more than a grain of truth. We may not be able to move as fast, but we learn how to accomplish more through economies of motion and exertion that only experience teaches. My dad used to say an old man can rarely outrun a young man, but he often can outsmart one.

Dr. Bob thinks so, too. Why then, do old people seem so forgetful? Dr. Bob once explained it this way:

"As we get older, we accumulate more information, and our brains become overloaded. So what appears to be forgetfulness may just signify that we must sift through a larger file before coming up with the right information."

The second reason mental capacity has a tendency to increase with age has to do with a remarkable physical fact about the brain. It appears that even though we lose some 50,000 nerve cells a day after age 21, the brain continues to grow for all of most people's lives.

Except for victims of Alzheimer's disease, the advance of age does not mean decline in mental capacity. What we once thought of as senility is now recognized as the result of side effects from strong medicines and sometimes malnutrition, but there is no scientific support for the notion that the mind automatically declines with age.

Given a choice of brain or brawn as we advance in age, most people would probably choose brawn. Here again, Dr. Bob, who heads the unique geriatrics center at Mt. Sinai Hospital in New York, argues against conventional wisdom.

Do we have to decline to flabby invalids after age 65? Dr. Bob argues there is nothing magic about 65 that means our physical decline has begun and the wheelchair is next. If we stay in shape, watch our diet and practice sensible health habits, physical decline is far more gradual than most people realize.

Dr. Charles B. Huggins is 81. In 1966, he won the Nobel Prize in medicine and physiology. Dr. Huggins agrees with Dr. Butler. In an interview in *The Wall Street Journal*, Dr. Huggins said:

"It's commonly held that age is a shipwreck, but that need not be so. You can be young at 90 or old and washed up at 35. The important thing is whether you use your bean. If you don't use it, you lose it."

The *Journal* reported in March that Dr. Huggins continues his daily laboratory work at the University of Chicago, still using his "bean."

Often, too often, we hear of instances in which people retire at age 65, cease being mentally and physically active, and go into a rapid decline. The reason for the decline often has less to do with the age 65 and more to do with the lack of mental and physical exercise.

Why is 65 the point of change for most people? Is it because a body clock says so? No. Otto von Bismarck said so 100 years ago. He was chancellor of the German Empire and a reformer who recognized that workers often toiled to the last days of life.

As a humane gesture, Bismarck instituted the idea of retirement at 65. It seemed a good idea at the time, but that progressive reform has come back to haunt us by inculcating in all of us the notion that we are one thing at age 64 and something else on the day we turn 65.

In fact, the only thing that changes is our attitude about ourselves, and that is a pity, because we are living longer. Soon a fifth of all Americans will be past 65. It is high time we revised our concept of our possibilities by remembering Dr. Huggins's warning to keep on using that "bean."

My Aunt Maude and Charles Huggins would have had no difficulty understanding each other. She knew nothing of medicine and physiology, but she understood human nature. She refused to visit doctors for her ailments in the belief that doctors were the cause of most people's problems.

Long before our increased awareness of preventive medicine, Aunt Maude believed that if you remained healthy and vigorous you could beat the need for a doctor. She regarded organized medicine as a form of dependency that tended to encourage illness.

When her contemporaries would complain of an illness and say they were going to the doctor, Aunt Maude would chastise them as only she could.

"If there weren't so many doctors waiting for you to get sick," she would say, "you wouldn't know you weren't well."

That is why I say she and Charles Huggins would agree. They both start from the premise that you are as old as you permit yourself to feel.

In the case of Aunt Maude, there must have been something to it. She lived to be 100.

Being 80 Soon Won't Be Rare

July 2, 1987—When Aunt Maude was due at our house, the air crackled with tension from the first light of dawn. My mother, ever the picture of poise, often seemed jittery as the appointed hour drew near.

As for us children, it was always a good idea to have our rooms spick-and-span. It also helped to be neatly groomed. The reason our household went on meticulous alert was simple. Aunt Maude, in her 80s when I knew her best, was a formidable figure in our lives.

Actually, she was my mother's aunt, not mine. That made her our great-aunt. Somehow that extra layer of generation made her even more fearsome in our eyes.

Thoughts of Aunt Maude come back often these days. Her visits always coincided with big family events or the changes of the seasons, especially the start of summer. Also, my friends in the field of gerontology tell me Aunt Maude was the precursor of a new breed of American, people who will commonly live to be 100.

"It won't be long," said one prominent student of human development, "before death at 80 will be regarded as premature. Death at 110 or even 120 will not be regarded as extraordinary."

The reasons for this optimism are not hard to recognize. Average life expectancy has lengthened considerably over the course of this century, from about 47 in 1900 to about 75 today. Over the next half-century, changes in science and behavior all but guarantee the elimination of several of today's common killers—heart disease, many forms of cancer and hypertension.

If vital 80-year-olds are about to become commonplace, they were most uncommon in the 1950s. And Aunt Maude might have been the least common among them. In fact, she was a holy terror.

Upon reflection, what made her so remarkable was her phenomenal energy, her extraordinary memory and her sharp eye. She missed nothing. She would walk in the house and take in the entire scene in a flash. Then her stream of critical commentary would begin.

I'll never forget the June Sunday she appeared right after church. She looked at one of my sisters and declared: "You look fat. You aren't pregnant, are you?" All my sisters, then unmarried, reacted in horror.

The old woman, always dressed in black, was never married. She was unfazed by my sisters' collective indignation. Instead, she launched into one of her commentaries:

"You girls may squirm, but somebody has to ask these questions. Men today are only out for one thing. They take advantage of young girls. Somebody has to remind you it's easy to get pregnant and ruin your life."

My sister said she was certainly not pregnant but she also vowed to go on a diet so as to avoid such a question in the future. Aunt Maude had that effect on our family. Once she raised a question in her incomparably acerbic fashion, you made sure she never had a reason to raise it again.

She was a thin woman, almost wiry. Her admirers often told her she had the figure of a young girl. Her detractors muttered that she looked like a witch.

Being the youngest, I was her favorite. She showered me with small gifts, but that was not the greatest honor she bestowed on me. As far as I can recall, I am the only one of the six children she never threatened to cut out of her will.

Aunt Maude's will was something of a running family joke. Each of my siblings was cut out at one time or another, sometimes for the tiniest of infractions. One evening she was grilling one of my brothers on his progress in school. He gave one of her questions a curt, cute answer.

"If you don't know any better manners than that, I'm going to remove you from my will. You get nothing," the old woman declared with a majestic gesture.

In truth, we children always believed Aunt Maude's most modest home in Barbados had grown in her mind into a lavish plantation as the years progressed.

It did not matter if her estate was big or small. Aunt Maude's declarations of disinheritance were her way of expressing displeasure and getting our attention.

She gave us many gifts in her years of visits. None was more important than what she showed us an 80-year-old human being could do. She was not just a role model for the '50s. She remains a role model even for the '80s, and beyond.

In The End

My older brother and I lost our parents somewhere in the Kaiser Oakland Hospital one evening in July 1993. I had been out running errands. Dad had left his studio and gone for tests at the hospital. Hours later we could not find him or Nancy.

Finally, an admitting nurse agreed to help me. Flipping through her charts she casually asked, "Oh, is he terminal?"

In the six years since my father had been diagnosed with inoperable cancer, we had never used that word. Seeing the look on my face, she quickly searched for another description. "Chronic," I supplied. "My father has chronic cancer."

We never treated Dad's cancer as a death sentence. "The disease must be managed properly," my father would say. He never did ask the doctors how long they thought he might live. Instead, he read all he could about cancer, its causes and its cures, meditated, tried to adjust his diet and worked closely with his doctors.

For years that approach worked well enough to keep Dad out of the hospital. Right after Christmas 1992, Dad went into the hospital for the first time. During the next six months, he was hospitalized with increasing frequency and for longer duration. Hours after I spoke to the emergency-room nurse, we found Dad. He had been admitted for what would turn out to be the last time.

There are those, I know, who hate hospitals. I am not one of them. Our family essentially moved into Dad's room, with my older brother and me taking turns spending the night.

I loved the noisy camaraderie of hospital life. Side by side with the nurses and nurses' assistants, we made sure Dad was as comfortable as possible. We brought his favorite down comforter from home. We catered his meals from his favorite restaurants. The days fell into a comfortable routine.

In the gentle murmur of the night, Dad and I outlined our future work plans. My older brother showed us the best way to mop Dad's brow or get him to eat. During the day, Dad detailed what he expected me to do in his absence. We didn't dwell on his death. He just wanted to make sure I understood what he wanted done with his papers and his work.

Nancy would bring over his breakfast. Then the two of them would settle in for a day of talking and reading together, frequently interrupted by various medical tests. Our younger brother, back from camp, came to the hospital for his writing tutorials with Dad. Our cousin was always there with a fresh sunflower.

Then there were other visitors. The author Ishmael Reed came by to discuss the Bible in connection with a libretto he was writing for the San Francisco Opera. Former *Tribune* managing editor Eric Newton, despite having a sick newborn baby, came over regularly to talk and play the word games they loved. Pastor J. Alfred Smith Sr. came by with some hospital ministration. Former *Tribune* executive editor Roy Aarons came to discuss the book he had just begun. Dad's right-hand person, Jan Snyder, with the dry humor Dad loved, was always there with a quick quip to make him smile. Seeing as Jan's jokes were usually at my expense, I rarely saw the humor.

His brother, Edward, and sister, Sybil, came to visit. Two of his best friends, Bob Butler and Myrna Lewis, came for the weekend. Decades ago, Dad had met "Dr. Bob" when he was Dad's therapist, a connection that had been hazy in my mind until that weekend.

"It was," my father proclaimed, "one of the best weekends of my life. You can't imagine what it means to have your old friend and therapist to talk to at this time in your life."

Not long after that, right before Dad went home, I had to go back East briefly. Because he was paralyzed and unable to negotiate the steps to his studio, Nancy fixed up a room on the ground floor, bringing down much of the furniture and many of the pictures and memorabilia from his studio.

We were on the phone one afternoon and he was telling me how good it was to be back home. He loved his new space, and said he was looking forward to motoring his wheelchair to the partner's desk right down the hall where we planned to work. Suddenly, out of the blue, he said, "I have to go now. I don't want to, but I fear I must." Then, as was our routine, we both said "I love you," before hanging up the phone.

D.J.M.

The Kindness of Neighbors
and Strangers

December 2, 1991—Disasters can have deceptive beginnings. Nothing about our peaceful morning forewarned us of the conflagration that was to come. Nothing except the wind. I went to open a French door.

The wind blew it back in one fierce gust.

Our youngest would be playing a Little League game around noon. We were reading the Sunday papers when the phone rang around 10 A.M. A friend told my wife there was a fire up on Grizzly Peak. That is more than a mile from our home in Upper Rockridge.

From a vantage point on our roof, I could see a thick plume of smoke rising on the horizon. A helicopter was making a water bombing run about every five to seven minutes.

As the day turned out, the image of that helicopter would form the basis for a bitter irony. It would be eventually the equivalent of thimbles of water trying to quench the flames of Hades.

Hell came to the neighborhood at a little after noon. A house on the hill above our house burst into flames. Then, as my older son and I took pictures on the roof, we watched the flames come roaring over the hill and down the Broadway Terrace corridor toward Lake Temescal.

My wife took a tour of the neighborhood and drove home with an urgent message. "We have to get out. Now," she said, "Let's just go."

We grabbed the dog and one of the three cats, TommyCat. Percy, the black Persian, and Abigail, the calico cat, were nowhere to be found, but they were streetwise cats so we were confident they would avoid harm on their own.

After Nancy and the children were settled in our office, my older son and I went back to the neighborhood. It was like a visit to Hell at Ground Zero. Cross Road, the little street on the north boundary of our property, was a ball of flame. Every house on both sides of the street, more than a dozen in all, was engulfed in flame.

It was an eerie scene. The wind howled down Cross Road and the flames sprang from tree to tree, from roof to roof. This little street, the one my Little Leaguer and I use to head to school every day, was now a blazing inferno.

Earlier in the afternoon, Jeff Langer called. His parents, our neighbors Bob and Michael Langer, were traveling. They have lived here for a quarter century in a house that was built in 1912. Could I look out for their house? he asked.

I told him I would do what I could. Now I was standing transfixed as the flames roared through the Langers' lovely home. They were already beginning to devour the Fujitas' house. Ours was next in the path of the inferno.

What added to the eerie nature of the scene at Cross Road and Broadway Terrace was the total absence of any fire equipment. The neighborhood was going up in flames, and there was not a firefighter to be seen at that moment.

My older boy and I were trying to decide if we dared try to rescue any family valuables by going back into the house. It hadn't caught yet, but it was bound to go at any minute.

Just then, two Oakland police officers came screaming to a halt in front of our home. "You only have five minutes," said Officer Smith. "Come on, I'll help you get some of your valuables out."

Smith and I raced up the stairs. I headed to our bedroom. Without electric power I was grabbing things in the dark. I reached for a suitcase to pack them.

"No, no," said Smith, "there's no time for that. You have to do it as if you were a burglar robbing the place."

I stood dumbfounded. "Like this," Smith said. He began helping me pile valuables and clothing onto the bed. When we had everything worth grabbing, Smith showed me what a burglar does. He grabbed the four corners of the bedspread and it became one huge bundle. Away we went.

Outside, Peter Haidt was in his car with his wife, his dog and a few valuables. Theirs was a particularly touching story. Their house, at the top of Cross Road, a few hundred yards above ours, had been vacant until last weekend. The Haidts bought it and moved in eight days ago.

"I'm trying to get a picture of the house we never got a chance to live in," Haidt said. With that, he went charging up Cross Road, his wife shouting at him to come back. In seconds, the flames, the heat and the heavy smoke drove him back.

Neighbors came to ask how they could help. When I told a total stranger about two large paintings I was afraid would be lost, he said, "I was an art major. I can't stand the thought of losing valuable paintings."

He and I ran into the threatened house. We saved two master-pieces by Elizabeth Turner Hall, one of our favorite painters. My wife, who had returned to the house, joined our son and me in shoving those paintings in the truck as our last family act before we fled.

On the day last week of the anniversary of the terrible Loma Prieta earthquake, we had made no particular mention of it in our house. It was not a memory we wanted to relive in any prolonged manner.

Instead, on that day, we were engaged in an act of supreme optimism. We erected a scaffold to begin painting our 81-year-old house. This is a remodeling and redecorating job we have been planning for more than five years.

Now my son and a friend of our family were using the scaffolding to get water on our roof. I watched their heroic effort. It was similar to the efforts I had been witnessing all afternoon. Hundreds of my neighbors were out with garden hoses, pouring water on their roofs.

I called them down from the scaffold. It was a futile effort. The temperature of the flames rose so high as to disdain something as inconsequential as a damp roof. The sun was hidden by the smoke. The howling wind and the crackling flames in the trees and the houses next door seemed out of this world. It felt as if we had visited Dante's Inferno.

As we made our way out, still uncertain of the fate of our own home, some firefighters were struggling with a hydrant, trying to get enough water pressure to fight at Broadway Terrace and Clarewood Road.

It was another display of that old futility. I remembered that first helicopter I had seen at 10:30 that morning. These paltry human efforts, a garden hose here and a bucket of water under a helicopter there, were no match. This was a disaster of extraordinary proportions that began on an otherwise ordinary Sunday morning.

Miracles and Mysteries

October 24, 1991—My father preached often when I was young on the theme of "divine mysteries," the events no mortal can explain. My mother, too, would quote to us children from the hymn that begins, "God moves in a mysterious way."

We have been pondering these mysteries in our family since last Sunday night. With a firestorm bearing down upon us at 60 miles an hour, we evacuated our neighborhood. We expected never again to see our home. We reflected on the profound impact of losing so many precious possessions, most of them representing family memories.

It would be nearly five hours before we would discover that our home stood virtually untouched. More important, it would be daylight before we would discover we had lost virtually all of our neighbors.

Their homes, for blocks and blocks, were heaps of smoldering ash. Some of the most elegant urban residential architecture in America had been wiped out by the roaring inferno.

We walked up our hill on Cross Road above Broadway Terrace. The further we went, the deeper our dread became. We beheld singular devastation. It resembled a massive cemetery, each chimney a stately headstone to mark the grave site.

We retreated in horror and despair back down the hill. We were following the easterly path the flames had taken. From the top of the hill down to our house, the flames consumed more than 100 homes. That is just in our immediate neighborhood. These were the homes of friends and associates, playmates and school chums of our children.

All the way from Grizzly Peak to Lake Temescal and then over the ridge above our home, the fire came on in a relentless advance east toward Broadway Terrace. That is where our home is located. I watched it with a television reporter Sunday night.

I imagine it might be something like the horror of watching your friends being mowed down by a madman. The flames rushed forward unimpeded. The Haidts had just moved into the house at the top of our street, four houses up from ours. The flames left one closet standing, a couple of dress shirts still on hangers.

Then the flames consumed the Langers' house. Mr. and Mrs. Langer were away on business. They didn't even have a chance to try to save one blessed object before the fire ate 135 Cross Road.

The last house before ours was the Fujitas' split-level. All there was left to recognize were the frames of two of Tiffany's little bicycles, still standing in what was the garage. They looked like the work of a sculptor whose medium was carbon.

Our house was next in line, the last home on the Cross Street corridor of flame. I watched the fire as it came through the Fujitas' house and crossed into our backyard. That is when my older son and my wife urged that we leave. We were worried about the flames leaping over our heads and encircling us on the ground.

When I looked at our home for the last time that night, I thought only a divine miracle could turn that wind from east to south. With my wife at the wheel, we gunned out at what we thought was the last safe moment to be in our neighborhood. We had no idea of the fate of our home, but we feared the worst.

As it happened, our escape route was to the south. What we could not know, and would not know for five hours, was that the wind, too, turned south. At the last possible minute, the flames took a hard right turn and cut across our backyard instead of continuing east into our home.

As they reached the south side of our lot, the flames headed down toward the garage. They burned the foliage six inches from the garage. That is where they were when a group of firefighters from San Mateo County came upon the flames. They doused the fire as it was about to gobble up the garage and then our house.

What miracle saved this one house at the end of a line of 100 or more? We will never know. The experts say our composition roof had a lot to do with it. My wife gives a lot of credit to the "old stucco," which she says is better than the stucco of today. Our house was built in 1910.

The miracle is a mystery, just as my parents said so many years ago. The tragedy of the massive loss of life and property is a much bigger mystery. Those of us who witnessed the great Oakland conflagration of 1991 will be pondering that mystery for some time to come.

The Trials and Triumphs of Percy

April 19, 1992—When we saw the flames come roaring over the ridge that Sunday afternoon, we bid our home farewell. Our concern was for the people and the animals. We were sure the fire would leave nothing standing. We were very wrong and very lucky. The wind shifted at the last possible moment, and our home was spared the devastation suffered by 3,000 other families last October 20.

A house without neighbors is a lonely place. If it is difficult for us, try to imagine what this devastation has been like for our four-footed friends. Take, for example, the trials of Percy the cat. Percy is a streetwise cat. He is a clever hunter. He has the thick black fur of an angora but the leap of a leopard. Many a blue jay discovered Percy's proficiency too late. And the word is out among the field mice and other rodents: Pass Percy's house by.

On the day of the fire, Percy and Abigail, his colleague in crime, disappeared. We were sick with worry for days. Percy and I have had our share of disagreements over the years, especially concerning his cruel treatment of his catch. The fire made those differences seem very small. We wanted our cats back.

Abby showed first. She seemed unharmed and happy to be home. Percy was a different story. We did not see him again for days. He seemed so spooked it was hard to be sure he even recognized everybody in the family.

In a day or so, he disappeared again. It was clear that all the new noises from chain saws, bulldozers and fire trucks were driving him away. My wife was concerned enough to put out an all-points-bulletin for Percy. Of our three cats, he is her favorite. Finally, late one evening after we had given up hope, he came strolling into the kitchen. Did I say strolling? Wobbling would be a better description. He looked a mess. He had been mauled.

Percy spent a few days in the hospital. The vet took care of the physical trauma. The mental trauma was ours to deal with. It has not been easy. We speculate that the fire sent the whole animal world into the same disarray felt by the humans.

In the course of the upheaval, the laws of the jungle took hold in earnest. A possum, somewhat larger than Percy, was displaced by the fire. He has been living in our backyard for several years. His hiding hole was under a giant Monterey pine that burned and caved in his house. We think he then challenged Percy for a space in which the cat hid to wait for unsuspecting birds to visit in search of figs. The fig tree burned, but the birds still came. As near as we can tell, Percy and the possum got into a fight over the space. I haven't seen what Percy did to the possum, but what the possum did to Percy shouldn't happen to a cat.

Percy came home from the hospital wearing a lamp shade. It was a hood to protect the stitches in his scalp. After he healed enough to run, he was gone again. A beautiful house cat seemed on the verge of turning feral. It was a little like watching a beautiful kid turn into a teenage brat. He would come and go as he pleased, most unlike his former, lovable self.

My wife would not give up on that cat, just as you can't give up on a wayward kid you love. She kept going to his hiding place to bring him back home. She hugged him even when he didn't want to be held. She showed she cared. He finally began to yield. He stays home for longer periods now. He allows himself to be held by select members of the family, not including yours truly. Not yet anyway.

Little by little, six months after the fire, Percy has become a domestic cat again. His travail must be multiplied by the thousands in the hills of Oakland and Berkeley. Their fire stories are rarely told. That's too bad. They have much to tell.

The Earth Shook, Time Stood Still

October 19, 1989—Soon after we moved to California, exactly 10 years ago, my wife and I went back East to a professional meeting. During idle cocktail hour chitchat, I was approached by a colleague. Why, he wanted to know, had I decided to "risk your family's safety" by moving to California?

An engineer by training, he went on to describe to me in chilling detail his doomsday scenario. One day, he said, a massive earthquake will shake a freeway overpass from its moorings. The whole thing will come tumbling down.

From then on, whenever we saw him at a conference, I would whisper to my wife: "There's simple Simon. He thinks our California engineers are too dumb to know how to build freeways to withstand earthquakes." After all, I reasoned, we have hundreds of earthquakes a year in this state. I remember only one incident in which a major piece of freeway fell. No fatalities occurred.

At 5:04 P.M., on Tuesday the 17th of October, all that changed. A freeway deck near downtown Oakland fell on the motorists below. I am writing this more than 18 hours afterward. We do not know now what the death toll will be. No one doubts it will be high, surely in the scores, possibly the hundreds. After all, it was the peak of rush hour.

The third World Series game that never was might turn out to have saved many lives. Because the game was due to begin in Candlestick Park only 26 minutes later, throngs of Eastbay residents had passed that spot an hour or so before the fatal event. We all know exactly what we were doing at 5:04.

It had been a long day of meetings for me. The last one was winding up. A colleague and I were conversing quietly when my conference room began to roll. I pointed out to him in a casual voice that my chandelier serves as my Richter scale. I was about to tell him all the things I can tell about an earthquake by watching the sway of the chandelier.

At that instant, the chandelier stopped swaying. Instead it began a violent upward and downward movement. The entire room felt as though massive hands had put it into a whiskey shaker and then jolted it vigorously up and down. We jumped into the doorway. I grabbed the door frame and held on for dear life. I felt as if I were riding a bucking bronco at the rodeo.

Fear? Yes, I felt a little. But I am so accustomed to earthquakes, I never felt that cold anticipation of imminent death. When we heard the snap, I thought it was all over. The snap sound seemed to come from the far corner of the office. As the building shook and the chandelier gyrated as never before, the sharp snap made me certain the entire Tribune Tower was about to drop to earth. The moment is a frozen frame engraved in my mind for life.

When finally I loosened my grip on the door frame, I looked out on the street and saw the debris that had fallen off the faces of buildings in downtown Oakland. The first wave of realization hit me in that instant.

Somewhere, I heard myself saying, someone just was killed. It would be a few minutes before the word filtered into our building. The Cypress section of the Nimitz Freeway had crushed those below it.

That is the most commonly used piece of highway in the Eastbay. Upon hearing that news, a colleague said she was moving back to New York after 25 years in the Bay Area. "I've seen enough," she said. "I don't intend to stick around for the next one."

She was referring to what we call The Big One. Seismologists have been forecasting an earthquake of 7.5 Richter or higher along the San Andreas fault. They have been saying for years it is inevitable. This earthquake, disastrous as it was, does not qualify as The Big One. That experience still awaits us some time in the next 30 years.

Wherever my "simple Simon" colleague might be, he has been vindicated in my mind. Perhaps our vaunted California engineers aren't as great as I'd thought.

For those who experienced it, 5:04 P.M., October 17, 1989, will stand out in our minds for years to come. In our fears and anxieties, we begin rebuilding our confidence with what we share. Strangers for days will begin conversations by telling each other what it was like for them at that special, terrible moment when the Earth shook and time stood still.

Facing Up to the "C" Word

November 1, 1987—My mother and father believed in the philosophy that people of faith thrive on challenges. That Tuesday morning, as I was driving to work, I thought about my parents and a wry thought crossed my mind. I never did ask them if there was ever such a thing as feeling your faith is just too challenged.

I could imagine my father shaking his head, vigorously denying the existence of such a thing as too much challenge. I remember him saying once, "You don't get more than you can handle. If you think you have, perhaps you should look to see if you are handling the burden properly."

All right, I thought to myself, I sure hope he was right because today is the day you find out just how much of a challenge you may have to handle. A few days before, I had the excruciating experience of a prostate biopsy. This was the day on which I was to receive the results.

What made this morning particularly poignant for me was an odd contradiction. Only weeks before, just as I turned 50, I had one of those thorough physical examinations. When it was all over, the doctor was pleased.

"You're one healthy guy for 50," the doctor said with admiration in his voice. "You still have the body of a kid." Then, almost in passing, he said, "Have you had a urologist look at your prostate lately? I notice it's enlarged."

My urologist suggested a biopsy. He had made that suggestion before, but both of us thought it somewhat improbable that it was cancer. Now, after months of speculation, the time to know for certain had arrived. When he called, my urologist was not his usual, jovial self.

"It's cancer," he said simply.

Thus was I introduced to my latest challenge, facing up to the "C" word. As it happened, I had plenty of time to adjust to the idea. My wife was just about to take the California Bar examination. I decided she could do without such news, although she knew something was amiss. After all, as she pointed out later, it doesn't take three weeks to get the results of a biopsy.

During that time and since, I have learned a great deal about the challenge of cancer. I suppose I learned what millions of Americans learn about this disease each year. It seems a strange and dread occurrence when you read about it or see a story about it on television.

That all changes once you know you have the disease. Then, instead of some alien happening, it is your disease, your challenge. It becomes personal. It's your fight.

More than that, it became a family affair. My wife and I have always faced our problems and our opportunities as a team. This would be no different. We both went to work on the best strategy for conquering the disease.

After finding excellent medical care, my wife and I decided we were not going to allow fear to do what disease could not do, dampen our enthusiasm for our lives, our children and our work.

Mind you, when you undergo radiation therapy, life is not exactly normal. Large doses of radiation have a way of making themselves felt in your system.

All the same, we found ourselves doing some of the same things we did while my wife was in law school. We made sure we had set aside family time so that we kept sharing and gaining the energy that only love can provide.

Odd now when I hark back to that first morning when I was thinking about my parents. Again, they were right. Once we made up our minds on a strategy for meeting the challenge, it hardly seemed difficult after all.

Since virtually nothing is known with respect to the possible causes of prostate cancer, it remains a mystery how this ailment wound up on my doorstep. It certainly came as a shock to discover that 50 is not too young to get prostate cancer. Since it has few noticeable symptoms, regular checkups are the only hope of detection.

The radiation treatment is nearly over, and my doctor feels very good about the progress and my prognosis. So do my wife and I. And if anything our family feels even closer from having to face the ordeal.

My kind and capable physician tells me the hardest part is behind me. My wife, noticing my itching to get back to a full schedule, has quietly padlocked my datebook and hidden the list of my next 3,000 chores.

Meanwhile, I am as enthusiastic about my work at the *Tribune* as ever. My colleagues and I have been working on the design of our newspaper and our company as we hope it will be into the next decade and on to the year 2000. Much exciting work remains to be done. And it is true: After this kind of challenge, the taste for life is richer than ever.

Just the same, my wife said, "I'm still keeping an eye on that schedule." The last time I looked at her studio, she was studying Hawaii travel brochures. That's what my dad meant, I suppose, when he said if you're having trouble with a challenge, you probably aren't handling it right.

Overcoming Fear of the "C" Word

November 27, 1988—We spoke her name in hushed whispers around the dining room table. Always, the speaker's voice took on a dread tone. Each utterance conveyed the aura of a shroud, as if in our minds the curtain had already been drawn. We were on this side, she on that. She had cancer.

Our neighbor, also a member of our church, had been diagnosed as having a malignancy. This was in the 1940s. As the youngest child in our family, I had the least comprehension of what this news meant. In careful, precise terms, the rest of the family was explaining it to me. The heart of the message was that people with cancer were doomed to death. Just that simple.

I suppose I am like most Americans in that respect. That is how most of us first learn of cancer. In the days of my childhood, there was an inexplicable stigma attached to the idea of cancer, perhaps in large measure because of the pervasive belief in its near total fatality.

Beyond that, there was then and still is a power in the mystery, perhaps even mystique, of cancer. So many of its causes remain unknown. Its effect is potentially so devastating. All the same, we generally do not hide away cancer victims as we did in the days when cancer carried a label of shame for a whole family. Then it was something akin to having a relative in the asylum.

Science and common sense have brought us a few insights regarding cancer, although no cures of the sort we have seen with some other dreaded diseases during that time, such as polio and smallpox. Yet the cancer myths remain.

I found that out when I wrote, almost exactly a year ago, that I was undergoing treatment for cancer. Many people reacted generously and thoughtfully. But I found out that the fear and mystique of cancer remain as powerful as when I first heard the word as a child.

Some readers wrote to say they didn't believe the subject should be discussed in public. Period. More poignant were those who had relatives or acquaintances suffering from cancer who denied they had it. They were so sure that to do so would be to acknowledge they were going to die.

"To some people," my doctor said one day, "to hear the word cancer is the equivalent of a sentence of death." You are so brave, one woman said, "to admit you have it."

My doctor again: "People's attitudes can be their worst enemy. They hear the word cancer, and they immediately prepare themselves to die." And so they don't rally their inner resources to fight back. If, instead of planning to die in the face of cancer, they planned to live in spite of it, many patients would do much better.

The Cancer Society of Oakland inaugurated the Thanksgiving season with a wonderful, if somewhat unusual, dinner. Its purpose was to celebrate the lives of four people who found out there is plenty of life left after the doctors tell you that you have cancer. I was privileged to be included in this company: Alta Diamond, Jane Logan and Mike Gallego.

What our four experiences seemed to have in common above all else was our determination to see cancer as merely another life challenge to be faced, dealt with and overcome. That and a great deal of faith in God.

If given a choice, I am not sure I would repeat the experience of the last year. Yet, there is a life-enhancing benefit that people come to know when they conquer their fear of the "C-word."

That is the realization that even this dread thing called cancer can be overcome with early detection, good treatment, faith and determination. It is not an automatic death sentence, and it need not be spoken of in whispers. It is a disease to be fought. It is not a signal for surrender.

Understand that, my doctor said one day, and you will have a better chance. I learned this year that a disease can impair your body, but only you can impair your spirit. I would never say the word cancer in a hush again. The first sign of winning, they say, is believing you can. It is best, I have learned, to begin with faith and courage.

Lee Atwater's Conversion

March 25, 1990 —This happens to me from time to time. Strangers generously offer me constructive criticism. I was seated in my doctor's waiting room reading a book. Another patient, a woman in her 60s or so, tapped me on the knee. "I love your column," she said, ". . . except when you write about Lee Atwater. It's the only time you become mean. I wish you'd be less verbose about him."

As my father once said in another situation, I told her, Lee Atwater just does not bring out the best in me. Then, in an idle, joking attempt to extricate myself, I promised her I'd be on the lookout for something nice to say about Atwater.

That was back in January. I hope my fellow patient will forgive me for saying this: I forgot my promise almost as quickly as I made it. The chairman of the Republican party was not about to convert himself into a sympathetic figure in my mind anytime soon . . . or so I thought then.

My daughter, a reporter in Detroit, is familiar with my feelings about any number of public figures, not the least among them Lee Atwater. "Dad," she said one recent afternoon on the telephone, "have you heard about Lee Atwater?" I'd been in a meeting all day. "He collapsed delivering a speech in Washington."

It turns out he has a benign tumor in his brain and is undergoing radiation therapy. Having experienced radiation for a tumor of my own, I felt deep and instant empathy for anyone who must encounter it. Only those who have experienced that ordeal can appreciate fully its impact on body and soul.

For that reason, I was among the least surprised Americans to read the other day that Lee Atwater, "Mr. GOP Slash and Burn," had experienced a profound change of heart about his approach to life and politics.

The "pit bull" of national politics told a reporter for the *State* newspaper of Columbia, South Carolina, "I can't imagine me getting back into a fighting mood. I don't see how I'm ever going to be mean." The master of negative attacks in politics, the creator of the "Willie Horton syndrome" of anything goes, has changed?

"What I am going to do is take a new approach," Atwater told the reporter for the *State*, "because politics is people. I've always loved people. But I have a better sense of humanity, a better sense of fellowship with people than I've ever had before."

Then he said something that seemed hauntingly familiar for reasons I will explain shortly. Atwater said: "Forget money and power. I had no idea how wonderful people are. I wish I had known this before. What a way to have to find out. . . . Seventy percent of the things I was frantically pursuing didn't matter anyhow."

Well, how ironic. Lee Atwater and I finally had something in common. We both found out through major, frightening illnesses that we had to reorder our priorities. I'll never forget the day my pastor came calling after my diagnosis of cancer. I told him my priorities had changed dramatically in just 24 hours.

My family, I told him, was my first priority, our newspaper the second, and writing my third. Everything else would forever land in a new category of priorities called "other." The pastor listened and then said, "Isn't it odd what it takes for us to see the real priorities?" That was almost three years ago. My priorities have not changed. As a result, the quality of my personal and family life could hardly be better.

That is the bright side of major, frightening illness. It awakens us acutely to what is important. It is, as Atwater and my pastor said, the hard way to learn that lesson, but it is the sure way.

For that reason, I have little doubt Lee Atwater's conversion is sincere. I just hope he doesn't become so mellow as to be boring. Knowing him, I somehow doubt there is any danger Atwater will overdo goodness.

Now if I only knew the woman's name in the doctor's office . . . I could write and tell her I hardly expected to keep an idle promise so soon.

On Winking Versus Blinking

September 27, 1990—Six children in a household, my mother was fond of saying, saved her money on outside entertainment. Somehow there was almost always something hilarious going on among us. To be sure, what was funny for some members of the family was not always so cute to the butt of the joke.

As the youngest in what my mother sometimes called her "train of six" locomotives, I was the butt of more funny episodes than the rest. At least that is how I remember it. My siblings do not disagree on that point, even to this day.

By unanimous agreement among the rest, one of the funniest of our growing-up experiences was dubbed "Teaching Robert to wink." For some reason, winking came naturally to every member of the family except me. They would tell their little jokes and stories, spiced here and there by a knowing wink. I simply could not manage it.

By the time I was 10, I was desperate. Everyone in the world, it seemed, could wink. All except me. I would stand in front of my bathroom mirror for hours on end trying to get the hang of the wink. Nothing happened. I contorted my face into several awesome configurations that were pretty funny all right, but they weren't . . . well . . . a wink.

One of my brothers took sadistic pity upon me. Yes, I know sadistic pity is an oxymoron. You would have to know my brother to appreciate it fully. He decided the problem was with my eye-muscle motor control, and that I needed to quicken my eye-muscle reflexes. He decided to assist me in this with a game we called "Think fast!"

In "Think fast!" the aggressor chooses the least opportune moment to toss an object at the unsuspecting target person. Only after the object is in midflight does the aggressor shout, "Think fast!"

Now if the object was a baseball or a football, the worst consequence was a beaning, possibly a black eye. If, on the other hand, we were washing the Sunday night dishes and the object was my mother's crystal salad bowl, the consequences were considerably more dire. Since the essence of "Think fast!" put the onus on the would-be recipient to catch the object, no matter what, the outcome of a disaster was always the same: "Robert dropped the salad bowl."

Whether this game ever helped my reflexes, I'll never know, but it did nothing constructive for our service wares and even less for my ability to wink. Needless to say, I found my proclivity toward blinking sharply reduced. In that house, you never seemed to have time to blink.

Neither "Think fast!" nor any other helpful overture from my family improved my ability to wink. What did it was love. In my freshman year in high school, I fell seriously in love for the first time. My sisters enjoyed teasing me about my "puppy love" romance. I resented such belittling of my first true love. We wrote each other an endless series of passionate declarations of undying devotion.

One Sunday in church, my true love's eyes and mine met for a fleeting instant. To us, our love was our own private, delicious secret. We liked to pretend no one, especially our parents, had any idea of our true relationship. So, when our eyes met, she blew me a furtive kiss. Then she winked. With not a second's thought or hesitation, I winked back.

It took me a few seconds to realize what I had done. Naturally, I tried it again. It worked. I did it again. This time my father leaned over and asked me if I had something stuck in my eye. I shook my head no and buried my eyes in my hymnal, first testing with one eye and then the other. A miracle! I could wink!

At home, I made a beeline for the bathroom mirror. It was true. No longer need I scrunch my whole face into some awful contortion. I had joined the rest of the world with secrets to share. I could do what every other member of the family could do. I had come of age. I could wink with the best of them. Those for whom a wink comes naturally might never know what a triumphal sensation it is to be able to wink at the world at will.

The Last Word

Our godfather, Earl Caldwell, broke it to me gently. "It doesn't get easier," he said a few months after Daddy died. "In some ways it even gets harder as time goes on." His was the voice of experience. His elderly parents had died a few years earlier.

One of Dad's best friends ever since they were cub reporters at two different Pennsylvania newspapers, Caldwell is known for his flights of fancy. He once told my younger brother, and his namesake, that he played for baseball's Negro Leagues and basketball for the New York Knickerbockers. Some took everything he said with grain of salt. This time he was right on the mark.

The first year after my father's death, I was in shock. Even though a "terminal" diagnosis may prepare you for some hypothetical inevitability, death still comes as a searing shock.

Everything looked the same, except it was a little grayer and farther away. I could not stop crying during the three days that lead up to my father's funeral. Then I decided my grieving was over. I began to think about the work he had left me to complete.

A month later, driving across the country, I lost it in Kansas. I was almost numb by the time I met up with my Nieman Fellow classmate, independent radio producer Sandy Tolan. Sandy had buried his father when he was 18. He looked almost relieved when I met him at a Boulder restaurant. "It's so good to see that you're finally allowing yourself to grieve," he said. I spent the next three days walking around in an almost comatose haze, saying the dumb things you say when you're sad. I vowed never to speak to anyone who had a father.

By the time I left I felt better, but better than that was still not good. The simplest things, once accomplished with ease, took on Herculean proportions. I tried Christmas shopping in September, so I wouldn't notice Dad's absence in December. It didn't work, of course. Close to Christmas, I cried my way through department stores.

The second year I hurt. I knew my father was dead, never to return. I just don't think I understood that forever is a long time. A year earlier I felt guilty about being able to watch Nightline without Dad. Now I felt grief stricken that I could never again argue the issues of the day with my father.

It was about that time that someone tried to tell me that along with the pain, the death of a loved one also brings gifts. Even as I secretly wondered about her sanity, I could easily see my father agreeing with her. "Well, aren't you the lucky one," I could hear him say. "Some people always have their daddies right there to help them out. Now you have the opportunity to see what you can do on your own."

It's hard to say when I noticed the change. The world had been turned upside down, but our family had survived. Knowing this did not make me grieve less for my father, only have greater faith in our own strength and inner resources.

Then, something else happened, something I tried to explain to Caldwell. There was a major crisis in his family, the first since his mother's death. Feeling responsible for helping the family cope, he lamented about the absence of his mother. "She would know exactly what to do," he told me.

It reminded me of what Dad said to me years ago. "Whenever I run into a sticky situation," he once told me, "I think about my father and what he would have done, and soon I have the answer."

I finally got it. It took awhile, but I understood what everyone was trying to tell me. There are some voices you hear forever.

This past year, I have found myself listening more and more to the internal voice of my father. Death has not mellowed Dad. We still bicker. It took weeks of wrangling over who would get the last word for our book before we agreed to share.

Sometimes, beneath all his determination that his family survive and grow, I see his softer side. Once, when I missed him so much I just wanted to hide under the covers, there he was. His eyes were twinkling and his voice was robust.

"Dori J. Maynard," I heard him say, gently pulling me to my feet, "there's nothing to it but to do it."

Then he winked.

D.J.M.